Behavior Modification
for the
Classroom Teacher

McGraw-Hill Series in Special Education
Robert M. Smith, *Consulting Editor*

Behavior Modification for the Classroom Teacher

Second Edition

SAUL AXELROD
Temple University

McGRAW-HILL, INC.
New York St. Louis San Francisco Auckland
Bogotá Caracas Lisbon London Madrid
Mexico Milan Montreal New Delhi Paris
San Juan Singapore Sydney Tokyo Toronto

Behavior Modification for the Classroom Teacher

Copyright © 1983, 1977 by McGraw-Hill, Inc. All rights reserved. Typeset in the United States of America. Except as permitted under the United States Copyright Act of 1976, no part of this publication may be reproduced or distributed in any form or by any means, or stored in a data base or retrieval system, without the prior written permission of the publisher.

10 11 12 13 14 15 DOR DOR 9 9 8 7 6 5 4 3 2

ISBN 0-07-002572-X

This book was set in Baskerville by Black Dot, Inc. (ECU).
The editor was Kaye Pace;
the designer was Joseph Gillians;
the production supervisor was Phil Galea.
Project supervision was done by The Total Book.

Library of Congress Cataloging in Publication Data

Axelrod, Saul.
    Behavior modification for the classroom teacher.

    (McGraw-Hill series in special education)
    Includes bibliographies and indexes.
    1. Classroom management.   2. Behavior modification.
I. Title. II. Series.
LB3013.A93   1983   371.1′024   82–9958
ISBN 0–07–002572–X   AACR2

Printed and bound by Impresora Donneco Internacional S. A. de C. V. a division of R. R. Donnelley & Sons, Inc.

Manufactured in Mexico.

To Robie and Randy

Contents

CHAPTER V Modifying Academic Behavior **166**

Carolynn C. Hamlet

Preface

The problems of educating today's children have been noted both formally and informally. One study found more than 12% of the 17-year-old students in this country were functionally illiterate; only 34% could determine the most economical size of items sold in retail stores; and only 10% could calculate a simple taxi fare (Gallagher and Rambotham, 1978).

A number of reasons have been proposed for the failure of students to acquire basic academic and social skills. Included are claims of unsupportive homes and parents; inadequate university training; the misuse of intelligence, achievement, and personality tests; and excessive sugar in children's diets. Speculating on the reasons for failure can be a time consuming and unproductive task. More important is devising the means for producing the type of learning that students must acquire in order to succeed in their daily environments.

Developments in behavior modification provide reason for optimism. Behavior modification with respect to school problems, refers to applying learning theory principles to improving the academic and social development of students. The precepts were initially developed in laboratory settings and then validated in hundreds of studies in real-life situations. The principles not only explain why certain behaviors exist, but also offer teachers and other educators a methodology to produce desirable changes.

A behavior modification approach provides specific recommendations on what teachers should do in given classroom situations. The ultimate judgment as to whether the procedures are effective, however, is based on what the *students* do. If the students learn at an acceptable level and behave in a socially appropriate manner, the procedure was a successful one; if not, the procedure was a failure and must be changed.

A number of factors characterize a behavior modification approach. First, behavior is directly observed in the setting in which it occurs, rather than being inferred from a standardized test or described in a counsellor's office. Second, it concentrates on solving problems in the here and now, rather than delving into a student's past. Next, a behavioral approach stresses actionable procedures that directly change the environment so as to prevent future problems or remediate existing ones. Many recent studies accomplish this with minimal disruption to the teacher's routine and without requiring unreasonable financial expenditure.

Although the book is directed mainly toward teachers, it is also intended for use by other educators, such as school psychologists, guidance counsellors, and principals. The range of examples varies from preschool to secondary school, and encompasses both regular and special education.

The first chapter describes basic behavioral principles and means of applying them in the classroom. In the second chapter less basic but important and useful procedures are discussed. Chapter 3 presents means by which teachers can accurately and conveniently measure students' behavior. There is also a description of the research designs educators can employ to isolate the factors which cause a change in student performance. In the fourth chapter, several case studies are presented, dealing with the management of disruptive classroom behavior. In the fifth chapter, my colleague, Carolynn C. Hamlet, describes procedures that can be used to increase academic proficiency. In the final chapter, some of the most commonly asked questions about behavior modification are discussed.

Saul Axelrod

REFERENCE

Gallagher, J.J., and A. Rambotham: "Competency Program in North Carolina," *High School Journal, 61,* 302-312, 1978.

Behavior Modification for the Classroom Teacher

1

Basic Processes and Principles

There are two assumptions governing the present book. First, it is assumed that all children can learn. Second, it is assumed that learning will not take place automatically—that it is most likely to occur when it is programmed for by teachers.

College and university courses of the past have provided teachers with altruistic, but impractical philosophies on how to teach. Teachers provided the hard work. The result was not always effective teaching. What has been lacking is a collection of general principles and specific procedures that teachers can use when they walk into their classrooms.

The problems that teachers face today are similar to those of the past. These include teaching academic skills, reducing disruptive behavior, increasing attendance, and so on. Until recently, teachers had no consistent framework with which to choose a procedure. One day they would ignore a problem on the supposition that a child would outgrow the behavior. Another day they might deal with the same problem by counseling the youngster or sending her to the principal. Some approaches worked and others did not. In many cases teachers did not even know whether or not their techniques had worked. Sometimes teachers simply concluded that Fridays were usually rough days and consoled themselves with the thought that Monday would be better.

As a result of much hands-on research in classroom settings, this situation is changing. There is now a set of learning principles, more popularly known as behavior modification principles, that will help teachers to achieve the kinds of classrooms they want. Once they have mastered the principles and successfully applied them a sufficient number of times, they will enter their classrooms with a specific plan of attack that leaves them confident of future success. The procedures they develop can be used in regular and special-education classrooms, with students ranging from preschool to high school levels.

Developing expertise in using behavior modification principles will not relieve teachers of the necessity to work hard. In fact they will need to change many of their own behaviors. They will have to keep daily records of the students' performance. They will have to be systematic. They must be willing to fail and try again. Sometimes teachers will find the process difficult, but the rewards are great—the academic and social growth of their students.

In this chapter, the basic procedures and principles that teachers can use to make favorable modifications in their students' behavior are presented. First, however, it is necessary to have an understanding of what behavior is, the types of behaviors that exist, and the conditioning processes associated with each type of behavior.

TYPES OF BEHAVIOR AND CONDITIONING

When behavior modifiers use the term *behavior*, they are referring to anything a child does. This is in contrast to the manner in which other educators have used the term. To some educators, the term "behavior" refers only to a child's deportment, that is, whether she follows a teacher's directions, whether she talks without permission, and so on. The term as used in this book not only refers to deportment but also includes the whole gamut of students' school activities, such as their reading, writing, and arithmetic performance.

Skinner (1938) pointed out that there are two kinds of behavior. One type is called *respondent* and refers to reflexive or involuntary behaviors. It is said that respondent behaviors are elicited by known stimuli. In other words, a stimulus is presented and the response automatically follows. An example of a respondent behavior is eye-pupil dilation when an individual enters a dark room. The pupils spontaneously become larger. Other examples of respondents are shivering in cold weather, perspiring in hot weather, and blinking when a cinder enters the eye.

Associated with respondent behaviors is a process known as *respondent* or *classical conditioning*. The operation which was initially noted by the Russian psychologist, Pavlov, allows a neutral event to acquire the ability to produce a reflexive behavior. For example, the presence of food in the mouth produces salivation. Shining a light initially does not produce salivation. However, if the light continually precedes the presentation of the food, the light alone will eventually produce salivation. This is shown on the following page.

The solid arrow indicates that food automatically produces salivation. The broken arrow indicates that the light, which precedes the delivery of food, *acquired* the ability to produce salivation. If one were to continually present the light and not follow it with the food, salivation in the presence of the light would eventually cease.

In addition to respondent behaviors, another type of behavior is known as *operant behavior*. These behaviors are considered to be voluntary behaviors. Operant behaviors are said to be emitted, unlike respondent behaviors, which are elicited. Examples of operant behaviors include reading a book, raising a hand, hitting classmates, and complaining to the teacher.

Respondent behaviors are ones that are controlled by events that precede the behavior. For example, a light is presented and pupillary constriction occurs. Operant behaviors, on the other hand, are controlled by events that follow the behavior. These events are called the *consequences* of behavior. The word "consequences" might be confusing to some people because they associate the term with something negative. Actually, consequences can be positive or negative. If the consequences of a behavior are positive, the chances are that the behavior will recur at a high rate. Suppose a teacher consistently smiles at a student who says "hello" to him. Since most students enjoy their teacher's smiles, it is likely that the child will continue to say "hello" to the teacher in the future. On the other hand, a teacher might scold a student for something the youngster did wrong in the past, each time the student greets him. In this case the consequence is negative, and it is likely that the student will cease saying "hello" to the teacher in the future. The process by which the consequences of behavior increase or decrease the future rate of that behavior is known as *operant conditioning*.

Operant conditioning is but one technique available to the behavior modifier. At the present state of knowledge, however, operant-conditioning methods are the most thoroughly investigated and useful techniques which the behavior modifier can offer to educators. This book will therefore concentrate on behavior modification techniques which involve operant-conditioning procedures. At times, however, mention will be made of other techniques which are helpful in teaching desirable classroom behavior.

Operant conditioning can bring about an increase or decrease in student behavior. When a desirable behavior does not occur, or when it occurs too seldom, teachers will be concerned with the means by which they can bring about increases in behavior. This can often be accomplished with the operations discussed in the next section.

MEANS OF INCREASING THE RATE OF BEHAVIOR

POSITIVE REINFORCEMENT

The behavior modification procedure that is most commonly used in school studies is known as *positive reinforcement*. The process involves presenting a reward to a child after he performs a behavior. If the future rate of that behavior increases, positive reinforcement is said to have occurred. The reward is then considered a *positive reinforcer*. A positive-reinforcement procedure might consist of placing a star on a student's paper whenever he reaches 80 percent accuracy on a weekly spelling test. If the youngster's spelling accuracy increases over what it was before stars were used, the stars are considered positive reinforcers for spelling accuracy. If the student's spelling performance does not improve, the stars cannot be regarded as positive reinforcers. Similarly, if a pat on the back following a hand raise increases the rate of hand raising, the pat on the back can be considered a positive reinforcer.

In order for a reward to increase a behavior, certain conditions must be met. First, the reward must be delivered *contingent* on the desired behavior. In the case of positive reinforcement, this means that *if* the desired behavior occurs, *then* a reward is provided. Simply increasing a class's free time is unlikely to improve student behavior, unless the free time is delivered contingent upon an increase in the desired behavior.

A second important point is that a reinforcer should be delivered as soon as possible after the desired behavior occurs. If not, some other behavior may intervene and be reinforced instead. Thus, it is better for a teacher to walk around a classroom complimenting desirable behavior, than for a teacher to sit at his desk. A common error occurs when a teacher is interested in improving a student's attentiveness. The student may have been attentive for an hour, yet the teacher neglected to compliment her. The student later becomes disruptive and the teacher says, "Oh, Lydia, you have been so good today. Try not to misbehave now." In this case the compliment came right after the youngster misbehaved. Immediate reinforcement is most important in the early stages of learning. Once learning has progressed satisfactorily, delays in reinforcement are usually not harmful.

A third point is that an object or event may be a reinforcer for a person at one point in time, but not at another. Thus a student who has received a great deal of a consumable reinforcer at the beginning of the day, may not work for it at the end of the day; or a student who receives a great amount of a reinforcer at home, may not work for it, at all, in school; or a child's preferences for reinforcers may change over time, due to a variety of other, unidentified processes. Meanwhile a teacher should provide a sufficient amount of a reinforcer that a child finds it appealing, but not so much that he is quickly satiated.

Fourth, Egel (1981) found that when a teacher alternated three different reinforcers, students did better on an academic task and were on-task at a higher rate, than was the case when only one reinforcer was used.

Finally, there is no event that is rewarding to all children. Sometimes a teacher uses a single event as a reinforcer and all students work for it. At other times, she is not so fortunate and additional choices must be offered as reinforcers. Even an M&M lacks ubiquitous power and can melt in a teacher's hand, before a student deserves to have it placed in his mouth.

Tribble and Hall (1972) provided a successful example of a positive-reinforcement operation. The study involved John, a youngster who completed only a small portion of his daily math assignments. During Baseline$_1$ (a period of days in which no special procedures are used), the percentage of problems John completed each day never exceeded 25 percent, and his average for the fifteen days of Baseline$_1$ was only 21 percent (see Figure 1-1).

Following Baseline$_1$, Ms. Tribble told John that if he finished 60 percent of the assigned problems, she would mark a "+" on his paper; John could take papers with a "+" to his mother and exchange them for a "surprise." During the first day of the "Surprise at Home" stage, John completed 100 percent of his assignment; joy turned to disappointment, however, as John's performance deteriorated during the remaining days of the phase. Undismayed, Ms. Tribble tried again, this time with the knowledge that John could do the work if she could only keep him motivated. On day 20, she announced that if John completed his mathematics problems within twenty minutes of the beginning of the period, the entire class would go outside to play a game, and that John could be the engineer leading the "train" of students to the school playground. For the eleven days of "Engineer$_1$," John finished his entire assignment on all but one day. On many occasions John's classmates would cheer for him after he completed his assignment.

For scientific reasons, to be explained in more detail in Chapter 3, Ms. Tribble reinstated baseline conditions in the fourth phase of the study. During this period, John was no longer earning the extra free time for the class. For the five days of Baseline$_2$, John completed an average of 21 percent of the math problems. This decrease in behavior showed that the improvement that occurred during the Engineer$_1$ phase was due to the privileges John was able to earn for himself and his classmates. When games were again made contingent on John's finishing his work during Engineer$_2$, John completed 100 percent of the problems each day.

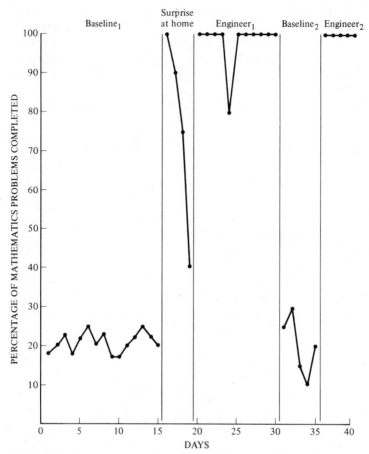

FIGURE 1-1 The percentage of arithmetic problems John completed on daily assignments. (*Adapted from A. Tribble and R. V. Hall, "Effects of Peer Approval on Completion of Arithmetic Assignments," in F. W. Clark, D. R. Evans, and L. A. Hamerlynck (eds.)* Implementing Behavioral Programs for Schools and Clinics: Third Banff International Conference. *Champaign, Ill.: Research Press, 1972, pp. 139-140. By permission of the publishers.)*

The positive reinforcer for completing assignments in the Tribble and Hall (1972) study was the opportunity to play games. The reinforcer was administered not only to John but to other members of the class. As a result, John's classmates provided additional reinforcement by applauding and praising him after he completed his arithmetic problems.

It should be pointed out that the first procedure that Tribble and Hall used was ineffective in improving John's performance. This is not surprising, since behavior modification techniques, like other techniques, sometimes fail to help a child overcome his difficulties. The important point is that when one procedure does not work, the teacher should attempt alternative techniques until an effective one is found.

Kazdin (1980) described various types of reinforcers and the characteristics of each. Three of the most prominent types are (1) food and other consumables, (2) social events, and (3) favored activities. Food is recommended on the basis of its great strength, particularly for children who reject social events as reinforcers. The effectiveness of food, of course, is affected by the degree to which an individual has been deprived of it. Therefore, if a particular type of food is an intended reinforcer, the teacher should attempt to limit a student's access to it at other times. Other considerations that Kazdin delineates are that delivery and consumption of food can disrupt behavior and that it can be cumbersome to deliver and carry. In addition, teachers must be concerned with student allergies and parental dietary preferences. Some teachers oppose the use of food on the basis that it is too primitive to use in classrooms. Yet, when an immediate and large change in behavior is called for, food or other consumables can be extremely useful. Willis, Hobbs, Kirkpatrick, and Manley (1975) found, for example, that rewarding students with a piece of candy for remaining in their seats greatly reduced disruptions on a school bus.

A second kind of reinforcer is a social reinforcer. Examples are compliments, pats on the back, nods, smiles, winks, and so on. Kazdin points out that advantages of social reinforcers are that they are easy to administer, can be delivered immediately, and require no preparation. Also they usually do not disrupt ongoing behavior.

A popular social-reinforcement technique consists of giving a disruptive student attention only when she is behaving properly. Thus, a teacher may walk up to a student when she is doing an assignment, whisper "You do nice work," smile at her, and squeeze her shoulder. When she is misbehaving, the teacher would ignore her. A study by Hall, Lund, and Jackson (1968) which successfully used this procedure found that it did not require that teachers give the students more attention. What was important was providing the attention for appropriate behavior, rather than for inappropriate behavior.

In spite of numerous demonstrations of social-reinforcement procedures, a study by White (1975) found that teachers seldom use such tactics. The study showed that in every grade after second, teachers used disapproval statements more than approval statements, and that teachers almost never complimented students for managerial-type behaviors. When students were complimented it was usually for academic work.

It may be that teachers do not compliment students more frequently because appropriate behavior does not call attention to itself. In such cases periodic reminders might be helpful. This was demonstrated in a study by Van Houten and Sullivan (1975) in which an audio cue was intermittently delivered through the school's public address system to three classrooms. When the teachers heard the sound they were to look around the room and praise students who were doing their work. In all three cases the teachers learned to use social reinforcement and retained their new skills even after cues were removed. Instead of using a public address system, teachers might find it more convenient to use an oven timer or a tape recorder to deliver audio cues.

Although praise and smiles are effective consequences for some students, other youngsters will become agitated when complimented or hugged. In these cases, a friendly conversation is probably a superior tactic to use. This is particularly true for children who have reached adolescence.

Some teachers are reluctant to use social reinforcers because they feel insincere about the process. Sometimes this problem is temporary, diminishing with experience. In other cases it might be helpful to practice in front of a mirror or to role play with a child who is well known to the teacher, but not a student of hers.

A third type of reinforcer is an activity reinforcer. Examples include extra free time, field trips, the opportunity to listen to records or to read a magazine, the privilege of being a classroom messenger, and so on. Many activity reinforcers are extremely powerful, yet are cost-free. In many cases students will never satiate on an activity reinforcer (for example, extra free time). Problems with activity reinforcers include the difficulty of delivering them immediately (for example, a field trip) and disruptions that occur in the transition between activities. Nevertheless, the great power of activity reinforcers makes them worth using. Givner and Graubard (1974) describe some means teachers can use to choose activity reinforcers. First they suggest observing a student and noting what he does frequently. High-frequency activities (for example, reading science-fiction stories) can often be used as reinforcers. In certain cases the activities are considered inappropriate in some classroom situations, but can be used as reinforcers if properly arranged. These include reading comics, talking with a particular student, and leaving the classroom.

Another procedure a teacher can use for identifying reinforcers is to note whether certain events consistently follow a particular behavior. Such events may be reinforcing the behavior and can be engineered to solve classroom problems. For example, a nursery school teacher may notice that he consistently picks up a youngster who cries. Picking up the youngster may reinforce crying behavior. In this case it would be better to pick her up when she is *not* crying.

Finally, teachers can ask students what they would like to work for. After requests for illegal or prohibitively expensive events are discarded, reasonable requests are often made. In many cases similar information can be obtained from parents and with questionnaires (Raschke, 1981).

NEGATIVE REINFORCEMENT

When a teacher uses a positive-reinforcement technique, a student performs a behavior and the teacher gives him something he likes. A second type of reinforcement procedure is known as *negative reinforcement*. This is an operation in which a student performs a behavior and the teacher removes something the student dislikes. That which is removed is known as a *negative reinforcer*. An example of negative reinforcement would involve students who work at a faster pace after their teacher states that she will relieve them of homework if they complete a certain assignment. The homework is the negative reinforcer. Another example of negative reinforcement would be a child who cries, "Uncle!" in order to escape the arm twisting of a classmate. In this case the arm twist is a negative reinforcer, since it increases the probability of the child yelling, "Uncle!"

Positive and negative reinforcement are similar in that both procedures result in an increase in the frequency of the target behavior. The difference between the two operations is that when positive reinforcement is programmed, a behavior will add something desirable (for example, extra recess, toys, or praise) to the environment. With a negative-reinforcement procedure, a behavior will remove something aversive from the environment (for example, a detention, a scowl, or an arm twist). The behavior performed in a negative-reinforcement operation allows a student to avoid or escape an unpleasant event.

Teachers should avoid the mistake of negatively reinforcing undesirable behaviors. For example, a student may frequently complain that his assignments are too difficult. If the teacher responds to the complaints by consistently reducing the difficulty of the assignments, she has negatively reinforced complaints (by making the task easier) and should expect complaints to increase. Similarly, a student may have frequent outbursts during an assignment he dislikes. The teacher may attempt to reduce outbursts by placing the youngster in a corner of the room. The student, however, may prefer isolation to doing the assignment. In this case, the teacher has negatively reinforced the youngster, by allowing him to avoid the work he dislikes. The teacher should then expect outbursts to occur at a high rate.

A common error is to consider negative reinforcement as an operation that produces undesirable behavior and positive reinforcement as an operation that produces desirable behavior. Actually either process can produce either type of behavior. Negative reinforcement can produce desirable behavior when a teacher informs a class that there will be no final examination in chemistry class for students whose prior average exceeds 85 percent. If the procedure is effective, the desired goal of improved performance on chemistry assignments has been achieved. On the other hand, positive reinforcement can produce undesirable behavior. A teacher, for example, might give a student access to a preferred activity whenever she cries. This process should strengthen the undesirable behavior of crying.

SHAPING

Reinforcing a behavior that has just occurred is an effective means of increasing the rate of that behavior. Teaching a new behavior, however, cannot be achieved by reinforcing it, since one cannot reinforce a behavior that does not exist. A procedure that *can* be used to teach a new behavior is known as *shaping*.

The shaping process involves reinforcing the existing behavior that most closely resembles the desired (that is, target) behavior. Once the original behavior is occurring dependably, the teacher only reinforces a behavior if it more closely resembles the target behavior than the previous behavior does. Progressively, behaviors that increasingly approximate the desired behavior are reinforced, until the student consistently emits the target behavior.

An example of shaping might involve a five-year-old girl who does not know how to draw a circle. Initially, the teacher might reinforce her if she draws any kind of line, for example, $\sim\!\!\curvearrowright$. Next the teacher might only reinforce the girl if she draws lines that come nearer to closing, for example, $)$. Next the requirement might be that the girl draw a figure that closes completely, such as, $\mathcal{S}\!)$. Later, the teacher might require that the figure be rounder, until the girl ultimately draws an acceptable circle. Each new behavior that approaches the target behavior is called a *successive approximation*.

Shaping a new behavior can be a difficult task. The process can be facilitated, however, by observing some rules. First, the starting point of a shaping program should be a behavior which the student can easily perform, even if it has only a slight resemblance to the target behavior.

Second, changes in behavioral requirements should be small enough that the student can perform them without too much difficulty. When students make too many errors at a given step or when they frequently become upset at a certain step, it is an indication that the change may be too great. In such a case, it might ultimately be necessary to find a step of intermediate difficulty.

Third, a student should repeat a successful step several times. There is no rule on how many times a student must repeat a step before moving on to a new one, but if a student is consistently succeeding at a certain step and appears relaxed, the signs are positive.

The importance of changing behavioral requirements in small units was clearly illustrated by Ayllon, Garber, and Pisor (1975). The study involved three educable mentally retarded youngsters who were given twenty minutes to complete math problems. It was suspected that they could complete the work in less time, perhaps in as little as five minutes. When the time limit was abruptly reduced to five minutes, however, their math performance deteriorated and the students exhibited undesirable emotional behaviors. Next, the students were again given twenty minutes to do their work and their performance returned to its original level. The next strategy was to gradually reduce the time limits to fifteen minutes, then to ten, and finally to five. With the gradual reduction in time limits, math performance increased markedly and adverse emotional responding did not occur.

Shaping procedures can be used to gradually increase the amount of time a student spends working productively. A study by Egner, Babic, and Kemel (1973) involved Brett, a seventh-grade boy, who seldom worked for more than a few minutes a period. During daily fifty-five minute reading- and language arts classes, Brett was initially given a short assignment. When he completed the assignment, he was permitted to engage in free-time tasks, such as leaving class for a drink, helping the teacher's aide staple papers, and so forth. When Brett was successful at this level, he was required to work for fifteen minutes and, when successful, had the rest of the period free. Gradually, the amount of time Brett had to be working increased, and the amount of free time decreased, according to the following schedule:

Days	Minutes of work time	Minutes of free time
1–8	30	25
9–35	35	20
36–37	40	15
38–45	50	5

By the end of the study Brett had been shaped into working fifty minutes for a five minute break.

It has been claimed (Miller, 1975) that all complex behaviors are acquired through accidental or intentional shaping. Included are playing an instrument, writing poetry, and riding a bike. Undoubtedly, programmed instruction textbooks use shaping principles, by having students begin at a level at which they are competent, prodding students with hints and questions, requiring student responses, and confirming correct answers.

FADING

In teaching a student to perform a behavior, a teacher might give the youngster detailed directions, show the student how to execute the response, give him hints as to what to do next, or physically guide him through the process. The aids a teacher provides to initiate the behavior are known as *prompts*. The use of prompts in the early stages of a teaching program is critical. Nevertheless, after a period of time, a teacher wants the student to perform the behavior with less assistance. In such cases the teacher can use the process of *fading*, which consists of the gradual removal of prompts.

A physical-education teacher could use fading to teach a girl to hit a baseball. Initially the teacher might instruct the student to hold the bat over her shoulder, bend her knees, and keep her eyes on the ball. As the youngster shows progress, he might drop one of the hints and only tell her to bend her knees and keep her eyes on the ball. As the student continues to progress, the teacher would drop the remaining prompts, until the student could hit the ball without his instructions.

Another example of fading involves a teacher who is reinforcing a student if he takes his seat within one minute of the beginning of class. Initially the teacher might make eye contact with the student, point to his seat, and remind him of the reinforcement program. Once his behavior improves, the teacher might only make eye contact and point to the seat. Later, eye contact alone could be used, until finally the student learns to go to his seat without prompting from the teacher.

There is a tendency to confuse fading and shaping. A major difference in the processes is that, in the case of fading, the behavior of interest remains the same while the conditions under which it occurs change. Thus, while the teacher gives the student fewer hints on how to hit a ball, the actual behaviors the child performs stay the same. In the case of shaping, the nature of the behavior itself changes as the student makes progress and approximates the target behavior. One element both processes have in common is the necessity to proceed slowly. Thus, prompts should be removed gradually in the case of fading, lest the behavior stop occurring.

Fading procedures can be used to teach children basic printing skills. In teaching a student to print the letter "A," a workbook might consist of the following exercises:

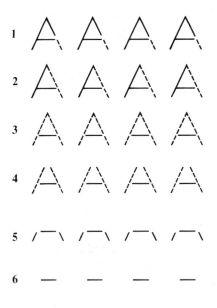

At each step the prompt is decreased slightly until the student can print the entire letter without assistance. If necessary the teacher could guide a student's hand in the early stages of learning and fade out the guidance as progress occurs.

Teachers typically use fading procedures to help students answer questions they are having difficulty with. For example, if a student had a problem recalling who the sixteenth president of the United States was, the teacher might give hints such as "His first name was Abraham," or "His initials were A.L." With success, such hints would be diminished. Sulzer and Mayer (1972) indicate that they used a similar procedure to teach a child with limited speech to identify items. Initially, the teacher would hold up an item such as a boat, and say "This is a boat." The child was asked to say boat and was reinforced if he did. Later, the teacher would hold up the boat and say "This is a bo——." Ultimately the student learned to say "boat" when the teacher simply held up a boat.

SCHEDULES OF REINFORCEMENT

A *continuous-reinforcement schedule* is an arrangement in which reinforcement follows every appropriate behavior. Some teachers probably feel that reinforcing each desirable behavior is a difficult, if not impossible, task. Fortunately, it is *not* necessary that a teacher use a continuous-reinforcement schedule in order to teach a student a new behavior or to maintain a behavior that already exists. When reinforcement follows only a portion of the desired behaviors, the arrangement is called an *intermittent-reinforcement* or *partial-reinforcement* schedule. In order to specify a schedule of reinforcement one must indicate the number of responses or the amount of time that must pass for a behavior to be reinforced.

Intermittent-reinforcement schedules are more representative of the conditions that exist in the natural environment than continuous-reinforcement schedules. A laborer is paid not for every appropriate behavior he performs, but for a series of behaviors at the end of a pay period. Certainly the behavior of people who fish or those who hitchhike persists in spite of a thin schedule of reinforcement. In school situations students are not reinforced every time they raise their hand or shoot a basketball.

There are some advantages in using intermittent-reinforcement schedules. First, since reinforcement is not delivered after every appropriate behavior, students are less likely to satiate on the reinforcer. Second, it takes less effort and is less expensive to reinforce *some* behaviors, rather than *all* behaviors. Finally, behaviors that experience an intermittent schedule of reinforcement continue occurring for longer, when reinforcement ceases, than behaviors experiencing continuous reinforcement. (The last point will be discussed in more detail under the topic of "Extinction.")

The four most popular schedules of intermittent reinforcement are: fixed-interval, variable-interval, fixed-ratio, and variable-ratio. When the two interval schedules are employed, a response is reinforced only after a certain amount of time has passed since the previous reinforced response.

The two ratio schedules deliver reinforcement after an individual emits a certain number of responses.

On a *fixed-interval* schedule, reinforcement is accessible at standard intervals of time. If a fixed interval of five minutes (FI5) is in effect, for example, reinforcement becomes available after exactly five minutes have elapsed since the last reinforced response. The first response that occurs after five minutes has passed is reinforced. Thus five minutes must elapse *and then* a response must occur in order to receive reinforcement. Following the response and the delivery of the reinforcer, a new five-minute cycle is begun. An individual who is exposed to an FI schedule eventually learns that responding before the time cycle has been completed does not lead to reinforcement. Thus, she ceases responding during the initial portion of the FI cycle, but responds very rapidly at the end of the cycle. This pattern of responding is known as a *fixed-interval scallop*. The long periods of inactivity during a fixed-interval schedule limit its usefulness.

A situation generating a fixed-interval pattern of responding is the practice of giving midterm and final examinations at set times to college students. At the beginning of the term there is little studying. As the midterm approaches the studying rate increases until it crescendos the night before the examination. In spite of vows to study at a steadier rate in the future, the exact pattern is repeated before the final examination. Another situation producing a fixed-interval scallop would involve a teacher who is told that her principal will watch her teach beginning at 1:00 P.M. Before noon she may look at her watch once an hour. Between noon and 12:45, she may look at her watch five times. From then on, she may check her watch every ten seconds.

An interval schedule which results in higher and more steady rates of behavior than the FI schedule is the *variable-interval (VI)* schedule. With a variable-interval schedule, the first response to occur after a period of time, which varies from one reinforcement to the next, is reinforced. If a variable-interval schedule of one minute (VI1) is in effect, for example, a reinforcer is available on the average of once a minute since the previous reinforced response. A VI1 schedule might consist of a sequence of reinforcers delivered for the first response to occur after 100, 2, 40, 60, 118, 20, and 80 seconds. (Note that the average interval is sixty seconds, or one minute.)

That is, the first reinforcer is available after 100 seconds has elapsed. The first time an individual responds after this period of time, he receives a reinforcer. The second reinforcer is available two seconds after the first reinforcer is delivered. The first response to occur after two seconds has elapsed will be reinforced. The third reinforcer is available forty seconds after the second reinforcer is delivered. Responses made before forty seconds have elapsed will not result in reinforcement, nor will they delay the availability of reinforcement; they will merely provide the individual with some exercise.

Since at least some responses are reinforced shortly after the previous reinforcement on a VI schedule, the pauses in responding associated with FI schedules are usually eliminated, and higher and steadier rates of responding generally develop. The game of musical chairs is played according to a VI schedule. Since a player is uncertain when the music will stop (making the reinforcer, in the form of an empty chair, available), he stays alert at all times. Similarly, the study patterns of college students would probably change radically if their professors gave "pop" quizzes (a VI schedule), rather than announcing the dates of midterm and final examinations (an FI schedule). In areas of the country in which the time of mail delivery varies from one day to the next, individuals who find mail reinforcing can sometimes be seen checking their mailboxes numerous times each day.

A study by Saudargas, Madsen, and Scott (1977) showed the superiority of VI schedules over FI schedules. Their study involved third graders who initially brought home a report every Friday (FI) indicating how much work they had completed the previous week. The reports also included comments on the quality of the work. In the next condition, a portion of the students was randomly chosen at the end of each day (VI) to receive a home report on work quantity and quality. The VI procedure resulted in substantially better student output than the FI procedure. Thus, teachers can enhance the excellent practice of frequent home reports by conducting them on an unpredictable schedule.

When the ratio schedules of reinforcement are used, an individual is reinforced for the number of responses she makes. A *fixed-ratio (FR)* schedule specifies the exact number of responses a person must perform to receive reinforcement. This number stays the same from one reinforcement to the next. With an FR5 schedule, for example, an individual is reinforced for every five responses she makes. This is similar to the practice of piecework in which a farm worker receives a certain amount of money each time she fills a basket with peaches. A teacher is using an FR10 schedule of reinforcement if she lets a student accumulate a minute of free time for every ten math problems he completes correctly. Individuals who are exposed to FR schedules of reinforcement tend to respond at a high rate, once they start responding. It has been found, however, that with large FR schedules, for example, FR50, people will often cease responding for a period of time following reinforcement (apparently taking a break before the long haul ahead). The decrease in response rate following a reinforcement on an FR schedule is called a *post-reinforcement pause*. The pauses are usually of shorter duration than those which occur on FI schedules.

The fourth type of schedule is the *variable-ratio (VR)* schedule. A VR schedule delivers reinforcement after an individual makes a certain number of responses, which varies from one reinforcement to the next. On a VR15 schedule, for example, reinforcement follows an average of one out of fifteen responses. Reinforcers may be separated from each other by 20, 1, 29, 10, 2, and 28 responses, but on the average one out of fifteen responses will be reinforced. (Note that the average of 20, 1, 29, 10, 2, and

28 is 15.) Hence, the first reinforcer occurs after twenty responses. The second reinforcer occurs after one more response is made. The third reinforcer occurs after an additional twenty-nine responses are made, and so on. An example of a VR schedule is betting that a head will come up when a coin is flipped. In this case, a VR2 schedule is in effect, and the bettor is reinforced on the average of one out of every two coin flips. VR schedules eliminate the post-reinforcement pauses which occur on FR schedules, and produce the highest and steadiest rates of behavior of the four intermittent reinforcement schedules discussed in the present section.

Miller (1975) points out that it is sometimes difficult to determine whether interval or ratio schedules are operating in everyday situations. The key, he points out, is whether the person controls how quickly she can earn a reinforcer. If a high rate of response produces a reinforcer more rapidly, a ratio schedule is in effect. If a high rate of responding does not lead to more rapid reinforcement, an interval schedule is operating. Thus, teacher paychecks are controlled by interval schedules, since teachers receive their pay at the same time, regardless of how well they have taught their students, since the previous pay period. The fact that interval schedules result in less productivity has obvious implications for education.

Teachers may wonder what relevance schedules of reinforcement have to classroom management. Admittedly, reinforcement schedules are difficult to implement in most classroom situations. Perhaps the points for a teacher to note are that it is usually possible to employ behavior modification procedures effectively by reinforcing only a portion of the correct behaviors, and that a child should be reinforced according to the number of appropriate behaviors he makes, rather than the passage of time. Also, it is better to reinforce behavior on an unpredictable rather than a predictable schedule.

CONDITIONED AND TOKEN REINFORCEMENT

The types of reinforcers mentioned earlier have varied from candy treats to teacher smiles. It is probably apparent to most readers that food reinforcers are different from social reinforcers such as smiles and praise. The distinction between the two types of reinforcers is the source of their reinforcing capacity, with some reinforcers classified as unconditioned reinforcers and others as conditioned reinforcers. An *unconditioned* reinforcer is one whose ability to reinforce behavior is *independent* of an association with other reinforcers. Such reinforcers are also called *primary* reinforcers. Examples of unconditioned reinforcers include food when an individual is hungry and liquid refreshment when one is thirsty. The ability of food and liquids to reinforce behavior is automatic when conditions are appropriate.

A conditioned reinforcer is one whose ability to reinforce behavior *results* from an association with other reinforcers. In order to establish a neutral event as a conditioned reinforcer, it is necessary that the event occur before or during the time an already established reinforcer is present. With frequent pairings of the two events, the neutral event becomes a conditioned reinforcer.

Praise is a commonly used reinforcer which acquires its ability to modify behavior through frequent association with other reinforcers. The process may take place when a parent often compliments his child for finishing a meal and then offers her dessert. If this combination of events occurs a sufficient number of times, praise becomes a conditioned reinforcer. Similarly, a teacher can establish praise as a reinforcer by often complimenting a student's academic achievements and then giving him the opportunity to perform a favored activity.

There is a tendency to regard conditioned reinforcers as something less than "real" reinforcers. In fact, conditioned reinforcers are a potent and important source of reinforcement, and teachers should always attempt to establish conditioned reinforcers for their students. This can be done by praising, smiling at, and making physical contact with children at the same time they are being awarded treats and privileges. Once such social events are associated with established reinforcers, they become conditioned reinforcers; it then becomes possible for teachers to withdraw privileges and treats as reinforcers and to maintain student progress with social reinforcers alone. This, of course, is desirable beyond classroom considerations, since students will eventually enter a world in which they work for conditioned reinforcers such as approval and money.

Some conditioned reinforcers are associated with many other reinforcers. Money, for example, is associated with treats, toys, and admission to favored events. Praise too can be associated with many other events if it has been paired with classroom privileges, staying up late, or a desired present. A conditioned reinforcer that is associated with a variety of other reinforcers is known as a *generalized* reinforcer.

A generalized reinforcer which can be effective in classroom management and instruction is the *token* reinforcer. A token reinforcer can be a poker chip, a checkmark in a notebook or on the chalkboard, a ticket, a gold star, or a smiley face. Tokens alone have little reinforcing power. They attain reinforcing value, however, by being exchangeable for a variety of items or events which are reinforcing. These items or events are called *back-up* reinforcers. Thus, a student may earn a point every time she reads a sentence correctly, and exchange the ten points she earns one day for five minutes of listening to the record player.

A token reinforcement system bears many resemblances to the monetary system in which an employee works and spends his money. Thus, an appropriately functioning token system requires that a teacher specify the behaviors to be performed, the number of tokens that will be provided for each behavior, and the cost of each back-up reinforcer.

There are several advantages in using a token reinforcement system over alternative reinforcement systems. First, since tokens can be exchanged for a variety of other reinforcers, it is less likely that children will satiate on the reinforcers than is the case when a single item or event is used. Second, tokens can be delivered immediately after a behavior occurs, as opposed to consumables or activities which are difficult to administer immediately. Third, tokens do not disrupt the classroom as do many other reinforcers. Fourth, token systems permit the use of expensive reinforcers (for example, a student can earn tokens for several weeks, and exchange the tokens for a trip to a ball game.) Finally, token systems have a tendency to be more powerful than social reinforcement and feedback (discussed in the next section) systems.

Ms. Kathleen Bodnar (Bodnar, 1974) used a token reinforcement procedure to reduce talk outs in a special-education classroom. As indicated in Figure 1-2, the average number of talk outs exceeded 130 during

FIGURE 1-2 The number of talking-out instances by 12 EMR children. (*From K. Bodnar, "Reducing Talk Outs in an MR class with a Token Reinforcement System." Unpublished manuscript, Temple University, 1974. By permission of the author.*)

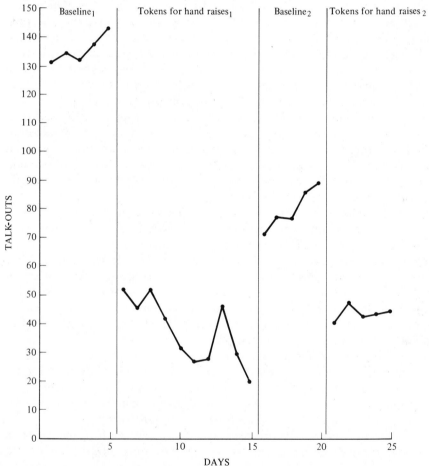

Baseline₁. In the second phase of the study Ms. Bodnar posted a chart listing the twelve most desirable jobs in the classroom and the number of points each would cost, as follows:

Jobs	Points
Washing boards	35
Cleaning chalkboard erasers	30
Taking trash can around	30
Emptying trash can	25
General cleanup	20

Next Ms. Bodnar taped a 3 x 5 inch card to each student's desk. If a child raised his hand and waited to be acknowledged before speaking, the teacher praised him warmly and gave him a star. (It probably would have been easier, but less personal, to keep one sheet at the teacher's desk and make check marks next to the appropriate student's name.) Only reasonable responses were rewarded, thereby preventing children from raising their hands for the sole purpose of attaining a star. As can be seen in Figure 1-2, talk outs declined to fifty-one during the first day in which tokens were used. Talk outs generally declined during the next nine days of the procedure and averaged thirty-six for the phase. During the five days of Baseline₂ there was an increasing trend in the number of talk outs with an average of seventy-eight per day. When tokens were again used in the final phase, the number of talk outs was relatively stable each day, averaging forty-three.

Token procedures can also be used to increase academic performance. Price and D'Ippolito (1975) set up the following program to improve a boy's reading skills:

1 token for every sentence read without errors

1 token for sounding out a word without teacher assistance

2 tokens for every correctly written response on his work pad

5 tokens for completing the reading of each page in the textbook

10 tokens for answering eight or more of the teacher's ten comprehension questions

The cost of back-up reinforcers was:

50 tokens for fifteen minutes of free time

100 tokens for a grab from a grab bag containing toys and trinkets

200 tokens for time to play any game of his choice with the teacher and two classmates

300 tokens for a Coke break

The procedure produced a substantial improvement in reading performance.

Although token reinforcement procedures are powerful, they frequently contain the problems that the bookkeeping is complex and the cost in teacher's time quite high. Also token procedures can be financially expensive and difficult to transfer to more naturally occurring reinforcers. For such reasons teachers may find the feedback procedures to be discussed in the next section a more reasonable means for modifying student behavior.

FEEDBACK

When a teacher delivers a reinforcer to a student, two functions are served. First, it motivates the student to work harder. Second, it informs the student that she performed a behavior correctly. A student who receives a reinforcer after a teacher grades a language arts answer, for example, realizes that her response is correct. The second function is known as "feedback"—information on the appropriateness of a behavior.

There is a great deal of evidence that feedback alone can improve student behavior. That is, simply informing a student that his answers are correct may be sufficient to improve his behavior. It is not always necessary to include a tangible, activity, or social reinforcer in the operation. The form of feedback can be a head nod, a statement, a note with relevant information, or a publicly displayed graph or chart. The fact that feedback alone can modify behavior raises the question of whether some behavior modification procedures have unnecessarily programmed rewards, such as candy (Drabman and Lahey, 1974).

A number of behavior modification studies have used feedback alone to improve student performance. Gross and Drabman (1979), for example, wanted to increase the participation in singing activities of preschool mentally retarded children. The teacher informed the youngsters that any child who took part in the activity would have his or her picture posted underneath a "Super Stars" poster. Their participation increased to 78 percent, as compared to 50 percent during baseline. Drabman and Lahey (1974) dealt with a ten-year-old girl, described by the principal as the most disruptive in the class. During social studies class the teacher used a feedback procedure to improve her classroom deportment. Four times during each class, a timer rang. At these times the teacher went up to the girl and whispered a rating from zero to ten, depending on how well behaved the student was. The procedure reduced disruptiveness to one-third of its baseline level. Finally, Fink and Carnine (1975) found that when students received a note indicating how many errors they made on math work sheets and then plotted the data on a graph attached to their desks, the number of errors was significantly below that which occurred during baseline.

There are a number of other ways in which teachers can use feedback procedures. Sometimes a teacher will be privately discussing a student's answer with him, when she notices that two other students have raised their hands. Rather than ignore the students, she should nod her head at each youngster and then say, "Michelle is next, and then it is Mike's turn." Failing to do this, the teacher may find the students leaving their seats for her attention or becoming otherwise disruptive. In another case, a teacher may ask a student the answer to a complex social studies question. The student might give the *correct* answer and have the teacher ask "Why do you say that?" It would be better if the teacher first informed the student that the answer was correct and then asked for an explanation. In the absence of feedback that her answer was correct, the student might interpret the teacher's question as an indication that she had responded incorrectly and, therefore, change her answer.

Feedback can be used in teacher training and supervision. A supervisor can sit in the back of a classroom and nod to the teacher when he correctly responded to a student. Supervisors can also take data on some aspect of a teacher's performance and present the figures to him at the end of the period (Piper and Elgart, 1979), or even hand slips of paper with relevant information to the teacher during the period (Parsonson, Baer, and Baer, 1974).

In order to be successful in the work market, it is not sufficient that an individual be able to perform a task accurately. It is also essential that the task be performed with reasonable speed (for example, typing). Van Houten (1980a, b) has shown how feedback can be used to deal with this important problem. The procedures he developed can be applied *without* great difficulty, to a number of academic behaviors, across all grade levels, and have been remarkably effective. Outlined below is a synopsis of the technique. In a given situation only a portion of the steps may have to be employed:

1 When new materials are presented, the teacher instructs students on how to do the task. Students then practice the procedure until they are sufficiently accurate. If the students make too many errors the teacher shows them a correct model and leaves the model in front of them.

2 Once the students have achieved sufficient accuracy, the teacher provides the students with the materials and prompts them to work.

3 To increase their work rate, the teacher times the students to see how much work they can complete in a set amount of time.

4 It is important that papers be graded immediately. This can be done by having the students in their classrooms grade the papers. To prevent cheating, the teacher can have the students do the assignments in red ink, put their pens away, and then have the students correct the papers in another medium, such as black pencil. At a later time the teacher can

spot check the papers and reward the class for accurate and honest scoring.

5 Next, the teachers should publicly post the student scores, no later than the next day. The chart should contain the names of the students, each day's score, and the highest score achieved so far for each student. The object for the students is to beat their *own* previous high. When a student exceeds a previous high, the score can be entered in a new color, or otherwise noted. The teacher can also note the scores and new highs for the class as a whole. If public posting with student names causes problems, students can be given code numbers or have their own charts at their own desks.

6 When students reach new highs, teachers should praise the students and appoint class captains to do the same.

7 If students are reaching their goals, the teacher can move them on to the next level. If not, further instruction and practice may be necessary.

A chart for a program to increase the rate at which students do an academic task in a given period of time might appear as follows. The data may represent the number of math facts done correctly per minute. Highlighted numbers are new best scores.

Name	Day 1	Day 2	Day 3	Day 4	Day 5	Day 6
Marie	29	28	**33**	**37**	36	**42**
Tony	17	16	**18**	**22**	22	19
Tommy	36	**38**	**42**	41	40	**45**
Kevin	•	•	•	•	•	•
Lee	•	•	•	•	•	•
Lynn	•	•	•	•	•	•
•						
•						
Class	892	**917**	**940**	938	**980**	970

The procedures can also be adapted to a management problem. A chart could be placed on an individual's desk to represent his daily performance, or in front of the entire group to represent the number of misbehaviors for the entire class, viz., a program to reduce a class disruption:

Day 1	Day 2	Day 3	Day 4	Day 5
62	**60**	**50**	51	**42**

Highlighted numbers represent a new best score for class misbehaviors.

Feedback procedures are often not as effective as token programs. Nevertheless, the effectiveness of feedback can be enhanced by delivery which is immediate and contains precise, quantitative information. Given the ease and low cost of operation, feedback is probably a greatly underused technique.

MEANS OF DECREASING THE RATE OF BEHAVIOR

Although educators are greatly concerned with means of teaching new behaviors, there are times when they find it necessary to decrease the rate of unacceptable student behaviors. Teachers who do not have behavior modification skills often must resort to sending disobedient children to the principal, demanding parent-teacher conferences, or referring students for psychological examinations in the hope that an alternative placement will be recommended.

Teachers with behavior modification skills, on the other hand, are usually able to deal directly with disruptive behavior and thereby help both their students and themselves. The present section will describe several procedures that teachers can use to obtain classroom control.

USING REINFORCEMENT TO DECREASE BEHAVIOR

Reinforcement has been described as a procedure to increase the rate of behavior. Therefore, it may seem strange that reinforcement is also listed as a technique to decrease behavior. Nevertheless, reinforcement can indirectly decrease behavior by rewarding a student for lowering the frequency at which he emits an undesirable behavior or by rewarding him for performing a behavior that is incompatible with the inappropriate behavior.

There are times when a teacher does not wish to eliminate a behavior, but merely to reduce its frequency. This would be the case when a student makes too many requests to leave the classroom for drinks of water or too frequently asks the teacher for assistance. In such a case a teacher can use a "differential reinforcement of low rate of response *(DRL)*" schedule. A DRL schedule provides reinforcement to a student for keeping the rate of his behavior at, or below, a certain level. An example of a DRL schedule would be offering a student the opportunity to be the classroom messenger if he talked out five or fewer times in a given morning. It is also possible to use a DRL schedule in a progressive manner to completely eliminate a behavior. For example, Dietz and Repp (1973) did an experiment in which high school girls could earn a free class on Fridays if they kept their rate of off-task verbalizations below a specified level during the first four days of each week. Figure 1-3 shows that once the girls were successful at one DRL level, the criterion was progressively lowered until the problem was eliminated.

A more stringent procedure for decreasing behavior entails the use of a "differential reinforcement of other *(DRO)*" behavior schedule. With a DRO schedule an individual must completely refrain from performing a behavior in order to receive a reinforcer. A common means by which DRO schedules have functioned involves reinforcing a student for not performing a behavior for a period of time. For example, a teacher might be interested in eliminating thumb sucking and employs a DRO 10 (minute) schedule of reinforcement. In most cases this means that if a student does not suck her thumb for ten minutes, the teacher reinforces her and a new ten-minute cycle is started (usually with the help of an oven timer). If she sucks her thumb before the ten minutes pass, she receives no reinforcer and a new ten-minute cycle is begun.

Homer and Peterson (1980) point out that a superior means of employing a DRO schedule is to use different time intervals, depending on

FIGURE 1-3 The number of inappropriate verbal behaviors per hour under baseline and different DRL conditions from a class of senior high school girls. In the first DRL condition there had to be six or fewer verbalizations, in the second DRL condition there had to be four or fewer, in the third, two or fewer, and in the final condition, there could be none. (*Adapted from S. M. Dietz and A.C. Repp, "Decreasing Classroom Misbehavior through the Use of DRL Schedules of Reinforcement,"* Journal of Applied Behavior Analysis, 6, *p. 461, 1973. Copyright 1973 by the Society for the Experimental Analysis of Behavior, Inc.*)

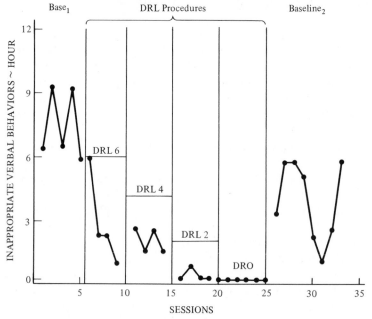

whether the individual performed the target behavior. For example, if the student did not suck her thumb and received a reinforcer, the DRO interval could be set for ten minutes. If she did suck her thumb, the next interval could be set for a longer period of time (for example, 15 minutes). They also suggest that DRO schedules can be made more effective by using a variety of reinforcers. A third factor that is important in using a DRO schedule is that a program be started with a brief time cycle. Longer cycles can be reached through a progressive process (for example, five minutes for a few days, then ten minutes, and so on).

Both DRL and DRO schedules have the advantage that they are constructive, noncontroversial procedures for reducing behavior. In addition there is a tendency for the procedures *not* to produce adverse side effects from students who experience them. A difficulty with both procedures, however, is that students are being reinforced for *any* behaviors other than the target behavior. Thus, a student on a DRO program for talk outs is reinforced for performing any behavior other than a talk out. The problem is that he may be performing behaviors *worse* than the target behavior (such as hitting others) and be reinforced for them. Teachers who use DRL and DRO schedules must be aware of this problem and change their program if they find that they are reinforcing undesirable behaviors.

A procedure used to decrease a behavior and at the same time require that an appropriate behavior be occurring is called *reinforcement of an incompatible behavior*. This means that a teacher reinforces a specific, desirable behavior that cannot coexist with the undesirable behavior. Hence if a teacher is concerned that her students are too frequently out of their seats, she might reinforce them when they are in their seats. Or, if a student spends too much time by himself, she can reinforce him when he is socially interacting with his classmates. Ayllon and Roberts (1974) used a procedure of reinforcing incompatible behavior with a classroom of thirty-eight fifth graders who were frequently disruptive. Rather than place a consequence on the disruptive behavior, the authors reinforced the students' reading behavior. There resulted both an improvement in reading performance and a near elimination of the disruptive behavior. Apparently it was more worthwhile for students to earn reinforcers through reading, than to misbehave.

It is possible to combine all three reinforcement procedures to produce an ideal program for eliminating a behavior. Suppose an inappropriate behavior is occurring at a high rate. A teacher could start to reduce it with a DRL procedure that is gradually made more stringent as progress occurs. When the DRL procedure reduces the behavior to a low level, the teacher could employ a DRO schedule that provides reinforcers for any behavior except the target response. Once the student is consistently receiving reinforcement on the DRO schedule, the teacher could reinforce a desirable behavior that is incompatible with the inappropriate behavior.

EXTINCTION

Another procedure for reducing the frequency of a behavior is to discontinue the reinforcement that follows the behavior. When the behavior decreases to the levels that existed before reinforcement was provided (not necessarily to zero), *extinction* has taken place.

Extinction is a process that affects individuals in their everyday dealings. People will stop putting money into a vending machine that doesn't work and will cease patronizing a store that does not carry their favorite items. Similarly, teachers will ignore students who irritate or interrupt them. At times, teachers will inadvertently and improperly use extinction by ignoring students who are working industriously.

Extinction refers to the discontinuation of any reinforcer—be it food, token, or attention—following a behavior. Nevertheless, the procedures have most often been used in classrooms when it was suspected that the attention a teacher showed to a student for misbehaving accounted for his inappropriate behavior. In these cases, the procedure involves ignoring the student's unacceptable behavior. One example of extinction might involve a preschool teacher who has responded to a child's temper tantrums in the past by ministering to the youngster's needs. An application of extinction would be to pay *no* attention to the child when he was having a tantrum, but rather to continue teaching in the usual manner. In another case, a high school teacher may have had a history of admonishing students not to use profanity in class. The teacher may surmise that the attention she is giving to the problem is responsible for the behavior. Remediation would then consist of carrying out teaching duties as if the problem behavior had not happened each time profanity did, in fact, occur. In both cases, extinction can only be considered to have occurred if the behavior decreased in rate.

An example of extinction was provided in a remarkable study by Wolf, Birnbrauer, Williams, and Lawler (1965). Laura, the student in the study, was a nine-year-old mentally retarded girl who vomited almost every day in class. Drug therapy proved ineffective in alleviating the problem. Whenever Laura vomited on her dress, the teacher dismissed her from class and sent her to the dormitory, where she was cleaned and comforted by the aides. The authors hypothesized that the child's vomiting was due to the possibility that the dormitory might contain more reinforcers for Laura than the classroom. Thus, it was considered feasible that vomiting was an operant (that is, voluntary) behavior which was reinforced by placement in the dormitory. Wolf et al. (1965) tested their suspicion by having the teacher ignore Laura whenever she vomited in class. During the extinction procedure, Laura had to remain in class regardless of the amount of vomit that accumulated on her dress. For the first twenty-nine days of extinction, vomiting occurred seventy-eight times. On one day, twenty-one episodes were recorded. Beginning with day 30, however, vomiting ceased entirely and stayed at the zero level for a period of more than fifty days.

Before ignoring behavior, teachers should be aware of some characteristics of the extinction process. First, a behavior undergoing extinction decreases slowly in rate. Thus, teachers should not use the procedure unless they can afford to tolerate a gradual change in behavior. Second, in many cases, when reinforcers no longer follow a behavior, the behavior first occurs at a greater rate before it diminishes. This process, known as *extinction burst*, could occur, for example, when a student interrupts a teacher who is no longer attending to his intrusions. In response to this, the youngster may interrupt his teacher at an even greater rate, before he gives up. If a teacher relents during this period, she will be reinforcing a more unfavorable level of the behavior. Perhaps this information will help teachers to endure the storm before the lull. Meanwhile, it should be recognized that extinction is not for the weak.

A third characteristic of extinction is known as *spontaneous recovery*. This is a process in which a behavior that has apparently disappeared through extinction, suddenly reappears. If the behavior is ignored it usually diminishes again in a short period of time. Nevertheless, teachers may not be prepared for the recurrence of the behavior and might reinforce it again. In such cases, the behavior can quickly return to its previous high level.

In addition to being aware of the characteristics of extinction described above, teachers should be cognizant of some problems in conducting the extinction operation. First, the procedure must be carried out with great consistency, since even occasional reinforcement may cause the behavior to recur at a high rate. This will often mean that peers must participate in the program, since they may be reinforcing the undesired behavior in some manner. Reinforcing students for their cooperation might facilitate their participation in ignoring the behavior. Second, it can be difficult to determine exactly which event is reinforcing a behavior. A teacher may suspect that his attention is maintaining a behavior, only to find that withdrawing his attention does not reduce the level of the behavior. Identifying the reinforcer to be withdrawn can be a trial-and-error process that is time consuming. A third problem is that some behaviors may themselves be reinforcing. Maintenance of these behaviors would be independent of additional sources of reinforcement. For example, if a teacher ignores a pair of students who are frequently conversing with each other at inappropriate times, her extinction procedure will probably fail because the students' conversation is itself reinforcing. In such cases, reinforcing nontalking behavior may solve the teacher's problem. A fourth difficulty is that some behaviors may be too dangerous to ignore (for example, behaviors that result in damage to self, others, or property). Such behaviors require direct teacher intervention. Finally, when some students see that their classmates are performing inappropriate behaviors without experiencing adverse consequences, they may imitate the misbehaviors.

In spite of many problems associated with extinction, its use should be considered by teachers, particularly since the process does not involve the use of aversive consequences. When using extinction, teachers should prepare themselves and others for the possibility that an extinction burst can occur or that students experiencing extinction may become angry or aggressive. The failure to prepare others for these possibilities can result in embarrassment and a lack of cooperation. Teachers should also be certain that there are no safety problems before using extinction. Last, it is extremely important that if teachers use extinction for an undesirable behavior, they also reinforce a desirable behavior. This should enhance the speed of extinction and prevent some of the problems associated with the process.

Resistance to extinction refers to the number of responses an individual makes once reinforcement no longer follows the behavior. A discovery which the reader may find surprising is that behaviors which have been learned on an intermittent-reinforcement schedule result in greater resistance to extinction than do behaviors which have been learned on a continuous-reinforcement schedule. Therefore, if a teacher wants a student to continue to perform a certain behavior (for example, study behavior) after reinforcement has been discontinued, it would appear that an intermittent-reinforcement schedule would be preferable to a continuous-reinforcement schedule. On the other hand, learning is generally more rapid with continuous- rather than intermittent-reinforcement schedules.

These findings produce a slight dilemma for a teacher who is trying to decide how often to reinforce a certain behavior. The solution to the problem is to initially reinforce the desired behavior as often as possible. After the desired behavior is well established, however, the teacher should use an intermittent-reinforcement schedule in order to increase the durability of the behavior.

PUNISHMENT

The reinforcement and extinction procedures described above are noncontroversial, constructive techniques for reducing the frequency of behavior. Educators and parents will typically not object to applying the tactics when management problems occur. Both procedures suffer from one main deficiency, however—they often do not work. In cases where they do work, they frequently work too slowly to be of practical value.

There *is* a class of procedures that acts more reliably and quickly to decrease the frequency of behaviors. These are *punishment* procedures. One might expect that the identification of procedures that can be used to diminish undesirable behaviors would be a cause for rejoicing. Such has not been the case. Instead, people respond suspiciously and reluctantly when the question of using punishment arises. In many cases a proposed punishment procedure is rejected and is not replaced with a feasible alternative.

It is not surprising that people react negatively to the notion of punishment. Popular connotations of punishment include corporal abuse, excessive detentions, and dunce caps. There will be no effort made here to defend such tactics; indeed they should be eliminated from school practices. Nevertheless, there are punishment techniques that do not involve physical abuse and that subject students to little, or no, public embarrassment. These procedures can be effectively and humanely used in classroom management.

My position is as follows: Given the choice of reinforcement or punishment, teachers should use reinforcement. When reinforcement proves ineffective, or appears unreasonable, because of the severity of the problem, punishment procedures should be considered. When punishment procedures are used, it is critical that they be applied in accordance with research indicating how their effectiveness can be maximized. That is, if punishment is going to be used, it should be used correctly. Once punishment has proved effective, teachers should attempt to substitute other tactics to maintain the improved behavior.

There have been a number of efforts to define punishment. Azrin and Holz (1966) proposed that punishment was a process in which the consequence of a behavior reduces the future rate of that behavior. Thus, if a teacher reduces a class's free time for talking out during study time and the future rate of talking out diminishes, loss of free time can be considered a punisher. If talking out does not decrease, loss of free time is not a punisher. Van Houten (1983) points out that a problem with this definition is that it does not take into account the relativity of punishment. That is, a given consequence will serve as a punisher only if it represents a less appealing condition than the one which existed during baseline. Thus, earning $10 an hour would be a punisher for someone who has been earning $15 an hour, but a reinforcer for someone who has been earning $5 an hour. Van Houten defines punishment as "an environmental change following a behavior that reduces the future rate of that behavior." He further states that for the sake of completeness, "it is necessary to specify the baseline and intervention conditions."

Punishment can take either of two forms. It can involve the application of an aversive consequence, such as requiring a student to repeatedly perform a task she does not like. Or, it can involve the withdrawal of a favored event, such as the opportunity to take part in free play. In either case, the consequences must decrease the rate of the target behavior in order to be considered a punisher.

Van Houten (1983) describes the factors that influence the effectiveness of punishment, as follows: First, the more intense the punisher, the greater the decrease in behavior. Obviously, the application of this fact has some limitations due to humane considerations. Nevertheless, it should be understood that when a punisher is delivered at full strength, it is more effective than when its intensity is gradually increased. When a punisher is gradually increased in intensity an individual may adapt to it and require a more intense punisher than was originally necessary. On the other hand, when an intense punisher is used and shows its effectiveness, it is often possible to switch to a less intense punisher and maintain the decrease in behavior.

Another factor influencing the effectiveness of punishment is the opportunity to avoid it. If a student can make up an excuse or lie to get out of punishment, the procedure is likely to be ineffective. Third, the more immediate the punishment, the greater the reduction of behavior. In accordance with this it is better to punish a behavior that occurs early in a series of behaviors than one that occurs late in the series. Thus, it is better to punish a student for name-calling than to wait until a fight erupts and then punish fighting behavior. Punishment is most effective if it follows all occurrences of the target behavior. Since continuous punishment also leads to quick extinction, once punishment ceases, it might be best to start a program with continuous punishment and then shift to an intermittent punishment schedule.

Reinforcement factors also influence the punishment process. Perhaps the most important, and often disregarded issue with respect to punishment, is that when a teacher applies punishment to one behavior, she should also reinforce a desired behavior. By using reinforcement in this manner there will usually be a quicker and greater decrease in the undesired behavior. It will also allow a teacher to use a less intense punisher without losing effectiveness. Thus, a teacher might reprimand a student for calling out in class, but she should also inform the student to raise his hand when he wishes to be called on, and then praise him when he does so. Or, if a teacher deprives a student of art time for not completing a homework assignment, she can add to the art time when improvement occurs.

Analagous to the situation for reinforcers, punishers can be unconditioned or conditioned. *Unconditioned* punishers reduce behavior independently of an association with other punishers. *Conditioned* punishers acquire their suppressive powers as a result of an association with other punishers. Suppose a teacher consistently warns a child to cease misbehaving or else lose physical-education time. As long as the warning is sometimes backed by the actual loss of physical-education time, it will become a conditioned punisher. As such, the warning will decrease behavior. On the other hand, if teachers make unreasonable warnings or threats (such as, "If you don't stop that, I will cut your gizzard out."), they will find such verbalizations ineffective.

A major criticism of punishment procedures is that they lead to adverse side effects, that is, they may produce undesirable changes in behaviors that were not the target for modification. Newsom, Favell, and Rincover (1983) reviewed literature on this topic. They found evidence that punishment is indeed associated with some undesirable side effects. One problem is the exhibition of emotional behavior such as crying, screaming, and fussing; another is aggression directed toward either the individual who administered the punishment or toward another individual who is not responsible for the difficulty (scapegoat). A third problem is that a punished child may avoid a teacher or school that has programmed punishment for her (for example, by playing hooky). In addition, punishing one behavior may lead to the substitution of other, perhaps even more undesirable, behaviors.

Newsom et al. (1983) stipulate that although such problems have occurred at times, their occurrence is relatively rare. They also indicate that such side effects tend to be short lived or respond readily to treatment. They further report that punishment procedures have also been associated with a number of *positive* side effects. For example, a punishment program that eliminates a student's aggressing toward peers may be associated with improved social relations. The most critical point of the review is that adverse side effects are least likely to occur in punishment programs that also contain a component that reinforces appropriate behavior. Thus, a student is less likely to become upset after being punished for performing an unacceptable behavior if he is reinforced for an alternative, acceptable behavior. Likewise, a student will not avoid a setting in which he is sometimes punished, if he is frequently reinforced for appropriate behaviors in the same setting. Finally, a student will not substitute an inappropriate behavior for a punished behavior, if he is being taught, through reinforcement, the correct way to behave.

Punishment should not be confused with negative reinforcement since the procedures have the opposite effect on behavior. In punishment an individual ceases performing a behavior in order to avoid an unpleasant consequence; in negative reinforcement an individual increases the performance of a behavior in order to avoid (or escape) an unpleasant consequence.

Four types of punishment techniques are in use in classroom management—reprimands, response cost, time out, and overcorrection. A discussion of each follows:

Reprimands The most common and *noncontroversial* form of punishment is the *reprimand*. Van Houten and Doleys (1983) indicate that a reprimand can be any expression of disapproval. A reprimand is usually a verbal statement, but according to this definition, can also be a gesture, such as shaking a finger, or a facial expression, such as a scowl. It appears that combining two or more of these actions, for example, verbal disapproval and a scowl, is more effective than using only one action. The advantages of reprimands are that they are easy to apply immediately after an undesirable behavior occurs, require no preparation, and result in no physical discomfort to a student.

Hall, Axelrod, Foundopoulos, Shellman, Campbell, and Cranston

(1971) report a study in which a verbal reprimand was used to reduce a serious misbehavior. The problem child was Andrea, a seven-year-old retarded girl, who bit and pinched herself, her classmates, the teacher, and classroom visitors. It is understandable that Andrea was not socially popular. Figure 1-4 shows that during the days of Baseline$_1$, the child averaged seventy-two bites and pinches per school day. The teacher used a punishment procedure that consisted of pointing at the child and shouting "No!" following each bite or pinch. When this contingency was in effect, Andrea's mean rate of bites and pinches immediately decreased and was rarely occurring at the end of the punishment phase. The average number of bites and pinches was only five. During a three-day Baseline$_2$ phase, the teacher made peace for the purposes of the experiment and discontinued the punishment procedure. Bites and pinches increased to thirty per day. When the reprimand procedure was reinstated in the final phase, the problem behaviors quickly decreased to low levels.

A study by McAllister, Stachowiak, Baer, and Conderman (1969) was superior to the Hall et al. (1971) study because approval for appropriate behavior was combined with disapproval for inappropriate behavior. The study involved twenty-five students in a low-track, eleventh- and twelfth-grade English class who frequently talked out or turned around without

FIGURE 1-4 The number of times Andrea bit or pinched herself or others each day. *(From R. V. Hall, S. Axelrod, M. Foundopoulos, J. Shellman, R. A. Campbell, and S. Cranston, "The Effective Use of Punishment to Modify Behavior in the Classroom,"* Educational Technology, 11, *1971, as reprinted in K.D. O'Leary and S.G. O'Leary (eds.),* Classroom Management: The Successful Use of Behavior Modification. *New York: Pergamon Press, 1972, p. 175. By permission of the publishers.)*

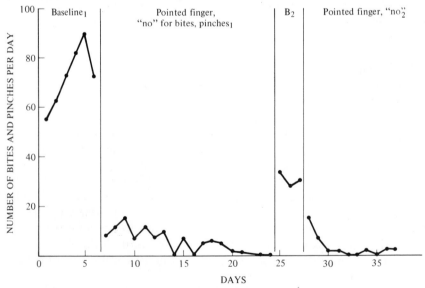

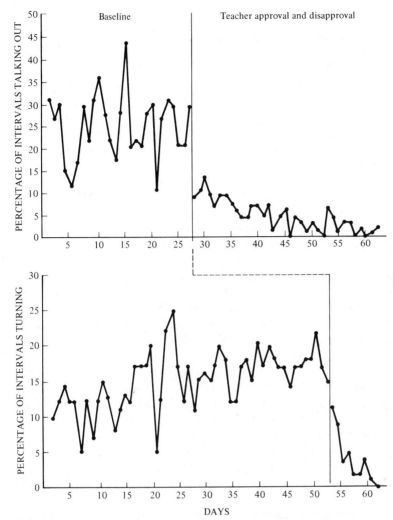

FIGURE 1-5   Percentage of intervals of talking out and inappropriate turning by twenty-five high school students in English class. *(Adapted from L. W. McAllister, J. G. Stachowiak, D. M. Baer, and L. Conderman, "The Application of Operant Conditioning Techniques in a Secondary School Classroom,"* Journal of Applied Behavior Analysis, 2, *p. 281, 1969. By permission of the publishers.)*

permission. As indicated in Figure 1-5, during baseline, talking out was occurring during an average of 25 percent of the intervals, whereas inappropriate turning occurred during 15 percent of the intervals. The teacher first applied the combination of procedures to talking out behavior. Typical comments were: "John, be quiet," "Jane, stop talking," "Phil, shut up!" When all students were quiet, the teacher made a statement praising the entire class, such as: "Thank you for not talking!" or "I'm delighted to see you quiet today!" After the procedure reduced talking out to low levels it was effectively applied to inappropriate turning.

Jones and Miller (1974) studied the components of a properly delivered reprimand. One critical factor was that reprimands be delivered right after a problem occurs, even if the behavior is only mildly disruptive. When teachers wait until a student becomes very disruptive before delivering a reprimand, the nature of the reprimand tends to be so intense that the entire class is brought to a halt. Thus, it is better for a teacher to say "Turn around!" as soon as a student turns to talk to a classmate, than to wait until the youngsters are engaged in conversation and then shout, "How many times have I told you guys to keep quiet!" Other important factors are that the teacher acquire the student's attention by making eye contact, that she be as close to the student as possible, and that she specify the problem. It is also important that reprimands be brief, be delivered firmly and frequently, and that approval occur after the behavior improves.

One caution is in order in using reprimands. Reprimands are a form of attention. If reprimands are the only form of attention a student receives, or if they involve lengthy explanations and discussion, they can serve to reinforce, rather than to punish an undesirable behavior. To avoid this problem, reprimands should be brief and incisive and should be combined with approval for appropriate behavior.

Response Cost A second punishment procedure is known as *response cost*. This is a procedure in which a teacher removes a reinforcer, or a portion of a reinforcer, contingent upon a specified behavior. The form of response cost can consist of fining a youngster for not returning library books on time, lowering a student's grade in science class for mishandling lab equipment, decreasing a class's free time for being too noisy, penalizing a football player five yards for being offside, or removing a token from a youngster for incorrectly answering a reading comprehension question.

Pazulinec, Meyerrose, and Sajwaj (1983) indicate that there are three variations of response-cost procedures. In one, students are given free reinforcers (for example, points) and can lose them for undesirable behaviors. In the second, students are working under a system in which they can both earn reinforcers for desirable behaviors and lose them for undesirable behaviors. In the third, a group as a whole can lose reinforcers for undesirable behaviors. Response cost can be used with either management or academic problems, but in most cases a management problem is the target behavior.

The first type of response cost in which students are given free points could be used by a teacher who is concerned that his students are mishandling science lab equipment. Rules could be posted and students informed that they are starting the term with a specified number of extra points on their final average. Each time a student breaks a rule, her teacher can cross off a specified number of points from her grade sheet. The final grade sheets might appear as follows:

Michelle	+X̶, +X̶, +3, +2, +1, 0, −1, −2 . . . .
Kevin	+X̶, +X̶, +X̶, +2, +1, 0, −1, −2 . . . .
Lance	+X̶, +X̶, +X̶, +X̶, +X̶, X̶, −1, −2 . . . .

According to the above, Michelle would have three points added to her average, Kevin would have two points added, and Lance would have one point deducted from his average.

Hundert (1976) provided an example of the second type of response-cost procedure involving earning and losing points. The teacher gave students tokens for correctly performing arithmetic problems and removed tokens for incorrect answers. This easily applied procedure almost doubled the student's work accuracy.

The third type of response-cost procedure involving group performance was used by Gallagher, Sulzbacher, and Shores (1967). In slightly adapted form the tactic might involve listing the numbers "15, 14, 13,......., 1, 0" on the board. The numbers might refer to minutes of extra free-play time available for the entire class. Each time a student violates a classroom rule, the teacher crosses the highest intact number off the board (see Figure 1-6) and places the name of the offending student next to the crossed-off number. With such a procedure, the author has often found that a teacher, without assistance, can quickly eliminate one or more inappropriate behaviors in a regular-size classroom. In addition, since free time can be used as the reinforcer, the procedure need involve no cost to the teacher.

The advantages of response cost are that it is an easily applied, precise procedure that can produce an immediate and large decrease in many undesirable behaviors. It also takes little time to administer, does not disrupt activities, does not require that students leave the classroom, nor does it involve physical intervention. One disadvantage with response cost is that students sometimes become disruptive when they lose points. Another problem is that when a student loses all her points, the teacher can no longer apply the response-cost procedure. Perhaps the main difficulty with response cost, however, is that it is so effective and easy to apply that teachers will overuse it, and thereby not develop positive alternatives for managing their classrooms.

Time Out   A third type of punishment procedure is known as *time out from positive reinforcement*, or more simply as *time out*. The procedure is defined as a period of time in a less reinforcing environment following a certain

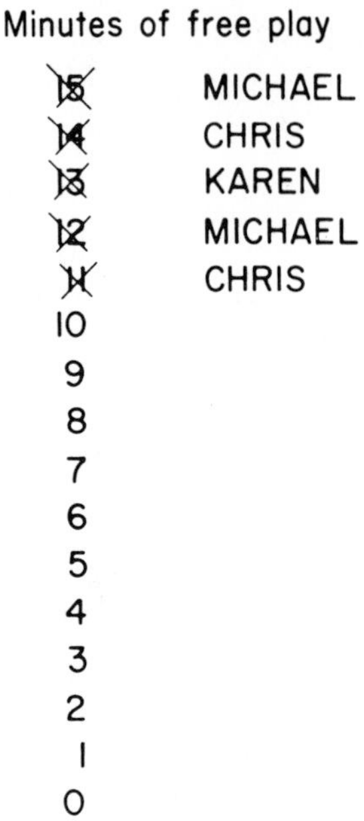

Minutes of free play

15	MICHAEL
14	CHRIS
13	KAREN
12	MICHAEL
11	CHRIS
10	
9	
8	
7	
6	
5	
4	
3	
2	
1	
0	

FIGURE 1-6 Hypothetical chart of a response-cost procedure.

behavior (Brantner and Doherty, 1983). It should be noted that a youngster's environment can be made less reinforcing either by removing the student to a less reinforcing environment or by making the existing environment less reinforcing.

Given the above definition, there are a number ways of implementing time out: A student can be deprived of the opportunity to earn tokens for fifteen minutes; a teacher can stop interacting with a student for five minutes; a teacher can turn off a record player for a few minutes; a student can be taken out of a ball game for several minutes (similar to the use of a penalty box in ice hockey); a student can be placed in an empty room for five minutes; an entire class of students can be required to put their heads on their desks for two minutes; a student can have her art materials removed for five minutes; a student can be required to sit in a corner of the room for ten minutes, and so on. In all cases an effort is made to create a less interesting environment for a period of time, following an inappropriate behavior.

Extinction and time out are frequently confused. Indeed the processes have much in common. The difference between the operations is that in the case of extinction the environment remains the same after the target behavior occurs; in the case of time out, the environment changes following the target behavior. Once example might be a case where a student calls out while a teacher is lecturing. If the teacher does not acknowledge the student's calling out, but continues to lecture as if nothing had happened, she is using an extinction procedure. On the other hand, if the teacher walks away from the youngster and refuses to talk to him for two minutes after he has talked out, the teacher is using time out. In the first case, the student's environment remained the same; in the second case the child's environment changed when the teacher walked away and did not talk to him for two minutes.

Another way to look at the distinction in the two operations is that extinction involves the nondelivery of a reinforcer that typically follows a behavior. Time out involves the temporary removal of a reinforcing event already present in a student's environment. Suppose the teacher typically plays a record if students enter the classroom quietly. If the students are rowdy one day and the teacher does not play a record, he is using extinction. On the other hand, suppose a record player is already on and the teacher turns it off for two minutes after the students become rowdy. The teacher is using time out. (I promise not to bring up this topic again.)

The most publicized examples of time out have involved removing a student to an isolation area for a period of time following a specific inappropriate behavior. Teel (1971), for example, dealt with a six-year-old boy whose crying behavior progressed to the point where he was crying six hours a day, every day. The problem became so great that the youngster was transferred to a learning-disabilities class, even though he did not exhibit the behaviors frequently attributed to the population. The time-out procedure consisted of placing the student in an empty room for five minutes, or until he stopped crying, following each crying incident. Within six days crying completely ceased. Madsen and Madsen (1968) used a time-out procedure to reduce disruptive talking by six junior high school girls. Time out consisted of requiring each girl who talked out to leave the classroom and sit in the hallway for a period of time. The procedure reduced talking-out behavior to one-eighth of its baseline level.

In using time-out procedures that involve a change in the physical environment, a number of factors must be considered. One important issue is the location of time out. Gast and Nelson (1977) described three types of locations. The first is "contingent observation" in which a student moves away from an activity, sits on a nearby chair, and observes her classmates behaving appropriately. The teacher attends only to the students who are behaving appropriately. The second location is known as "exclusion" time out. The student moves from the activity, but is *not* able to observe her classmates. Having a child sit in and face the corner of the room would be an example of this type of time out. The third kind of time out is known as "seclusion" time out. This consists of physically removing a student from the classroom and placing her in an empty room. Given the greater absence of reinforcers in seclusion time out, it is probably more effective than the alternatives.

Another important factor may be the duration of time out. Reports of successful durations of time out have varied from less than a minute to thirty minutes or more. At this point it is unclear what the optimum duration of time out is. Most recommendations are that time out be applied for no more than five or ten minutes, since longer durations do not necessarily increase effectiveness. A further factor that is critical in determining the effectiveness of time out is the contrast between the time-out and time-in (that is, regular) environments (Solnick, Rincover, and Peterson, 1977). If it is important that the time-out environment be as *uninteresting* as possible, then it is also important that the time-in environment be as *interesting* as possible. Teachers with exciting classrooms should find time out to be an effective procedure.

Properly applied, time out can be a quick-acting, effective procedure for reducing inappropriate behaviors. It also tends to work in situations in which alternative procedures such as extinction and reprimands fail. In using seclusion time out, however, teachers should be aware of a number of problems. First, it is not always easy to find an appropriate location for seclusion time out. An appropriate seclusion room is one that has an absence of interesting activities and also prevents a student from injuring himself or the property. Second, seclusion time out often requires physical intervention. In some cases this can lead to injury; in other cases students may find the struggle reinforcing. Third, teachers may find it embarrassing to be seen dragging a student to a time-out room or to have the youngsters act out during time out. Preparing other personnel for these possibilities is important. Fourth, time out should not be applied so much that it interferes with educational programming. If a student is spending a great deal of time in seclusion, the procedure is probably not working and should be discontinued.

In recent years, courts have ruled on various aspects of seclusion time out. Issues include the amount of time that a student can be in seclusion and the environmental conditions of the seclusion setting. Readers interested in more details on the subject should consult an article by Gast and Nelson (1977). Meanwhile, it is important that teachers consider procedures, such as reinforcement, extinction, reprimands, and response cost, before using seclusion time out. It is also critical that seclusion time out only be used when parents and principals have been informed of and agree with the necessity to use the procedure.

Overcorrection A fourth type of punishment procedure is known as *overcorrection* and is the most recently developed form of punishment to be discussed in this text (Foxx and Azrin, 1973). There are two types of overcorrection—*restitutional* and *positive-practice*. Restitutional overcorrection would be used in a situation where a student damaged the environment by knocking over desks and chairs. In accordance with restitutional overcorrection, the student would be first required to restore the environment to its original state by picking up the books and desks he knocked over (correction). He would then be required to improve the environment over its original condition (overcorrection) by straightening up other desks and the class bookcase, for example. Positive practice would be used in a situation where a student performed a behavior incorrectly. Positive practice might consist of repeatedly performing the behavior correctly. If a child had difficulty with certain math facts, for example, she might be required to repeatedly practice the appropriate exercise in a correct manner until she mastered the task.

The rationale behind overcorrection is that an offending individual be taught responsibility for his misbehavior (for example, by improving an environment he disturbed) and that people practice correct forms of a behavior, in order to re-educate themselves. Overcorrection procedures have typically been used with institutional populations and have shown great success in remediating a wide range of problems including self-injury, aggression toward property and others, consumption of unsafe items, and incontinence (see Axelrod, Brantner, and Meddock, 1978; and Foxx and Bechtel, 1983 for review articles). There have only been a few examples of applying overcorrection procedures to school problems—two of the studies follow.

Azrin and Powers (1975) used a positive-practice procedure to decrease the talking-out and out-of-seat behaviors of six boys, aged seven to eleven, in a special summer school class. During recess, offending students had to remain in class, state classroom rules, practice raising their hands until the teacher recognized them, and ask permission to speak or leave their desk. The process was repeated several times, for a period of at least five minutes. The problem behaviors decreased to 2 percent of the baseline level.

Foxx and Jones (1978) used positive practice to increase the spelling scores of twenty-nine elementary and junior high students. During baseline the teachers encouraged the students to spell correctly through various reinforcement procedures. The intervention included a pretest in mid-week, positive practice on words spelled incorrectly on the pretest, the regular weekly test, and positive practice on incorrectly spelled words on the weekly test. Positive practice on misspelled words included spelling the word correctly, spelling it phonetically, specifying the part of speech, writing the dictionary definition, and using the word correctly in five sentences. The average increase in spelling scores exceeded one letter grade.

Given the fact that overcorrection procedures have seldom been applied in classroom situations, it is difficult to evaluate their usefulness. Applications in other settings provide reason for encouragement. Two problems that do have to be dealt with in overcorrection are that the procedures are time consuming and that it is sometimes difficult to prompt people to perform the required behaviors.

A Concluding Comment on Punishment   The preference that teachers have for reinforcement techniques over punishment is understandable and commendable. The conflict is that punishment procedures often work where reinforcement techniques do not. The failure to use punishment under these conditions can be contrary to a student's long-term best interests. Consider a child who is frequently aggressive toward other students. Minimally, the youngster will have a disrupted social life; maximally he will be placed in a class for the "emotionally disturbed." A response-cost or time-out procedure that quickly reduces the problem is a preferable alternative.

It should also be understood that punishment is as natural a learning process as reinforcement. Through punishment students learn not to run into walls or to dress inappropriately. The question often is how to maximize the benefit of the punishment process while decreasing the discomfort. Again, this can be done by collaterally reinforcing appropriate behavior, in conjunction with a program to punish inappropriate behavior. This will serve to produce a quicker, more dependable reduction in behavior, while avoiding many of the undesirable side effects associated with punishment.

ADDITIONAL BASIC PROCESSES AFFECTING BEHAVIOR

The principles and procedures discussed in the earlier parts of the chapter account, in large measure, for the behavior of human beings. There are, however, additional factors and processes affecting human behavior. The reader may wonder, for example, what influence the behavioral traits of adults and peers have on children. Or the reader might wish to know how children learn that it is appropriate to perform a behavior in one situation but not in others, or be curious as to how behavior transfers from one situation to another. There is also the question of how complex behaviors are formed. The remaining portions of the chapter will be devoted to describing processes that lend answers to each of the above questions.

IMITATION

One of the most common means through which children learn new behaviors is by observing and *imitating* the behaviors of other people. Casual observation of children indicates that many youngsters have the same idiosyncratic facial mannerisms and speech patterns as their parents.

Adults are well aware of the influence that children have on each other and, therefore, encourage their youngsters to associate with some children and to avoid others. Imitation is a process in which an individual learns a behavior by observing another person perform that behavior. The person initially performing the behavior is called the "model". The learner neither performs the behavior nor experiences a consequence during the observation period. Imitation can produce either an increase or decrease in the rate of a behavior, depending on the consequence the model receives.

A number of studies have shown that reinforcing the attentiveness or productivity of one student will increase the rate of similar behaviors from students who observe the process. In other cases it has been shown that punishing the behavior of one student reduces the same behavior of other students. Wilson, Robertson, Herlong, and Haynes (1979) found, for example, that when one student received time out for aggressive behavior, the aggressive behavior of his classmates also decreased. One means by which teachers can increase the likelihood of imitation is to make the delivery of consequences obvious to all students.

There are a number of ways in which teachers can use the imitation process to improve student performance. In teaching a new academic behavior, for example, a major component of Van Houten's (1980b) system is to have a teacher do all steps of an example in view of a student, and then leave a correct model in front for the students to imitate. O'Connor (1969) found that when preschool children with a history of isolate behavior observed a film depicting social interaction, they later displayed substantial amounts of social activity. The film showed preschool youngsters interacting with each other at a high rate and receiving reinforcers for the social activities. When an apparently shy child in the film found his peers in play, for example, the other children would offer him toys, talk to him, and smile at him. The social gains which accrued to the youngsters who watched the film were maintained throughout the school year. Modeling can also be used in teacher training. Brown, Reschly, and Wasserman (1974), for example, dealt with a teacher who seldom moved out from behind her desk or praised students. After another adult was introduced into the classroom and moved about the room socially reinforcing students, the teacher did likewise.

Role-playing procedures with an imitation component can be used to teach both students and teacher trainees. The procedure might involve having the teacher play the role of a student and show the appropriate means of responding in a given situation. After observing the teacher's behavior, the student then imitates the teacher's responses and receives feedback from the teacher on the appropriateness of her behavior. This approach was used by Poché, Brouwer, and Swearingen (1981) in teaching three preschool children how to avoid being abducted by adults. The authors cited data that in the vast majority of child abduction cases, the youngster is *not* led away by force, but by lure, such as, "Would you like to go with me for a walk? Your teacher said it was all right for you to come with me," or "I've got a nice surprise in my car. Would you like to come with me and see it?" During baseline an adult acting like an abductor approached all three children and found that they were susceptible to the lures. During training the teacher modeled the correct behaviors in the presence of a "suspect" and then had the children confront the same situation. The teachers socially reinforced correct student responses. All three students learned how to reject the lures within a week, and were still behaving appropriately in a test situation twelve weeks later.

Jones and Eimers (1975) used role playing in an after-school training program for in-service teachers. The trainer would model the appropriate way to respond to different classroom problems. Participants then alternated roles in which they played the "teacher," the "good" student, and the "bad" student. Participants received feedback on how well they used praise, reprimands, instructions, and time out, after seeing the procedures used appropriately. Results showed that children in the participant's classrooms became less disruptive and more academically productive after their teachers experienced the program.

Kazdin (1979) points out that programs based on modeling have not always been effective. Even when desirable effects have been demonstrated, they have sometimes been short lived. One way to regard modeling is that it is a good procedure to initiate a behavior, but that for long-term maintenance of improvement, reinforcement of desirable behavior is necessary.

DISCRIMINATION

So far the book has concentrated on the means by which events that follow behavior (that is, consequent events) affect the future rate of behavior. It is also true that events that precede behavior (that is, antecedent events) can influence the future occurrence of behavior. For example, teachers will give students instructions on how to complete a task, hints on how to spell a word, or demonstrate how to perform an arithmetic problem, with the intention that these antecedent actions will prompt desirable behavior.

Events that precede behavior, influence behavior if they have been associated with reinforcement. For example, if a teacher assigns students homework, collects the work, and then reinforces students for doing their work, it is likely that students will do their homework when the teacher places the assignment on the board (an antecedent event). On the other hand if a teacher writes an assignment on the board, but does not collect the work nor reinforce students for compliance, it is unlikely that writing an assignment on the board will influence students to do their homework.

Children learn to respond differently in disimilar situations, through a combination of reinforcement and extinction. A youngster may learn that if she asks her father for permission to stay up late when he is in a happy mood, her request will be granted. She may also learn that if she requests such permission when her father is in an unhappy mood, her request will be rejected. Situations (that is, stimuli) in which a behavior has a chance of being reinforced are called *discriminative stimuli* and are denoted "S^D" (pronounced "ess dee"). Situations in which a behavior has no chance of being reinforced are denoted "S$^\Delta$" (pronounced "ess delta"). When a student performs a behavior in the presence of S^D, but does not perform the behavior in the presence of S$^\Delta$, a discrimination has been formed. In the present case, the father's happy mood is an S^D, his unhappy mood is an S$^\Delta$, and the child has formed a discrimination because she only makes her requests when her father is in a happy mood.

There are many cases in which it is necessary to teach students discriminations. For example, a preschool teacher may wish to teach a boy to discriminate the "Boys" room from the "Girls" room. She might do this by repeatedly presenting him with signs saying "Boys" and "Girls" (with the order randomly alternated) and praising him every time he points to the correct sign. If a college professor wishes to make 4:30 P.M. an S^D for her students to be in class, she should start to lecture at 4:30 P.M. and present the most important information at the start of class. If she starts class when most students arrive, she might find that 4:30 has become an S$^\Delta$ for entering class, and that her students arrive at a later time. If a teacher wants the flashing on and off of classroom lights to be an S^D to begin class, he should reinforce his students if they are ready to work within one minute (for example) of the time he flashes the lights.

There are times when a faIlure to discriminate can cause a school problem. For example, a girl who yells and runs in class the way she does on the playground has failed to make an appropriate discrimination. The discrimination can be brought about by reinforcing the girl for such behaviors on the playground, but not in the classroom. At other times a problem will exist because a student *did* make a discrimination. Speech therapists, for example, should not be surprised when a child who is being reinforced for verbal Behavior emits certain speech behaviors during a therapy session, but does not exhibit the same sounds outside therapy. The problem is that the child has learned to discriminate the situation that will lead to reinforcement (speech therapy) from the situation that does not (any environment other than speech therapy). The solution to the problem is to use one of the stimulus-generalization strategies discussed in the next section.

STIMULUS GENERALIZATION

It sometimes happens that a behavior which is learned in one situation also occurs in other situations. For example, a student who learns to park a car in a driver's education course may also park the family car appropriately in front of her house. When a behavior that has been reinforced in one setting also occurs in settings in which the individual has *not* been reinforced, "stimulus generalization" is occurring. The more similar the new situation is to the one in which the original learning took place, the more likely it is that stimulus generalization will occur.

Examples of stimulus generalization are common in daily life. Sometimes the occurrence is desirable; sometimes it is not. Desirable examples include cases in which a student learned to put his coat on in nursery school and used the same procedure when he was home; or a case where a youngster learned to do long division in math class, and then went home and figured out her favorite team's winning percentage. Undesirable examples would include cases in which a child learned that his sister's name was "Nancy" and then called several girls of similar age the same name; or when a child learned that T-O-Y spelled "toy," but also read the word "top" as "toy." When it is undesirable that generalizations occur, a discrimination program in which appropriate responses are reinforced, and inappropriate ones are not, is called for.

Behavior modification has often been criticized because behavior that has improved in one situation does not always improve in other situations. It might be found, for example, that students become more orderly in social studies through a reinforcement program, but that the youngsters continue to misbehave in science class. In fact, the specificity of change should be expected. That is, generalization should not be expected to occur automatically; it should be programmed (Baer, Wolf, and Risley, 1968).

Several strategies for extending behavior change have been developed. One strategy is to train the behavior in the new setting, employing a procedure similar to that which was originally used. Usually the behavior will change more quickly in the new environment than it did in the original one. Stokes and Baer (1977) deal with the topic of generalization in depth. One suggestion they make for achieving generalization is that teachers modify behaviors that are likely to be reinforced by the natural environment. Thus, a teacher may initially reinforce a shy student for social interaction. Once the behavior is occuring at a suitable rate, she might prompt classmates to reinforce the same behavior. Other suggestions are that several people carry out the original training, that instructions vary, that different cues precede the behaviors, and that various reinforcers be used. Also if behavior generalizes automatically, they suggest that teachers reinforce it.

BEHAVIOR CHAINS

So far, when a behavior has been mentioned, it has been described as if it were a singular act. Actually, a behavior is a complex act composed of many simpler responses. For example, a breakdown of walking might consist of the following:

Raise foot off ground⟶ Extend foot for a distance ⟶

Balance oneself on the other foot ⟶ Place ball of foot on ground⟶

Place heel of foot on ground ⟶ Raise other foot.

The series of behaviors comprising a larger act is called a *behavior chain* or a *chain*. Each link in the chain serves as an S^D to perform the next response. For example, raising a foot off the ground serves as an S^D to extend one's foot for a distance. The element that maintains the links in the chain is the reinforcer at the end of the chain. In the case of walking the reinforcer would be reaching the destination after taking several steps.

Performing a new behavior often involves combining already learned responses in a chain. Thus, a girl named "Robie" might be able to write every letter in the alphabet but not be able to write her name. The child must first learn to write an "R," that the "R" is a cue to write an "O," that "O" is a cue for a "B," and so on. Similarly, students may be able to enunciate every word in the "Gettysburg Address" but must learn to link each of the words together in a behavior chain.

Chaining will take place most efficiently if students already know how to perform each link in the chain. Thus, Robie should already know how to write each letter in her name before she is taught to link the letters together in the proper order. Similarly, the reading process for some children may be facilitated if they are taught, in advance, all words they will encounter in their reading text.

The reinforcer at the end of a behavior chain most strongly reinforces the last link in the chain. Nevertheless it still reinforces earlier links in the chain, albeit to a lesser extent. This point was made clear in a study by Kazdin (1977) who found that reinforcing an attentive behavior which was preceded by another attentive behavior, improved performance more than reinforcing an attentive behavior preceded by an inattentive behavior. This point also has implications for applying the recommendation that teachers punishing an undesirable behavior also reinforce a desirable behavior. Although this suggestion should be carried out, it is important that a teacher *not* reinforce a student *immediately* after punishing her, lest both the undesirable and desirable behaviors be reinforced. It is common, for example, for parents to comfort their children after their children have misbehaved, been punished, and then become compliant. In so doing, they may be reinforcing a chain of behaviors that includes inappropriate links. It is better not to immediately reinforce appropriate behavior, after punishing inappropriate behavior. The processes should be separated in time.

The examples of the chaining process cited above have all involved *forward* chaining. This is a process in which a student initially learns the first link in the behavior chain, then the second one, the third one, and so forth, until she can perform the entire chain. Another way of learning a task is through *backward* chaining. With such a procedure a student first learns the last link in the chain, then she learns the next-to-last link, until finally she learns the initial link. This might sound like a comedy routine, but many behaviors are naturally learned by backward chaining.

Consider the process by which a child learns the way home from his grandparent's house, which is five blocks away from his own. Early in life he learns to return home from a few feet away from his front door. A little later in life, he learns how to return home from the lawn in front of his house. At still later points in his life, he finds his way home from the sidewalk in front of his house, then from the neighbors' house, then from a block away, and so forth, until he learns to return home from his grandparent's house. With forward chaining, the learning process would begin by teaching the child the appropriate direction to take from his grandparent's house and guiding his path from there.

It is possible to teach a variety of school tasks through backward chaining. In order to teach Robie to spell her name with backward chaining, for example, a teacher might present the girl with the following work sheet:

ROBI-

If the youngster consistently filled in an "E," she would be reinforced and would receive the following worksheet:

ROB--

Later, it would be,

RO---

then,

R----

and, finally,

When she consistently writes "ROBIE" she would have learned to spell her name with backward chaining. In another case, Sulzer and Mayer (1972) describe how they taught a six-year-old boy in a special-education class to assemble a four-piece puzzle using backward chaining. First, all pieces but one were assembled and the youngster was required to replace only one piece. Each time he succeeded, he received a reinforcer. When the first step was mastered, two pieces were removed, then three, and finally all four pieces were removed and the child had to assemble the entire puzzle.

There is some controversy concerning whether a teacher should use forward chaining or backward chaining when both procedures are feasible. Although there is an absence of definitive experimentation on the topic, behavioral researchers tend to favor backward chaining. The question is still an open one, but one advantage in backward chaining is that the child who completes a step successfully experiences the reinforcer of observing a completed task. This is often not the case with forward chaining.

It is sometimes difficult to tell how chaining differs from shaping. Indeed both processes are techniques for producing new behaviors. Kazdin (1975) explains, however, that shaping involves gradually changing a behavior from its original form to a new one. In teaching a speech sound, for example, a teacher may initially reinforce a rudimentary sound and slowly require changes in the nature of the behavior, until the final form of the behavior does not resemble the original form. In the case of chaining, a teacher tries to link existing behaviors together to form a new behavior. Therefore, each of the links is still evident in the final version of the behavior. Even so, it may be necessary to use shaping to develop the links in the chain and many teaching programs involve both processes.

SUMMARY

There are two types of behavior—respondents and operants. Respondent behaviors are involuntary and consist of such responses as pupil dilation and sweating. Operant behaviors are voluntary and include behaviors such as hand raising and reading. Associated with each type of behavior is a conditioning process. In respondent conditioning, a neutral stimulus (for example, a light) is repeatedly presented before a stimulus (such as food) that automatically elicits a reflexive behavior (in this case salivation). Eventually, the stimulus that was originally neutral elicits the reflexive behavior. The other type of conditioning is operant conditioning. With this type of conditioning, consequences of the behavior alter the future rate of the behavior.

There are a number of operant-conditioning procedures that can be used to increase behavior. One procedure, known as positive reinforcement, involves presenting a student with a reward after he performs a behavior. If the behavior increases in rate, positive reinforcement is said to have occurred. It is important that reinforcers be delivered contingent upon a desired behavior and that they immediately follow the behavior.

Three types of reinforcers are food, social events, and activities. Ideas on choosing positive reinforcers can be obtained by observing what a child spends much of her time doing, and by interviewing students and their parents. Another process, known as negative reinforcement, involves the removal of something the student dislikes (for example, homework) if he performs a certain behavior. Positive and negative operations can both produce increases in appropriate or inappropriate behaviors. The difference is that in the case of positive reinforcement the target behavior results in the presentation of something desirable, whereas in the case of negative reinforcement the behavior results in the removal of something objectionable.

Shaping is a procedure that can be used to teach new behaviors. The process involves reinforcing behaviors that progressively approximate the desired behavior, until the target behavior occurs. Important aspects of shaping include beginning at a level where the student can perform, proceeding in small steps, and giving students practice once they are successful. Fading is a process in which the prompts that initially assist in teaching a behavior are gradually removed until the behavior occurs under more natural conditions. Shaping differs from fading in that the behavior gradually changes during shaping. In fading the behavior stays the same, while the conditions under which it occurs change.

When each behavior is followed by a reinforcer, a continuous-reinforcement schedule is in effect. It has been found, however, that it is possible to use an intermittent-reinforcement or partial-reinforcement schedule to maintain existing behaviors or to teach new ones. Some intermittent reinforcement schedules are known as interval schedules and provide reinforcement only after a certain amount of time has elapsed since the previously reinforced behavior. Another type of reinforcement schedule is a ratio schedule, in which reinforcement occurs after the student performs a certain number of appropriate behaviors. Ratio schedules tend to produce higher and steadier rates of response than interval schedules, especially if reinforcers are delivered according to an unpredictable pattern.

Reinforcers can be unconditioned or conditioned. Unconditioned reinforcers, such as food and water, operate independently of an association with other reinforcers. Conversely, conditioned reinforcers, such as praise and money, owe their effectiveness to an association with other reinforcers. When conditioned reinforcers are associated with many other reinforcers, they are known as generalized reinforcers. A type of generalized reinforcer which has been useful in classroom situations is a token reinforcer. Tokens are items or symbols (for example, checkmarks) which can be exchanged for a variety of reinforcers, known as back-up reinforcers.

Feedback is information indicating whether or not a student response was correct. When feedback is immediate and precise, it can modify a student's behavior even without being backed up by a reinforcer. Given the ease and low cost of feedback procedures, the techniques should be used more frequently than is presently the case.

There are three reinforcement procedures that can be used to decrease inappropriate behaviors. One procedure is to use a differential reinforcement of low rate of response schedule, in which a student is reinforced if the target behavior occurs below a specified rate. Another procedure is a differential reinforcement of other behavior schedule, in which a student is reinforced only for completely refraining from a behavior. A third procedure is the reinforcement of a specific behavior that is incompatible with the undesirable one.

Another procedure that can be used to reduce the rate of a behavior is to remove the reinforcement that has followed the behavior. When the behavior decreases to its pre-reinforcement level, extinction is said to have taken place. Although extinction is a slow process which has several problems associated with it, teachers can use it when safety factors have been accounted for and when the teachers simultaneously reinforce a desired behavior.

The most dependable procedure for reducing behavior is through punishment. This is a process in which an environmental change following a behavior reduces the future rate of the behavior. Punishment can involve the application of an aversive consequence or the withdrawal of a desired event. In order to maximize the effectiveness of punishment, it should be introduced at full intensity, rather than gradually, and immediately follow each misbehavior. In addition reinforcement should be provided for the desired behavior.

There are four common punishment procedures. One is a reprimand or an expression of disapproval. Reprimands should be delivered incisively and immediately after a misbehavior occurs. A second type of punishment procedure is response cost, in which positive reinforcers are lost for each misbehavior. Another punishment procedure is known as time out, which involves a period of time in a less reinforcing environment following a behavior. Time out can be brought about by making the existing environment less interesting, or by placing a student in a different environment which is less interesting. Time out is most effective when a student's normal environment is highly reinforcing. A fourth type of punishment is overcorrection. There are two types of overcorrection—restitutional and positive-practice. Restitutional overcorrection is used when a student commits an environmental disturbance. The youngster is first required to restore the environment to its original condition and then improve it. Positive-practice overcorrection is used when a student does not perform a behavior correctly. The tactic involves repeatedly performing the behavior in the appropriate manner.

There are other basic processes which affect the occurrence of a behavior. Imitation, for example, is a process by which students learn new behaviors which they themselves are not performing. By observing the consequences others receive, a student's behavior may increase or decrease in rate. In many cases, students learn to discriminate those conditions in which it is appropriate to perform a behavior from those situations in which the behavior is inappropriate. The process can be brought about by reinforcing student behavior in certain situations and extinguishing the same behavior in other situations. Discriminations do not always occur, however, and in some other cases a behavior which has been learned in one situation will occur in other, similar situations. The process is known as generalization and is a transitory one, unless specific measures are taken to ensure the maintenance of the behavior in the new situations.

QUESTIONS AND ACTIVITIES

1   Give two differences between operant and respondent behaviors.

2   Distinguish between operant and respondent conditioning.

3   Suppose a child says that she considers a star to be a reinforcer. What must occur before a teacher can be certain that the star really is a reinforcer?

4   Why is it important for a reinforcer to come immediately after a behavior?

5   Describe advantages and disadvantages of three types of reinforcers.

6   In what way are positive reinforcement and negative reinforcement the same? How are they different?

7   Devise a situation in which a teacher's behavior positively reinforces a student's behavior, at the same time the student's behavior negatively reinforces the teacher's behavior.

8   Describe a shaping procedure a teacher could use to get a withdrawn child to socially interact more with her classmates.

9   Devise a situation in which it would be appropriate to use fading. Describe the fading process. Do not use an example given in this book.

10 Why do ratio schedules produce more responding than interval schedules?

11 Consider a common academic problem and describe the steps you would go through using a feedback chart to remediate the problem. Do the same for a management problem.

12 Suppose an expression such as "Nice going" is not originally a social reinforcer for a student. How could a teacher make the expression into a social reinforcer?

13 Give five advantages and four disadvantages of token-reinforcement procedures. In each case two of the answers should not appear in the book.

14 Distinguish between using a DRO schedule and reinforcing an incompatible behavior.

15 Describe four problems that can occur when using extinction procedures and suggest means by which the difficulties can be avoided.

16 In using a punishment procedure to decrease an inappropriate behavior, what are the advantages in also reinforcing a desired behavior?

17 Summarize the findings on the question of whether punishment procedures produce undesirable side effects.

18 How does response cost differ from extinction?

19 Describe advantages and disadvantages of contingent observation, exclusion time out, and seclusion time out.

20 Distinguish between restitutional overcorrection and positive-practice overcorrection. Describe a problem for which each of the overcorrection procedures is appropriate.

21 Indicate the steps a teacher would use in a role-playing situation to teach a diabetic child to reject candy when offered some by an insistent classmate.

22 Suppose students do not follow a teacher's instructions. How can she make her instructions into an S^D?

23 Why is discrimination the opposite of stimulus generalization?

24 How would a teacher use backward chaining to teach the long division problem: $127 \div 3$?

REFERENCES

Axelrod, S., J. P. Brantner, and T. D. Meddock: "Overcorrection: A Review and Critical Analysis," *Journal of Special Education*, **5**, pp. 367–391, 1978.

Ayllon, T., S. Garber, and K. Pisor: "The Elimination of Discipline Problems Through a Combined School-Home Motivational System," *Behavior Therapy*, **6**, pp. 616–626, 1975.

Ayllon, T., and M. D. Roberts: "Eliminating Discipline Problems by Strengthening Academic Performance," *Journal of Applied Behavior Analysis*, **7**, pp. 71–76, 1974.

Azrin, N. H., and W. C. Holz: "Punishment" in W. K. Honig (ed.), *Operant Behavior: Areas of Research and Application* (New York: Appleton-Century-Crofts, 1966), pp. 213–270.

Azrin, N. H., and M. A. Powers: "Eliminating Classroom Disturbances of Emotionally Disturbed Children by Positive Practice Procedures," *Behavior Therapy*, **6**, pp. 525–534, 1975.

Baer, D. M., M. M. Wolf, and T. R. Risley: "Some Current Dimensions of Applied Behavior Analysis," *Journal of Applied Behavior Analysis*, **1**, pp. 91–97, 1968.

Bodnar, K.: "Reducing Talk Outs in an MR Class with a Token Reinforcement System," unpublished manuscript, Temple University, 1974.

Brantner, J. P., and M. Doherty: "A Review of Time Out: A Conceptual and Methodological Analysis," in S. Axelrod and J. Apsché (eds.), *The Effects of Punishment on Human Behavior* (New York: Academic Press, 1983).

Brown, D., D. Reschly, and H. Wasserman; "Effects of Surreptitious Modeling Upon Teacher Classroom Behaviors," *Psychology in the Schools*, **11**, pp. 366–369, 1974.

Dietz, S. M., and A. C. Repp: "Decreasing Classroom Misbehavior through the use of DRL Schedules of Reinforcement," *Journal of Applied Behavior Analysis*, **6**, pp. 457–463, 1973.

Drabman, R. S., and B. B. Lahey: "Feedback in Classroom Behavior Modification: Effects on the Target and Her Classmates," *Journal of Applied Behavior Analysis*, **7**, pp. 591–598, 1974.

Egel, A. L.: "Reinforcer Variation: Implications for Motivating Developmentally Disabled Children," *Journal of Applied Behavior Analysis*, **14**, pp. 345–350, 1981.

Egner, A., L. Babic, D. Kemel, J. Cross, P. Epifiano, M. Hampton, P. Leach, H. C. Lehouiller, H. Powell, and R. V. Lates: "Individualizing a Junior High School Environment: A Case Study," in A. Egner (ed.), *Individualizing Junior and Senior High School Instruction to Provide Special Education within Regular Classrooms* (Burlington, Vt.: University of Vermont Press, 1973), pp. 31–44.

Fink, W. T., and D. W. Carnine: "Control of Arithmetic Errors Using Informational Feedback and Graphing," *Journal of Applied Behavior Analysis*, **8**, p. 461, 1975.

Foxx, R. M., and N. H. Azrin: "The Elimination of Autistic Self-stimulatory Behavior by Overcorrection," *Journal of Applied Behavior Analysis,* **6**, pp. 1–14, 1973.

Foxx, R. M., and D. R. Bechtel. "Overcorrection," in S. Axelrod and J. Aspshé (eds.), *The Effects of Punishment on Human Behavior* (New York: Academic Press, 1983).

Foxx, R. M., and J. R. Jones: "A Remediation Program for Increasing the Spelling Achievement of Elementary and Junior High School Students," *Behavior Modification,* **2**, pp. 211–230, 1978.

Gallagher, P. A., S. I. Sulzbacher, and R. E. Shores: "A Group Contingency for Classroom Management of Emotionally Disturbed Children." Paper presented at the Kansas Council for Exceptional Children, Wichita, March, 1967.

Gast, D. L., and C. M. Nelson: "Legal and Ethical Considerations for the Use of Time Out in Special Education Settings," *Journal of Special Education,* **11**, pp. 457–467, 1977.

Givner, A., and P. S. Graubard: *A Handbook of Behavior Modification for the Classroom* (New York: Holt, Rinehart, and Winston, 1974).

Gross, A. M., and R. S. Drabman: "So You Want to be in Pictures: The Evaluation of a New Reinforcer for Children," *Child Behavior Therapy,* **1**, pp. 395–397, 1979.

Hall, R. V., S. Axelrod, M. Foundopoulos, J. Shellman, R. A. Campbell, and S. Cranston: "The Effective Use of Punishment to Modify Behavior in the Classroom," *Educational Technology,* **11**, pp. 24–26, 1971.

Hall, R. V., D. Lund, and D. Jackson: "Effects of Teacher Attention on Study Behavior," *Journal of Applied Behavior Analysis,* **1**, pp. 1–12, 1968.

Homer, A. L., and L. Peterson: "Differential Reinforcement of Other Behavior: A Preferred Response Elimination Procedure," *Behavior Therapy,* **11**, pp. 472–487, 1980.

Hundert, J.: "The Effectiveness of Reinforcement, Response Cost, and Mixed Programs on Classroom Behaviors," *Journal of Applied Behavior Analysis,* **9**, p. 107, 1976.

Jones, F. H., and R. C. Eimers: "Role Playing to Train Elementary Teachers to Use a Classroom Management 'Skill Package,'" *Journal of Applied Behavior Analysis,* **8**, pp. 421–433, 1975.

Jones, F. H., and W. H. Miller: "The Effective Use of Negative Attention for Reducing Group Disruption in Special Elementary School Classrooms, *The Psychological Record,* **24**, pp. 435–448, 1974.

Kazdin, A. E.: *Behavior Modification in Applied Settings* (Homewood, Ill.: Dorsey Press, 1975).

Kazdin, A. E.: *Behavior Modification in Applied Settings*, rev. ed. (Homewood, Ill.: Dorsey Press, 1980).

Kazdin, A. E.: "The Influence of Behavior Preceding a Reinforced Response on Behavior Change in the Classroom," *Journal of Applied Behavior Analysis*, **10**, pp. 299–310, 1977.

Kazdin, A. E.: "Vicarious Reinforcement and Punishment in Operant Programs for Children," *Child Behavior Therapy*, **1**, pp. 13–36, 1979.

McAllister, L. W., J. G. Stachowiak, D. M. Baer, and L. Conderman: "The Application of Operant Conditioning Techniques in a Secondary School Classroom," *Journal of Applied Behavior Analysis*, **2**, pp. 277–285, 1969.

Madsen, C. H., and C. R. Madsen: *Teaching/Discipline* (Boston: Allyn & Bacon, 1968).

Miller, L. K.: *Principles of Everyday Behavior Analysis* (Monterey, Calif.: Brooks/Cole, 1975).

Newsom, C., J. E. Favell, and A. Rincover: "Side Effects of Punishment," in S. Axelrod and J. Apsché (eds.), *The Effects of Punishment on Human Behavior* (New York: Academic Press, 1983).

O'Connor, R. D.: "Modification of Social Withdrawal through Symbolic Modeling," *Journal of Applied Behavior Analysis*, **2**, pp. 15–22, 1969.

Parsonson, B. S., A. M. Baer, and D. M. Baer: "The Application of Generalized Correct Social Contingencies by Institutional Staff: An Evaluation of the Effectiveness and Durability of a Training Program," *Journal of Applied Behavior Analysis*, **7**, pp. 427–437, 1974.

Pazulinec, R., M. Meyerrose, and T. Sajwaj: "Punishment via Response Cost," in S. Axelrod and J. Apsché (eds.), *The Effects of Punishment on Human Behavior* (New York: Academic Press, 1983).

Piper, T. J., and D. N. Elgart: *Teacher Supervision Through Behavioral Objectives* (Baltimore: Paul H. Brookes, 1979).

Poché, C., R. Brouwer, and M. Swearingen: "Teaching Self Protection to Young Children," *Journal of Applied Behavior Analysis*, **14**, pp. 169–175, 1981.

Price, M., and M. D'Ippolito: "The Effects and Side Effects of a Token Reinforcement System on Reading Behavior," unpublished manuscript, Temple University, 1975.

Raschke, D.: "Designing Reinforcement Surveys—Let the Student Choose the Reward," *Teaching Exceptional Children*, **14**, pp. 92–96, 1981.

Saudargas, R. W., C. H. Madsen, and J. W. Scott: "Differential Effects of Fixed and Variable-Time Feedback on Production Rates of Elementary School Children," *Journal of Applied Behavior Analysis*, **10**, pp. 673–678, 1977.

Skinner, B. F.: *The Behavior of Organisms* (New York: Appleton-Century-Crofts, 1938).

Solnick, J. V., A. Rincover, and C. R. Peterson: "Some Determinants of the Reinforcing and Punishing Effects of Time-Out," *Journal of Applied Behavior Analysis*, **10**, pp. 415–424, 1977.

Stokes, T. F., and D. M. Baer: "An Implicit Technology of Generalization," *Journal of Applied Behavior Analysis*, **10**, pp. 349–367, 1977.

Sulzer, B., and G. R. Mayer: *Behavior Modification Procedures for School Personnel* (Hinsdale, Ill.: Dryden Press, 1972).

Teel, S. K.: "The Use of Time-Out Procedures in Diminishing Crying Behavior: A Case Study," *School Applications of Learning Theory*, **3**, pp. 27–31, 1971.

Tribble, A., and R. V. Hall: "Effects of Peer Approval on Completion of Arithmetic Assignments," in F. W. Clark, D. R. Evans, and L. A. Hamerlynck (eds.), *Implementing Behavioral Programs for Schools and Clinics: Third Banff International Conference* (Champaign, Ill.: Research Press, 1972), pp. 139–140.

Van Houten, R.: *How to Motivate Others Through Feedback* (Lawrence, Kan.: H. & H. Enterprises, 1980a).

Van Houten, R.: *Learning Through Feedback* (New York: Human Sciences Press, 1980b).

Van Houten, R.: "Punishment: From the Animal Laboratory to the Applied Setting," in S. Axelrod and J. Apsché (eds.), *The Effects of Punishment on Human Behavior* (New York: Academic Press, 1983).

Van Houten, R., and D. Doleys: "Are Social Reprimands Effective?" in S. Axelrod and J. Apsché (eds.), *The Effects of Punishment on Human Behavior* (New York: Academic Press, 1983).

Van Houten, R., and K. Sullivan: "Effects of an Audio Cueing System on the Rate of Teacher Praise," *Journal of Applied Behavior Analysis*, **8**, pp. 197–201, 1975.

White, M. A.: "Natural Rates of Teacher Approval and Disapproval in the Classroom," *Journal of Applied Behavior Analysis*, **8**, pp. 367–372, 1975.

Willis, J. W., T. R. Hobbs, D. G. Kirkpatrick, and K. W. Manley: "Training Counselors as Researchers in the Natural Environment," in E. Ramp and G. Semb (eds.), *Behavior Analysis: Areas of Research and Application* (Englewood Cliffs, N.J.: Prentice-Hall, 1975), pp. 175–186.

Wilson, D. D., S. J. Robertson, L. H. Herlong, and S. N. Haynes: "Vicarious Effects of Time-Out in the Modification of Aggression in the Classroom," *Behavior Modification*, **3**, pp. 97–111, 1979.

Wolf, M. M., J. S. Birnbrauer, T. Williams, and J. Lawler: "A Note On Apparent Extinction of Vomiting Behavior of a Retarded Child," in L. P.. Ullman and L. Krasner (eds.), *Case Studies in Behavior Modification* (New York: Holt, Rinehart, and Winston, 1965), pp. 364–366.

2

Derivative Procedures For Modifying Student Behavior

The processes and principles described in Chapter 1 are of basic importance to an understanding of the practice of behavior modification and to the ability to apply the methods in classroom situations. A reader of the relevant literature will notice the operations recur consistently in behavior modification studies. The procedures described in the present chapter have been derived from the fundamental principles and have been found to be useful in classroom situations.

The initial section of this chapter will describe group contingencies. With this type of arrangement, student consequences are affected to some degree by the performance of their classmates. The second section of the chapter describes various ways in which students can be involved in the modification of their peers' behavior. One way in which this can be accomplished is through peer tutoring programs. The following section describes programs in which consequences are delivered at home, based on a student's performance in school. In the fourth section, there is a description of various means by which students can learn to control their own behavior. The concluding section discusses factors teachers should take into account in organizing their classrooms.

GROUP CONTINGENCIES

Many of the studies mentioned so far have been concerned with the problem behaviors of one or two children in a classroom. Some teachers, however, may have situations in which there is a general level of disruptive-ness, or poor academic development, and therefore prefer techniques which are applicable to an entire classroom. In another case, a teacher might have problems managing the behavior of only one or two students, but be reluctant to administer reinforcers to them alone, due to negative reactions from their classmates. In such cases teachers should consider using a *group contingency*. This is an arrangement in which the consequences for one or more of the group members depends, at least in part, upon the behavior of some other group members (adapted from Neumann, 1977). Group contingencies can be used to reinforce appropriate behavior or to punish inappropriate behavior.

The use of group contingencies may appear contrary to contemporary trends in education which emphasize the individualization of instruction. Nevertheless, teachers commonly use such procedures. For example, a teacher will inform his students that he will read them a story as soon as all pupils finish their work. In another case, a teacher will permit students to leave the classroom for free play only after they become quiet. At the college level, some professors grade students on a curve. As such, a student's grade depends in large measure on her classmates' performance. Group contingencies are also common outside the classroom. Players may stand on the sidelines waiting for a teammate to make or miss two foul shots at the end of a basketball game; the shots may spell the difference between a victory and a loss for all members of the team. Certainly, automobile safety and insurance rates are determined according to group contingen-cies.

Two types of group contingencies will be discussed in the present section. The first type is known as *consequence sharing* (Kazdin, 1980) and consists of one student's performance determining the consequence all students receive. Examples include having all students receive extra free time if one student achieves 85 percent or better on a spelling test, or allowing a class to listen to the record player if a particular student refrains from hitting classmates during a given day.

An example of consequence sharing appeared earlier in the book (see p. 5) when all students received extra free time if John completed 60 percent of his assigned arithmetic problems (Tribble and Hall, 1972). Another example was provided by Greenberg and O'Donnell (1972). The study involved Mike, a first-grade boy who frequently had temper tan-trums in class. The consequence sharing procedure consisted of awarding Mike and his classmates a piece of candy for every ninety minutes in which the youngster refrained from having a tantrum. There resulted a great decrease in temper tantrums.

The second type of group contingency is known as an *interdependent group contingency system* (Litow and Pumroy, 1975) in which the same contingencies are in effect for *all* group members. The behavior of all students determines the consequences the group receives. This type of group contingency is in effect when a teacher offers youngsters a day without homework, if *all* students pass a history test. Another example appeared earlier in the book (see p. 35) in a study in which the misbehavior of *any* student cost the entire class an extra minute of free-play time.

Switzer, Deal, and Bailey (1977) used an interdependent group contingency procedure for the difficult problem of reducing stealing in three classes. In order to estimate the extent of the problem, the teachers placed ten items such as money, pens, and gum at various locations in the classroom. After a lecture on the importance of honesty failed to reduce the problem, the teachers used a group contingency. They informed the students that if no items were stolen, the entire class would have ten extra minutes of snack time. If something was stolen, but returned within a specified period of time, students had their normal snack time. If all items were not returned, the students had to sit quietly while eating their snacks and put their heads on their desks when they finished. The stealing rate decreased to zero or near zero levels in all three classes. In another case (Wilson and Williams, 1973), a teacher offered the class five minutes of free time if all students completed their writing assignments within twenty minutes and made fewer than seven errors. There resulted a substantial improvement in work output.

A variation of the interdependent group contingency is to divide the group into two or more competitive teams. Consequences are then determined according to how each team scores in relation to the other team(s). This procedure was used by Axelrod and Paluska (1975). During Baseline$_1$, the teacher, Ms. Paluska, gave the students six spelling words each day and tested them on the words the next day. Figure 2-1 indicates that the average for this phase was 3.5 words correct (58 percent accuracy). In the Game$_1$ stage, Ms. Paluska divided the children into the Blue team and the Red team. The teams were matched according to their Baseline$_1$ scores. After giving the students their daily test, the teacher added the scores of the two teams and announced the team with the higher overall score. She then read aloud the names of the winners and permitted the winners to stand by their desks and cheer for themselves. Although the students were enthusiastic about the game, their average spelling accuracy increased only 3 percent—to 3.65 words correct. In the "Game plus Prizes" phase, the children on the winning team continued to receive social reinforcement, but each student was also awarded a prize, such as a candy bar, a pencil, or a toy car, after his team won. The class's spelling accuracy increased to 5.0 words a day, or 83 percent correct. Hence the awarding of prizes for the winners furnished the motivation for improved spelling performance that the game alone failed to provide. When the game alone and baseline conditions were later reinstated, the children's spelling accuracy decreased.

A competitive game was also used in a study by Barrish, Saunders, and Wolf (1969). The teacher was dealing with twenty-four fourth graders— many of whom were chronic discipline problems. When baseline observa-

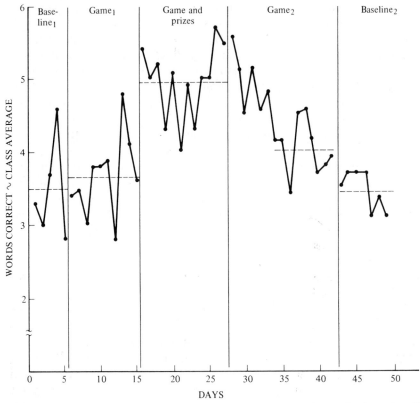

FIGURE 2-1 The average number of words the students spelled correctly on daily six-word spelling tests. *(From S. Axelrod and J. Paluska, "A Component Analysis of a Classroom Game on Spelling Performance," in E. Ramp and G. Semb (eds.),* Behavior Analysis: Areas of Research and Application, *Englewood Cliffs, N.J.: Prentice-Hall, 1975, p. 280. By permission of the publishers.)*

tions indicated that out-of-seat and talking-out behaviors were occurring more than 80 percent of the time, the authors devised a "good-behavior" game. The teacher divided the students into two teams, according to the rows in which they sat. She informed the youngsters that they were going to play a game in which there were some rules relating to out-of-seat and talking-out behavior. Each time a student violated one of the rules, the teacher placed a mark against his team on the chalkboard. The team that had the fewer marks at the end of the period was declared the winner. If both teams had five or fewer marks, they both won the game. Besides winning the game, the members of the winning team received victory tags, free-play time at the end of the day, and a star next to their names on the winner's chart. The procedure reduced misbehaviors to less than one-fourth of the baseline level.

There are several advantages in using group contingencies over individual contingencies. When consequence sharing is used (one student's behavior determines consequences for the group), it is common to see classmates encourage a student. For example, when a student earns a reinforcer for the entire class, peers often congratulate or otherwise socially reinforce a student for her successes. At other times students will laugh when a classmate clowns around. This reaction is likely to cease when a class's reinforcers are dependent on the reduction of the problem behavior.

There are also a number of benefits in using interdependent group contingencies (all students' behaviors determine group outcomes). As was true for the consequence sharing procedure, students will frequently tutor each other in programs involving academic improvement (for example, see Axelrod and Paluska, 1975; McCarty, Griffin, Apolloni, and Shores, 1977) or praise each other for improved classroom deportment. There are also a number of practical benefits in using this type of group contingency. Implementation of the procedure is relatively easy because the teacher need only keep one set of records and administer the same reinforcer to all students. This permits the use of reinforcers such as free time and class trips which are difficult to give to only a portion of the students in a class (as would occur with an individual contingency). A further advantage in the present type of group contingency is that a teacher need not determine who is responsible for a particular behavior, and yet can effectively modify the behavior. For example, a fight between two students may have been incited by a comment unheard by the teacher. Since the consequence is applied to both students, fighting should cease regardless of who initially caused the problem.

There are also some disadvantages associated with group contingencies. One problem is that students may place excessive pressure on a classmate to meet the conditions for reinforcement. It is even possible that physical force will be employed. As such, it is important that teachers *not* use group contingencies unless it is certain that all students are capable of performing the desired behavior. They should also monitor the behavior of the students as closely as possible. Second, the use of competitive games can lead to unpleasant social interactions. It is preferable to set up games in which the class competes to surpass its own previous high score, rather than have groups compete against each other. A third problem is that some students might intentionally subvert the system. This occurred in the aforementioned study (see p. 35) by Gallagher, Sulzbacher, and Shores (1967) in which a student repeatedly stood up and sat down (reducing group free time by two minutes for each instance) in order to deprive classmates of all their extra free time. When this occurs, a teacher might set up an individual contingency for the noncompliant student. Finally, it is possible that some students will find the common reinforcer used during a given group contingency program to be unappealing. This problem might be solved by using additional reinforcers but this adjustment would also make the procedure more difficult to administer.

The question of the fairness of group contingency procedures is frequently raised. To many it seems unfair to penalize an entire class because of the misbehaviors of one student. In making this judgment I ask the reader to evaluate the long-term effects of the procedure. A student who is generally well behaved will suffer in academic and social development if his classmates are continually disruptive. In a sense the students are unwilling participants in a group contingency that is not benefiting them. If a teacher uses a technique that will reduce inappropriate behavior, it is likely that all students will eventually profit. This should not be taken as a recommendation that group contingencies be used over individual contingencies. Research comparing the effectiveness of the two operations has found them to be about equally effective. For reasons of convenience, however, individual contingencies are sometimes unrealistic. In such cases, teachers should consider using group contingencies.

STUDENTS AS AGENTS OF BEHAVIOR CHANGE

McLaughlin and Malaby (1975) describe a number of ways in which students can be involved in classroom behavior modification programs. First, they can serve as observers and recorders of their own behavior. This might mean keeping a record of the number of times they raise their hand or call out in class; the number of pages they read in a day; or the number of tokens they gain and lose each period. In so doing, the teacher's workload is reduced and students receive frequent and immediate feedback on their behavior. This topic will be discussed in greater detail in the "Self-Control" section of the present chapter. A second role students can serve in is as observers of the behaviors of other children. Most measurement techniques used in behavior modification studies are sufficiently simple that students with minimal training can serve as reliable observers. In fact, due to their location in the classroom and the nature of their activities, students are sometimes in a better position to observe behavior than are teachers. Whether students serve as observers of either their own or their classmates' behavior, it is important that their data be checked at times to be certain it is correct. The youngsters should also be reinforced for their accuracy.

A third capacity in which students can serve is as tutors for their classmates or for younger children. As such, some children receive an inexpensive, and often effective, one-to-one teaching arrangement. Finally, students can act as researchers carrying out programs to modify the behavior of their schoolmates' or teacher's behavior. In order to serve in this role, it is necessary to teach students basic behavioral principles and to give them practice in carrying them out. The present section will discuss the means by which students can serve as tutors and researchers.

STUDENTS AS TUTORS

Before using one student to tutor another, a teacher must decide whether to employ a "cross-age" tutor or a "peer" tutor. A cross-age tutor is a student from a higher grade, whereas a peer tutor is a student from the same grade as the tutee (that is, the recipient of the tutoring). Possible advantages of cross-age tutors are that they may be more knowledgeable in the subject matter and may be better teachers than peer tutors.

Nevertheless, Dineen, Clark, and Risley (1977) point out that when older children are used as tutors, they must often leave their classes or come after school to offer their services. This can result in missing important classes, scheduling problems, and transportation difficulties. Also, Robertson, DeReus, and Drabman (1976) found that college students were no better than peers as tutors of reading for second-grade students. For reasons of convenience, it would appear that teachers should first seek peers in the classroom as tutors for their children; where this is not feasible, the teacher should consider using cross-age peers.

Conlon, Hall, and Hanley (1972) provided an example of using a peer tutor. The students, Tom, Dick, and Harry, were all nine-year-old boys in an ungraded class for youngsters who were behind in arithmetic and reading. Tom, however, was doing better in arithmetic than the other two boys and, therefore, served as the tutor. Each afternoon the students received a sheet of paper with thirty examples which they had twenty minutes to complete. Following baseline, the tutoring stage began. Tom had an answer sheet and a stopwatch. After six minutes he stopped his watch and graded the tutees' papers by placing a big red "C" on correct answers and ignoring incorrect answers. At the twelve-minute and twenty-minute marks, he repeated the process. Dick's accuracy increased by 27 percent and Harry's by 40 percent. In addition, Tom's performance reached almost 100 percent accuracy. The authors indicated that the teachers had to monitor Tom a great deal during the first two days, but after that he needed little help. Tom also ceased being a discipline problem.

Johnson and Bailey (1974) conducted a study using five fifth-grade students to tutor five kindergarten children in basic arithmetic skills. Tutoring consisted of presenting tasks to the children, showing the tutees how to perform the task, allowing them to do the work, giving them feedback on their work, recording and graphing scores, advancing them to new tasks upon perfect completion of the present task, and contingently reinforcing them with play activities. Results showed that the tutees made substantially greater gains in arithmetic achievement than their classmates who did not receive the program.

There are a number of advantages in student tutoring programs. First, they allow a one-to-one teaching situation. As such, a student can begin instruction at her own level, can be paced according to her own learning rate, can be given immediate feedback, and can be taught according to methods most appropriate to her. This is not possible when a teacher instructs all students simultaneously. (The effect of one-to-one instruction is discussed in more detail below.) Second, student tutoring reduces the need to employ expensive specialists. Third, it frees the teacher to work with other students in need of help. Fourth, students sometimes express a preference for tutoring over traditional teaching procedures and exhibit improved social behavior outside of tutoring (for example, see Dineen et al., 1977).

There are also several benefits for the tutor. First, it has been found that in the process of tutoring, the tutors themselves often experience academic gains. This has been noted with both peer and cross-age tutors. For example, Dineen et al. found that when elementary school students in the same grade tutored each other in spelling, the tutor learned almost as much as the tutees. More surprisingly, Cloward (1967) showed that when tenth- and eleventh-grade students tutored fourth-grade students, the *tutors* scored higher in reading tests than their classmates who had not served as tutors. Another advantage is that it gives the tutor an opportunity to learn how to teach (without the expense of a student-teaching course).

An important question is whether and how tutors should be taught how to teach. When tutors have received training, the sessions usually proceed in the manner described by Johnson and Bailey (1974). This included having the teacher model appropriate behaviors, such as praising desirable behavior, ignoring undesirable behavior, correcting incorrect responses, and giving students a chance to correct incorrect responses. There is also a great deal of role playing in which students alternately play the role of tutor and tutee and receive feedback on their performance.

In spite of the apparent desirability of training tutors, Harris and Sherman (1973) found that even without training, students could benefit from peer tutoring. In the study, fourth- and fifth-grade students were asked to form groups of two or three students and teach each other spelling and math work. The authors did not appoint specific tutors, nor request that they use a particular tutoring strategy. In spite of the lack of structure and training, the students made more gains than they had when they worked alone. Perhaps the best way to proceed is to train tutors when possible, but to still use peer and cross-age tutors when training is not feasible.

The remarkable importance of one-to-one instruction was illustrated by Jenkins and Mayhall (1976). Examine Figure 2-2 and note that students made an average of 11.7 correct responses under 1:1 instruction and 8.0 correct responses under 23:1 instruction. About 40 percent of their loss of learning occurred in moving from 1:1 to 2:1 instruction! Thus, there is a large difference in having a teacher teach one student and having the teacher instruct two students. Moreover, Jenkins and Mayhall report that cross-age tutors in a 1:1 situation are more effective than regular teachers

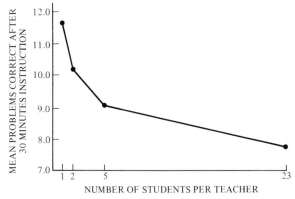

FIGURE 2-2 Mean correct performance under varying pupil-teacher ratios. *(From J. R. Jenkins and W. F. Mayhall, "Development and Evaluation of a Resource Teacher Program,"* Exceptional Children, 43, *p. 25, 1976. By permission of the publishers.)*

are in small group teaching. Thus, a case has been made for schools to increasingly adopt students as tutors as a teaching strategy, especially since the procedure is inexpensive and can be effective without the training of tutors.

Peer and cross-age tutoring are not without their problems. First, it should be understood that students are not experienced teachers and, therefore, may become impatient or even cruel when working with other children. Conversely, they might grade their classmates too easily or provide them with answers before giving the tutee an opportunity to respond. Thus, it is important that teachers monitor student tutoring. Also, since peer tutoring departs from usual school practices, teachers should inform parents and relevant school personnel of their plans, before proceeding.

STUDENTS AS RESEARCHERS

Most studies presented in the book have involved a teacher modifying the behavior of a student. Thus if Michelle is constantly teasing Sandy, the teacher might devise a program to eliminate Michelle's teasing behavior. Although there is much merit to this approach, one might wonder whether Sandy could be taught to modify Michelle's behavior? If Sandy learned such skills she might be able to apply them when other children teased her and would, therefore, not be dependent on her teacher's intervention. Similarly, suppose a student encounters a teacher who constantly reprimands and seldom compliments him. Is it possible for the student to modify the teacher's behavior so that the teacher will reinforce the student more and punish him less? These questions will be discussed in the present section.

Students as Modifiers of Student Behavior   It is obvious that students strongly influence each other's behavior through both reinforcement and punishment. Thus students are pleased when their classmates compliment their achievements or appearance and are distraught when ridiculed in these regards. The question becomes whether teachers can engineer peer influence in such a manner as to produce desirable changes. The process usually involves teaching the students some basic behavorial principles and then allowing the children to apply them.

One program was based on the assumption that peer influence is greatest when the modifiers are somewhat older than the youngsters whose behavior is being modified (Long and Madsen, 1975). In this case the behavior modifiers were five years old and the students were three years old. The younger children were in a day-care center and had exhibited problems including not responding to teacher questions, talking-out behavior, and throwing food. The older children were in a kindergarten class at the same day-care center and were considered socially mature. The young behavior modifiers experienced a training program in which they learned how to identify appropriate behavior and to administer approval and disapproval. In the classroom they would reinforce appropriate behavior with praise, affectionate touching, holding the hand, kissing, and smiling. Disapproval involved a grimace and a statement such as "You're irresponsible," or "That's bad." The procedure resulted in a great decrease in inappropriate behavior.

Grieger, Kauffman, and Grieger (1976) used an interesting procedure to increase prosocial behavior and reduce aggressive behavior among kindergarten children. They surmised that if children reported friendly and cooperative incidents involving their classmates, such behaviors would increase, and aggressive behaviors would diminish. During sharing time, each youngster was asked to name a classmate who had been friendly to her and to identify the friendly behavior. Each child who was mentioned could choose a happy face badge. This procedure resulted in more cooperative and fewer aggressive behaviors. With some modifications it would be interesting to see if such a tactic could improve social interactions among older students and even among adults.

It is also possible to train older children to modify each other's behavior. For example, Mosier and Vaal (1970) worked with an eleven-year-old boy who frequently called a classmate a name he disliked. The latter child was instructed to ignore the former and walk away from him if he was called the name (thus, using time out). If the teasing child spoke to him without calling him the name, he was to express his satisfaction. The problem was eliminated in a few days.

A more extensive program for dealing with teasing behavior was conducted by Graubard, Rosenberg, and Miller (1971). The study involved special-class children who were frequently taunted by schoolmates in regular classes. The regular-class children would call the special-class children "tardos," "rejects from the funny farm," and so on. It was common for some children to throw one child's hat while he tried to reclaim it. Such problems can be devastating to the victims. They may cry, avoid social contact with other children, or run to their parents and teachers for help. Although it is important to teach students not to taunt other children, it is also important to teach the recipients of such misdeeds how to deal with the problems. The tactic used in the present study was to show the special-class children how to walk away from the chase-the-cap game, and not make eye contact with the children who were provoking them. They also taught the youngsters how to reinforce desirable behavior by sharing desired objects and giving compliments. As a result, teasing decreased and desirable social interactions increased.

Having students carry out behavior modification programs with their schoolmates has some obvious advantages. First, the students learn which factors cause behavior to change and thereby develop skills they can use in many situations. Also, as was mentioned earlier, students can frequently observe behaviors that teachers miss. Finally, students may sometimes have a stronger influence on their classmates than do teachers. As was the case with student tutoring, it is important that teachers monitor student behavior modification programs and inform relevant individuals of the details and progress.

Students as Modifiers of Teacher Behavior   It should be recognized that just as teachers modify student behavior, so do students modify teacher behavior. For example, a student who does not become orderly when a teacher politely requests that he do so, but does become orderly when the teacher yells at him, is teaching the teacher to yell at him. If this pattern is repeated frequently, it can be expected that the teacher will control the student's behavior through yelling. Also, some teachers may be aware of an incoming student's reputation as a troublemaker. The teacher's approach from the outset may be to use disapproval to control the student's behavior. The question then becomes whether students can modify their teacher's behavior, so as to produce more favorable social interaction.

An example of this approach was shown by Polirstok and Greer (1977). The student in the study was an eighth-grade girl who was regarded as an extreme discipline problem. Data indicated that the teachers' use of approval in four academic classrooms was low, whereas their use of disapproval was high. The student experienced a program in which she learned how to reinforce her teachers when they approved of her behavior. In role playing situations, she learned to use statements such as, "I appreciate that," "super," "thank you," and "right on." When she used such statements in response to desirable teacher behavior in the classroom, there was an overall increase in teacher approvals, and a decrease in disapprovals.

A comprehensive program for modifying teacher behavior was provided by Graubard et al. (1971). The study involved seven seventh- and eighth-grade special-education students who were being reintegrated into regular classes. The teachers were resisting the mainstreaming program and were using disapproval comments at a greater rate than approvals. The students were taught how to make eye contact with the teacher and to ask for academic help. They also learned to compliment their teachers with comments such as "Gee, it makes me feel good and work so much better when you praise me," and "Ah hah! Now, I understand; I could never get that point before." The students also showed up early for class and asked for extra assignments! Not only did more favorable interaction between teachers and students take place, but the amount of time spent in the regular classes greatly increased.

Two points concerning the modification of teacher behavior by students should be noted. First, some teachers may object to having their behavior unknowingly modified. This problem was handled in the Polirstok and Greer (1977) study by having the teachers agree to allow a research project to take place in their classrooms. The teachers were not informed of all details of the program in order to prevent bias. Second, it is not clear whether classroom programs should concentrate on modifying student or teacher behavior. Perhaps the best approach is to modify the behavior of both parties.

HOME-BASED PROGRAMS

There are times when teachers may be willing to carry out behavior modification procedures, but cannot identify effective reinforcers for their students. This may be particularly true for students in secondary schools for whom desired reinforcers are often expensive. Other teachers may be concerned that awarding reinforcers to some students will upset classmates who are not on special programs. Still other teachers may be reluctant to engage in behavioral programs because they see the administering of reinforcers as time consuming and disruptive to their teaching routines. In all such cases, teachers should consider using *home-based programs*, in which teachers rate student performance and send the reports to the parents. As such, parents can discuss their children's program with them, help them with their work, and reinforce them for suitable achievement. Parents have traditionally received report cards from teachers, but the reports come so infrequently that they can be meaningless.

Dougherty and Dougherty (1977) used a home-based reinforcement program in a private school involving 15 fourth graders. Although none of the students was seriously disruptive, they frequently failed to submit homework assignments and tended to talk out in class. After baseline, the authors devised a daily report card in which teachers rated the students from one to four on "Behavior," "Schoolwork," and "Homework." Students received a four on homework when all homework was completed and totally accurate. They received smaller scores for work that was less complete and less accurate. Similarly, they received high scores for not talking out and low scores if they did. One week before the program was implemented, the parents received letters describing the daily report card system. After a student brought home a report card, the parents were to discuss the ratings with their children, praise them for high ratings, and work on areas requiring improvement. If a student did not bring home a report card, the parents were to consider the ratings to be poor. As a result of the program, talk outs were nearly eliminated and homework was completed more regularly.

The information provided on the daily report cards can be extensive or limited. One card might only give "Yes" or "No" information as to whether students obeyed classroom rules (see for example, Bailey, Wolf, and Phillips, 1970) or the ratings can be more precise. Also the report card can include information on different aspects of a student's performance in various academic subjects (see for example, Schumaker, Hovell, and Sherman, 1977) or a report can simply indicate a student's behavior in one area. Decisions as to the precision that will be attained and the number of areas that will be rated depend on the amount of time a teacher can devote to the effort and the number of areas that are problematic for the student. Figure 2-3 depicts a simple daily report, whereas Figure 2-4 shows a report conveying a great deal of information.

Two matters that must be dealt with in setting up a home-based system are how much parent training there should be and how often reports should be sent home. It appears that home-based programs can be successful with minimal amounts of parent training. For example, Ayllon, Garber, and Pisor (1975) were successful after conducting only one two-hour meeting to inform parents of the program. In a study requiring even less parent training, Lahey, Gendrich, Gendrich, Schnelle, Gant, and

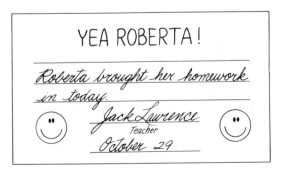

FIGURE 2-3 A hypothetical home report card to encourage a girl to bring in her homework each day.

Daily Report Card

Name_____   Date_____

Period	Homework Completed? (1-5)	Quality of Homework (1-10)	Class Participation (1-5)	In-Class Work (1-20)	Follow Classroom Rules (1-10)	Behavior toward other Students (1-10)	Assignment Copied Down (1-5)	Teacher's Initials
Math								
Social Studies								
English								
Physical Science								
Social Science								
Health Ed.								
Physical Ed.								

Parent's Signature_____

FIGURE 2-4 A hypothetical daily report card in which several aspects of a student's performance are rated each day. Some aspects of performance can be rated from one to five, others from one to ten, and another from one to twenty.

McNees (1977) simply sent parents a letter describing the prospective program. At times it may be necessary to supplement initial training with follow-up phone calls to provide parents with feedback and further instructions.

In most home-based studies, teachers send parents reports on a daily basis. Bailey et al. (1970) found, however, that after an initial period of daily reports, it was possible to shift to a twice-weekly system, without losing progress. Also (as described in the "Schedules of Reinforcement" section of Chapter 1, p. 15) Saudargas, Madsen, and Scott (1977) found that students performed well with only one report per week. Progress was better when the students could not predict who would receive a report on a given day, than it was when all students received reports on Fridays. Also the teacher indicated that it was easier to write seven reports each day, than to write the entire class's reports at the end of the week.

There are several advantages in home-based programs. First, they allow the awarding of very appealing reinforcers that are not feasible in school settings. Reinforcers such as staying up late, weekend movies, and trips can be provided at no expense to the school. Such activities may even enhance parent-child relations. Second, the programs can be effective even with minimal time spent on parent training. Paralleling this is the fact that many of the rating systems take only a few minutes of teacher time. Third, parents who receive frequent feedback on their children's performance can become actively involved in their programs. Thus a parent can tutor a child in a particular academic subject before she falls too far behind. Fourth, providing desired rewards outside of class usually does not irritate students who are not on reinforcement programs. Fifth, the programs can be tailored toward the academic and management problems of individual students, yet operate on many children at the same time (Millman, Schaefer, and Cohen, 1980). Finally, home-based programs encourage a positive association between the home and school, supplanting the traditional relationship in which parents only hear from school personnel when their students have a problem. This can produce a beneficial communication in which each party provides the other with useful information on dealing with the child.

There are two problems that must be considered in setting up home-based programs. First, parents may not always conduct the programs properly. They may either deliver reinforcers when their children did not earn them, or they may fail to provide reinforcers that *are* merited. Secondly, it is possible that students who bring home unfavorable reports may be subjected to verbal or physical abuse. Thus, it is important that teachers stress the positive intention of the home reports and monitor the programs with meetings and telephone calls as much as possible.

SELF-CONTROL

Some educators admit to the effectiveness of behavior modification procedures but object to the fact that the teacher rather than the child himself modifies the youngster's behavior. Thus, although a teacher might devise and conduct a reinforcement system that enhances the academic development of the student, some educators would prefer that the child learn to modify his own behavior.

Several reasons have been proposed for having students learn to control their own behavior, as described in work by Kazdin (1980) and O'Leary and Dubey (1979). First, behaving independently is a valued characteristic in the present culture. Second, the youngsters will be less dependent on their teacher's management skills, and there will be less demand on teacher time. Third, due to conflicting activities, teachers miss many behaviors. Fourth, if a teacher administers a program to change a certain behavior, it is possible that in her absence students will revert to their old behaviors. Fifth, it has been found that performance is sometimes better when students participate in the structuring of their own program.

Self-control consists of any procedure which an individual engages in, in order to change some aspect of her behavior (Sulzer-Azaroff and Mayer, 1977). Examples of self-control endeavors are common. People will make a New Year's resolution to be more punctual, will leave a note on the dashboard to have the oil checked, and will set the alarm on their watch to remind themselves of an appointment. Similarly, teachers will promote self-control among their students by encouraging them to recall expressions, such as "Look before you leap," and "Thirty days hath September, ... " Even without instructions, children will attempt self-control by turning their heads to avoid an unpleasant sight, or bite their lips to avoid laughing during religious services.

One popular view of self-control is that "some people have it, and others do not." A behavioral position, on the other hand, is that self-control can be learned in the same way as other kinds of behavior. Efforts, therefore, concentrate on the best means to teach students to develop self-control. As such, programs have been devised which involve self-recording of behavior, self-selection of goals and consequences, and self-administration of consequences. The present section will describe self-recording and contingency contracting. Contingency contracting encompasses the practices of selecting goals and consequences, and self-administering consequences.

SELF-RECORDING

It has been found that *self-recording*—the practice of keeping a record of one's behavior—can alter the rate of the behavior. Thus, noting the number of cigarettes one smoked may decrease her rate, whereas keeping a record of the number of times an individual complimented others may increase his rate of compliments. In classroom settings, self-recording has increased attention to task, academic output, and class attendance, and has decreased talking out and aggressing toward others (O'Leary and Dubey, 1979).

Broden, Hall, and Mitts (1971) provided an early example of self-recording. The case involved Liza, an eighth-grade girl who had received a D− in history and seldom engaged in "study behavior." Study behavior, which consisted of attending to classroom assignments and following teacher directions, was occurring 30 percent of the time during baseline. The school counselor requested that the history teacher use a praise procedure to increase Liza's study rate, but the teacher felt this was not feasible due to the lecture format of his class. As an alternative, the counselor worked out a self-recording procedure with Liza. Her instructions were to rate her behavior as "study" or "nonstudy," "when she thought of it," during history class. She was to place a "+" in one of the boxes if she had been studying for the previous few minutes, and a "−" if she had not been. With the self-recording procedure, Liza's study rate increased to an average of 78 percent and her history grade increased to a C.

In some cases it might be helpful to signal students to record their behavior; Glynn, Thomas, and Shee (1973), for example, had a beep sound periodically. At these times, the second graders were to put a check on their papers only if they were working on assigned tasks. Similarly, Hallahan, Lloyd, Kosiewicz, Kauffman, and Graves (1979) had a tone emitted from a tape recorder. When the sound occurred, an eight-year-old boy was to check "Yes" or "No" under the title, "Was I Paying Attention?"

In order to attain a self record of behavior, a student could use a pencil and paper (see Figure 2-5) or a wrist counter. (See Figure 3-2, p. 99). Maletsky (1974), for example, dealt with a student who furiously waved his hand in response to teacher questions, even when he did not know the answer. The youngster wore a wrist counter which he pressed each time the undesired behavior occurred. Within a few weeks hand waving was no longer a problem.

Teachers can use similar procedures to attain a record of their own behavior. Teachers who wish to increase their rate of praise might use a wrist counter or put several tokens in a pocket. The object of the latter would be to get rid of all the tokens by removing one each time the teacher praised a student. Whether dealing with student or teacher behavior, self-recording might be enhanced by graphing daily scores and setting goals which require progressive improvement.

It is difficult to say why self-recording procedures are effective. It is possible that when an individual keeps a record of her behavior she becomes more aware of it and is more capable of changing it. Also, when a person has a record of her behavior, she can show the measure to others and presumably derive reinforcement from them. Even though the reasons for the effectiveness of self-recording are unclear, its advantages are evident. It is an inexpensive way of teaching students self-control and it can be used in situations in which teachers are unwilling or unable to implement programs involving external control.

There are several factors that must be taken into account when using

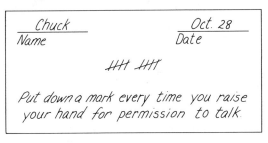

FIGURE 2-5 Sample self-recording sheet that could be used to increase the rate of handraising.

self-recording. First, recording is more likely to be accurate if the behavior of interest is clearly defined and if student records are checked for accuracy. The latter point is critical both for detecting errors and dishonesty. Second, self-recording tends to produce only a temporary improvement in behavior, unless a reinforcement component is added. Third, Komaki and Dore-Boyce (1978) found that only those students who had indicated a strong motivation to change their behavior were likely to benefit from a self-recording procedure.

CONTINGENCY CONTRACTS

A more encompassing effort to achieve self-control consists of a *contingency contract*. This is a written agreement between a teacher and a student (and sometimes a parent) that specifies the privileges a teacher will provide if a student behaves in a certain manner. Depending on the complexity of the contract, it may specify bonuses for outstanding performance, penalties the student or teacher must pay for failing to meet the terms of the contract, the conditions under which the contract may be negotiated, and an expiration date. Contracts may be used for virtually any aspect of student performance, including academic work, classroom deportment, and homework. Contracts may also be set up in a home-based manner in which parents provide the reinforcing activities.

Homme (1969) states some guidelines for writing an appropriate contract. Many of the suggestions are applicable to any behavior modification program:

1 The payoff should be immediate. This is especially important in the early stages of learning when the student is first becoming familiar with contracting.

2 The contract should provide frequent, small rewards for slight improvements in behavior, rather than one large reward for a great change in behavior. Thus, it is better to give a student one piece of candy after completing two arithmetic problems than to reward him with an entire box of candy for doing twenty-five problems. This also is most important during the early stages of learning.

3 Both sides of the agreement should be of relatively equal weight. Hence, a student should not receive a trip to the zoo after working for a minute, nor should he be required to spell fifty words correctly for two minutes of free time.

4 The terms of the contract should be clear. A student should know, for example, that he is required to do *five* arithmetic problems for a certain reward rather than to do *some* problems for the reward.

5 Because of the different learning levels and learning rates of children, it is better to devise individual rather than group contracts.

6 The tasks should be short enough so that they can be completed in the allotted amount of time.

As implied by the term itself, contracts should involve negotiation between the student and teacher. The negotiation process should not only occur prior to the initiation of the contract, but also during the time the contract is being implemented. In this manner, adjustments can be made when it is learned that the work is too easy or too difficult, that the rewards have lost their effectiveness, or that the terms of the contract are unfair in some manner. It is also important that teachers be sensitive to the student's input as to how much work she should be required to perform, and the amount and kind of reinforcement she should receive. At the same time, the teacher must guard against contracts that are biased too much in a student's favor.

Figures 2-6 and 2-7 represent possible contingency contracts. The former contract is a home-based program designed to increase homework completion, whereas the latter is a classroom program intended to decrease hitting incidents.

Self-control can be achieved through contingency contracts by gradually transferring control of the terms of the contract from the teacher to the student. Sloane, Buckholdt, Jenson, and Crandall (1979) described the steps that a teacher could use to achieve the shift of control. The amount of time each step lasts depends on student progress:

FIGURE 2-6 A sample contingency contract devised to improve a student's homework performance through a home-based program.

Homework Contract

We agree that whenever Liza does her homework and it is at least 80% correct, she can stay up an extra 15 minutes. If she meets the terms of her contract every school day, she can have a friend sleep over on the weekend.

September 30
Date

October 21
Expiration Date

Liza Melton
Child's Signature

Mike Melton
Parent's Signature

Carla Robinson
Teacher's Signature

Behavior Contract

We agree that whenever Charles goes an entire

day without hitting another student, he will receive

one point. Whenever he receives a total of five

points, he can be the classroom messenger for

one day, and move his desk for a day.

Whenever he hits a student, he will spend 10

minutes in the corner of the room.

January 18
Program Starts
January 31
Program Ends

Charles Gomez
Child's Signature
Heidi Marks
Teacher's Signature

FIGURE 2-7 A sample contingency contract to reduce hitting behavior.

1 Initially the teacher writes the contract.

2 The next step is the same as the first, except that the teacher specifies the reinforcement and asks the student if the amount is too large or too small.

3 The teacher writes the part of the contract describing the required behavior, but asks the student to indicate what he feels is an appropriate amount of reinforcement. If the teacher agrees with the student's suggestion, the contract is approved.

4 The teacher writes the contract, but asks the student to approve the amount of work that is required.

5 The teacher specifies the amount of reinforcement the student will receive and asks the student to suggest the amount of work that should be required.

6 The student writes the entire contract and the teacher signs it, if he approves.

To summarize the fading approach, the teacher initially writes the contract. With progress, the student is given more control over the amount of reinforcement she should receive, then is given more control of how much behavior is required, and finally constructs her own contract, pending teacher approval.

One advantage of contracting systems is that they promote self-management skills that are maintained even when contracts are no longer used (Cantrell, Cantrell, Huddleston, and Woolridge, 1969). Second, students learn negotiation skills in the process of arriving at a contract. Third, as a result of receiving student input in the negotiation process, teachers receive valuable information on potential reinforcers and the capacity of students to achieve desired goals. Fourth, students and their parents, particularly at the secondary school level, seem not to object to behavior modification procedures that come about through negotiation. This may be because contracting allows a student to be a mature contributor to her own education. Finally, by setting up contracts for each student, teachers can individualize instruction.

There are at least two problems teachers can encounter in using contracting procedures. First, some students may be unreasonable in negotiating a contract. Some will make unfair demands for reinforcers and others will complain vigorously when asked to accept less reinforcement after behavior improves. (Adults have been known to behave in the same manner.) Second, it is difficult to use contracting systems with low-functioning students, due to the complexity of the process.

CLOSING COMMENTS ON SELF-CONTROL

Self-control procedures are used when individuals are attempting to respond to long-term, rather than short-term reinforcers. Thus, an individual who tries to stop smoking is giving up the immediate reinforcement associated with smoking, for the long-term health benefits. It should also be understood that behaviors that are seen as under self-control are also controlled by external factors. That is, an individual may use a procedure that effectively reduces his weight. Although the reduced weight may be seen as a result of self-control tactics, external factors such as compliments from friends, increased social opportunities, and improved health are elements which are also operating.

CLASSROOM ORGANIZATION

Every day, teachers make important decisions that influence their instructional effectiveness. They decide how to arrange the desks in the classroom, which students should be placed next to each other, whether to write assignments on the chalkboard or mimeographed sheets, and how to schedule their day. The present section will offer information as to the effects some of these factors have on student behavior. In particular, there will be a discussion of the physical organization of the classroom and the means for scheduling a school day.

PHYSICAL ARRANGEMENT OF THE CLASSROOM

It is not unusual for a teacher to conjecture that a certain student's behavior is influenced by other pupils in the vicinity. In cases where there is a great deal of inappropriate interaction between neighboring children, the teacher might separate the students in the hope that the new seating arrangement will produce an improvement in behavior. A portion of a study by Burdett, Egner, and McKenzie (1970) showed that such manipulations will sometimes have a beneficial effect on student performance. The youngster in the study was a first-grade boy who will be referred to as Wayne. At the beginning of the study, Wayne sat at the base of a U-shaped desk arrangement. On one side of Wayne sat a boy, whereas a girl sat on the other side. Under this arrangement, Wayne attended to his work 68 percent of the time. During this time Wayne's teacher observed the tendency for Wayne and his boy neighbor to distract each other from classroom tasks. Thus, the teacher moved the boy who sat next to Wayne to another desk, and replaced him with a girl. With a girl on either side of him, Wayne's attending rate increased to 100 percent. (Different results might have been attained if the study had been done in a junior high school.)

Another factor that can influence student performance is the manner in which desks are arranged throughout the classroom. Traditionally, teachers have arranged the desks in a row formation as follows:

A   B   C   D   E

F   G   H   I   J

•   •   •   •   •

•   •   •   •   •

•   •   •   •   •

More recently, however, an increasing number of teachers have been arranging students in a "cluster" or table formation as follows:

A   B   E   F   • •   • •

C   D   G   H   • •   • •

Child A sits next to child B and directly faces child C. Child D faces B and sits next to C. A similar relationship exists for E, F, G, and H and the other clusters of children.

A study by Axelrod, Hall and Tams (1979) compared the talk-out performance of thirty-two seventh graders under the table and row formations. As indicated in Figure 2-8, there was an average of fifty-eight instances of talking-out behavior per period when the students first sat in the table arrangement. In the next phase when a row arrangement was used, talk outs decreased to an average of thirty. The authors speculated that there were more talk outs in the table arrangement because of the proximity of the students to each other and the ease with which the students could make eye contact with each other and start conversations.

In some school environments several teachers are present in the same classroom, while different activities are occurring simultaneously. This is frequently the case in preschool, special-education, and "open" classroom settings. The question may arise as to how best to deploy the available personnel. That is, is it better to have teachers stationed at one activity and direct different students as they come to the teacher's location; or would it be better to have a teacher move from one location to the next, with the same group of students? LeLaurin and Risley (1972) compared each of the above staffing arrangements in a day-care center with thirty-nine students and three teachers. They found that transition times from one activity to another were smoother (shorter) when teachers remained in the same location and were responsible for only one activity.

FIGURE 2-8 The number of talk outs exhibited by 32 seventh-grade children in a life sciences class during rows and tables seating arrangements. *(From S. Axelrod, R. V. Hall, and A. Tams, "Comparison of Two Common Classroom Seating Arrangements,"* Academic Therapy, 15, *p. 34, 1979. By permission of the publishers.)*

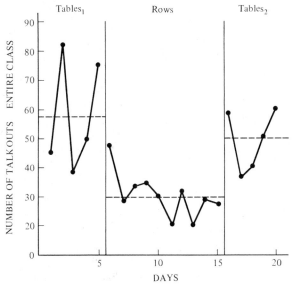

Ready access to reinforcers is an important factor in the teaching process. In providing training in fluent speech to a child who stutters, for example, a therapist who has reinforcers near her will generally be more effective than a therapist who must fumble around to locate the reinforcers. Likewise, it has been found that the sectioning off a portion of the classroom as a reinforcement area is an effective and convenient means of providing immediate rewards for desirable behavior.

Hopkins, Schutte, and Garton (1971) provided an excellent example of a reinforcement area with twenty-four first and second graders who were having difficulty completing printing and cursive writing assignments. Each day the teacher wrote on the chalkboard a printing assignment of about 200 letters for the first graders and a cursive writing assignment of approximately 250 letters for the second graders. She then passed out sheets of paper and asked the students to copy the lesson. During Baseline$_1$ the students gave their completed papers to the teacher and were instructed to return to their seats and to sit quietly. The children then had to wait for the last student to hand in his paper and have it graded before proceeding to the next subject. Under these conditions the group of first graders printed an average of six letters per minute, whereas the second graders wrote approximately seven letters per minute.

In the second phase of the study, the teacher gave the students in both groups fifty minutes to complete their assignments. If a child finished his assignment before the fifty-minute period was over, he was allowed to go immediately to the play area in the back of the classroom for the remainder of the session. The play area was separated from the remainder of the classroom by an L-shaped partition and consisted of a television set and a variety of games and toys. The children were allowed to bring toys and games from home to supplement those provided by the teacher (thus insuring that at least some items would be reinforcing to each of the children). When this procedure was in effect, the printing rate of the first graders went up by 25 percent and the writing rate of the second graders increased by 56 percent.

A later phase of the study consisted of allowing the students only forty-five minutes to complete the assignment and continuing to permit them to go to the play area. With less time to do their work, the first graders further increased their printing rate and the second graders their writing rate; both rates continued to increase when the assignment time was decreased to forty minutes and later to thirty-five.

I consider the procedure employed by Hopkins et al. an outstanding one. The main asset of their technique is the manner in which they provided reinforcement for the students as soon as they completed their assignments. Immediately after a student had finished his work, he could walk to the back of the classroom and engage in the reinforcing activities. In addition, the administering of the reinforcing activities required little effort on the part of the teacher, who was, therefore, able to continue with other classroom duties. Many other reinforcement systems do not contain these advantages. In a social reinforcement system, for example, teachers are not always able to praise students immediately after they behave appropriately. Other teachers find it difficult to administer praise to all children, particularly when the classrooms are large. Likewise, token reinforcement tactics are sometimes hampered by practical problems such as record-keeping chores, stealing of tokens and back-up reinforcers, and replenishing popular reinforcers.

There are at least two difficulties that can arise with the present procedure. First, it is possible that the children will be noisy during the time they are playing, thus interfering with the work of their slower classmates. In the Hopkins et al. study, the teacher avoided the problem by making a rule that if a child became particularly noisy, he would have to leave the play area and return to his desk. The authors reported only three incidents of this nature. Second, it is possible that the students will carelessly rush through an assignment in order to gain quick access to the play area. In order to avoid this difficulty, the authors kept track of the number of errors the students made during each condition. Suprisingly, they found that, in general, the faster the students completed an assignment, the *fewer* errors they made. During the final phase of the study with the first graders, however, an exception to this rule was noted: some of the first graders were making more errors as their speed increased. This situation was remedied by requiring the students to recopy a portion of their assignment if their error rate exceeded an individually determined criterion.

Homme (1969) gives detailed recommendations on the organization of a reinforcement area. First, he describes the layout of a classroom containing a reinforcement area. As illustrated in Figure 2-9, the teacher's and students' desks are on one side of the room and there is an L-shaped partition separating the reinforcement area from the rest of the room. He then lists events that can take place in the reinforcement area for various age groups. They are as follows:

(Three- to five-years-old)
    a Being read to
    b Looking at books
    c Playing with crayons
    d Painting
    e Working puzzles
    f Cutting and pasting
    g Playing with clay
(Six- to eight-years-old)
    a Reading stories
    b Playing with cards
    c Drawing
    d Painting

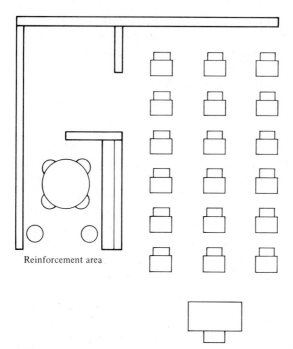

Reinforcement area

FIGURE 2-9 The suggested layout of a classroom containing a reinforcement area. *(From L. Homme, How to Use Contingency Contracting in the Classroom, Champaign, Ill.: Research Press, 1969, p. 84. By permission of the publishers.)*

    e Playing with Tinker Toys
    f Playing dominos
    g Working puzzles
(Nine- to eleven-years-old)
    a Reading comics
    b Reading science fiction, mystery stories, and so on.
    c Working puzzles
    d Playing chess
    e Playing checkers
    f Drawing
    g Painting
(Twelve- to fourteen-years-old)
    a Playing chess
    b Playing cards
    c Writing letters
    d Reading magazines, books, comics
    e Playing dominos
    f Talking
    g Playing tic tac toe
(Fifteen- to sixteen-years-old)
    a Talking

b Playing tic tac toe
c Playing chess
d Reading books, magazines, comics
e Working jigsaw puzzles
f Playing checkers
g Writing letters

Homme also makes the following suggestions with respect to reinforcement areas:

1 After determining the reinforcing events, the teacher should make up a reinforcement "menu." The menu consists of the activities the students may engage in while they are in the reinforcement area. It can also indicate the amount of time the students are permitted to participate in the activities. The menu should be posted adjacent to the reinforcement area so that it will be accessible to the students.

2 The children should spend no less than three minutes nor more than ten in the reinforcement area. With less than three minutes, the students cannot become sufficiently involved in an activity to make it interesting, and with more than ten, they may become satiated on the privileges.

3 In order to control the amount of time a student is in the reinforcement area, timing devices such as oven and memo timers can be used. Teachers can also use sign-in and sign-out sheets on which the students are required to state the time of entry and exit. The teacher can make periodic checks to make sure the students are not exceeding their time limits.

Undoubtedly, there are a variety of problems that might confront teachers in setting up a reinforcement area. It is usually worth the trouble that is involved, however, since the associated contingency is often effective with children at a variety of age and learning levels.

SCHEDULING OF ACTIVITIES

In scheduling classroom activities, teachers must make decisions on which activities to start the day with, which subjects should be taught in the morning and which in the afternoon, which subjects should follow each other, and so on. Sloane (1976) made some suggestions for the scheduling of activities:

1 Begin each day with an activity that students prefer. In this manner the youngsters are reinforced for coming to school promptly.

2 Alternate the least-preferred activities with the most-preferred activities. In this way students can be rewarded for completing the less-desired work with the opportunity to engage in a preferred activity. For example, suppose most students in a given class do not enjoy English grammar but do like to listen to stories. The teacher could then inform the class that when all students complete their grammar assignment, they will have a story read to them.

3 In many cases it is better to schedule two medium-length assignments during the day, than to have one large one. For example, one twenty-five–minute math period in the morning and another in the afternoon might be better than one fifty-minute math period.

4 It is often helpful to publicly post each day's schedule. This is particularly important when the schedule changes from one day to the next.

Another matter that must be dealt with in sequencing activities is what type of event should follow an event involving vigorous activity. For example, after students are engaged in a competitive dodgeball or volleyball game, should teachers schedule a quiet activity such as silent reading, or an activity of moderate intensity such as student oral presentations? A study by Krantz and Risley (1977) found the latter to be preferable. That is, after students are involved in vigorous activity, they should be allowed to wind down slowly with a moderately intense activity.

In addition to considering which activity should follow another, teachers should be certain that they present lessons to students in a smooth, continuous manner. When teachers pause in the midst of a presentation, students can become distracted with incompatible activities. This point was demonstrated in a study by Carnine (1976) which compared a faster-paced presentation of reading activities with a slower-paced presentation. In the faster-paced presentation, a teacher presented a new question or demonstration right after the students responded. In the slower-paced presentation, the teacher waited five seconds after the students responded before continuing with the lesson. The faster-paced presentation resulted in a more on-task behavior, more correct answers, and more class participation than the slower-paced presentation.

SUMMARY

There are numerous procedures for modifying student behavior that can be derived from basic behavioral principles. For example, teachers can use group contingencies in which student consequences are dependent to some degree on the behavior of their classmates. One type of group contingency is known as consequence sharing in which one student's behavior determines the consequences the entire class receives. An example would be awarding an entire class a privilege if a particular student exceeds a criterion for academic performance. Another type of group contingency is an interdependent system in which the behavior of all students affects the consequences for all group members. An example would be a class party following a week of perfect attendance by all students. Advantages of group contingencies include ease of record keeping and administration, student cooperation in producing desired goals, and the *non*necessity to identify students who cause problems. Difficulties with group contingencies include the possibilities of undue social pressure and intentional subversion of the system.

Students can be involved in programs to modify their classmates' or their teachers' behaviors. Many benefits have been derived when students have served as tutors for other students. The process often results in academic gains for the tutors and tutees, permits the teacher to spend more time with other students, and is inexpensive. Research has shown that both peer and cross-age tutoring is effective, but that peer tutoring is more convenient. Tutoring has been effective even when the tutors were not trained. What seems most critical is that students experience a 1:1 learning arrangement. Programs exist in which students have been able to modify the behavior of classmates. This has been done in order to reduce general classroom disturbances and to get provocative students to stop antagonizing certain youngsters. Students have also modified teacher behavior so as to make them more approving and less disapproving. Such programs have usually involved teaching the students basic behavioral principles and having them practice the procedures in role-playing situations.

An alternative to programs in which students receive reinforcement in school is to use a home-based program. With such a program, teachers rate some aspect of a student's performance and send reports home to the parents. Reports are usually sent home daily, but can be sent home less frequently and still be effective. The reports can center on one, or on many aspects of a student's behavior. Home-based programs are inexpensive to the schools, permit the use of a wide variety of reinforcers, do not disrupt the classroom, and allow parents to have ongoing involvement in their children's education. Such programs should be monitored closely to be certain they are properly implemented and to prevent abusive treatment when students do not do well.

Behavior modification programs usually involve a teacher modifying the behavior of a student. In some cases it is possible to have students learn to control their own behavior. Self-control is seen as desirable because it entails minimal teacher time, allows for improvement of behavior in the absence of the teacher, and because student involvement in structuring a program sometimes improves performance. One procedure for self-control is self-recording. Thus, a student can record the number of times he was punctual, with the intention of increasing his rate, or make a record of the number of times he hit other students, with the intention of decreasing his rate. Another means of achieving self-control is through contingency contracting. This is a written agreement between a student and a teacher, specifying the rewards the youngster will receive if she meets the criterion for reinforcement. The intention is that with progress, the student will take over more responsibility for setting the terms of the contract.

The physical arrangement of the classroom and the manner in which activities are scheduled can influence student performance. Research has shown that a student's neighbor can affect his behavior, that arranging students in clusters will sometimes produce more disruption than row arrangements, and that reinforcement areas in the classroom can serve as a convenient and powerful incentive for work completion. In scheduling activities, teachers should begin the day with a favored activity, alternate the least favored with the most favored, and have students wind down gradually from vigorous activities.

QUESTIONS AND ACTIVITIES

1 Describe each of the two types of group contingencies discussed in this chapter and identify a situation for which each would be superior to the other.

2 Give three advantages and disadvantages of group contingency procedures.

3 Name three precautions that should be taken when students are involved in programs to change their classmates' or teachers' behavior.

4 Under what conditions is it better to use a peer tutor over a cross-age tutor? When is the converse true?

5 Have a colleague play the role of a student who is frequently teased by his classmates. Indicate how you would teach the individual basic behavioral principles and to modify the behavior of the students who are taunting him.

6 Give five benefits that can occur when peer tutoring is used.

7 Describe three situations in which it might be better to use a home-based, rather than a school-based reinforcement program.

8 Devise a home-based reinforcement program for a student who is having management and academic problems in three subject areas. Include a diagram of the home report.

9 Use a self-recording procedure to improve some aspect of your teaching performance.

10 Set up a contingency contract to modify an academic problem in your classroom.

11 List six activities that are typically on your students' daily schedule. Describe the order in which they should occur during the day. Give the rationale for your order.

REFERENCES

Axelrod, S., R. V. Hall, and A. Tams: "Comparison of Two Common Classroom Seating Arrangements," *Academic Therapy*, **15**, pp. 29–36, 1979.

Axelrod, S., and J. Paluska: "A Component Analysis of the Effects of a Classroom Game on Spelling Performance," in E. Ramp and G. Semb (eds.) *Behavior Analysis: Areas of Research and Application* (Englewood Cliffs, N.J.: Prentice-Hall, 1975), pp. 277–282.

Ayllon, T., S. Garber, and K. Pisor: "The Elimination of Discipline Problems Through a Combined School-Home Motivational System," *Behavior Therapy*, **6**, pp. 616–626, 1975.

Bailey, J., M. M. Wolf, and E. Phillips: "Home-Based Reinforcement and the Modification of Pre-Delinquents' Classroom Behavior," *Journal of Applied Behavior Analysis*, **3**, pp. 223–233, 1970.

Barrish, H. H., M. Saunders, and M. M. Wolf: "Good Behavior Game: Effects of Individual Contingencies for Group Consequences on Disruptive Behavior in a Classrom," *Journal of Applied Behavior Analysis*, **2**, pp. 119–124, 1969.

Broden, M., R. V. Hall, and B. Mitts: "The Effects of Teacher Attention on Attending Behavior of Two Eighth-Grade Students," *Journal of Applied Behavior Analysis*, **4**, pp. 191–199, 1971.

Burdett, C., A. Egner, and H. McKenzie: "P 14," in H. McKenzie (ed.), *1968–1969 Report of the Consulting Teacher Program*, vol. II (Burlington, Vt.: Consulting Teacher Program, College of Education, The University of Vermont, 1970), pp. 218–227.

Cantrell, R. P., M. L. Cantrell, C. M. Huddleston, and R. L. Woolridge: "Contingency Contracting with School Problems," *Journal of Applied Behavior Analysis*, **2**, pp. 215–220, 1969.

Carnine, D. W.: "Effects of Two Teacher-Presentation Rates on Off-Task Behavior, Answering Correctly, and Participation," *Journal of Applied Behavior Analysis*, **9**, pp. 199–206, 1976.

Cloward, R. D.: "Studies in Tutoring," *Journal of Experimental Education*, **36**, pp. 14–26, 1967.

Conlon, M. F., C. Hall, and E. M. Hanley: "The Effects of a Peer Correction Procedure on the Arithmetic Accuracy for Two Elementary School

Children," in G. Semb (ed.), *Behavior Analysis and Education—1972* (Lawrence, Kan.: University of Kansas, Department of Human Development, 1972). pp. 205–210.

Dineen, J. P., H. B. Clark, and T. R. Risley: "Peer Tutoring Among Elementary Students: Educational Benefits to the Tutor," *Journal of Applied Behavior Analysis*, **10**, pp. 231–238, 1977.

Dougherty, E. H., and A. Dougherty: "The Daily Report Card: A Simplified and Flexible Package for Classroom Behavior Management," *Psychology in the Schools*, **14**, pp. 191–195, 1977.

Gallagher, P. A., S. I. Sulzbacher, and R. E. Shores: "A Group Contingency for Classroom Management of Emotionally Disturbed Children." Paper presented at the Kansas Council for Exceptional Children, Wichita, March, 1967.

Glynn, E. L., J. D. Thomas, and S. M. Shee: "Behavioral Self-Control of On-Task Behavior in an Elementary Classroom," *Journal of Applied Behavior Analysis*, **6**, pp. 105–113, 1973.

Graubard, P. S., H. Rosenberg, and M. B. Miller: "Student Applications of Behavior Modification to Teachers and Environments or Ecological Approaches to Social Deviancy," in E. A. Ramp and B. L. Hopkins (eds.), *A New Direction for Education: Behavior Analysis*, vol. I (Lawrence, Kan.: Department of Human Development, 1971), pp. 80–101.

Greenberg, D. J., and W. J. O'Donnell: "A Note on the Effects of Group and Individual Contingencies upon Deviant Classroom Behavior," *Journal of Child Psychology and Psychiatry*, **13**, pp. 55–58, 1972.

Grieger, T., J. M. Kauffman, and R. M. Grieger: "Effects of Peer Reporting on Cooperative Play and Aggression of Kindergarten Children," *Journal of School Psychology*, **14**, pp. 307–313, 1976.

Hallahan, D. P., J. Lloyd, M. M. Kosiewicz, J. M. Kauffman, and A. W. Graves: "Self-Monitoring of Attention as a Treatment for a Learning-Disabled Boy's Off-Task Behavior," *Learning Disability Quarterly*, **2**, pp. 24–32, 1979.

Harris, V. W., and J. A. Sherman: "Effects of Peer Tutoring and Consequences on the Math Performance of Elementary Classroom Students," *Journal of Applied Behavior Analysis*, **6**, pp. 587–597, 1973.

Homme, L.: *How to Use Contingency Contracting in the Classroom* (Champaign, Ill.: Research Press, 1969).

Hopkins, B. L., R. C. Schutte, and K. L. Garton: "The Effects of Access to a Playroom on the Rate and Quality of Printing and Writing of First- and Second-Grade Students," *Journal of Applied Behavior Analysis*, **4**, pp. 77–87, 1971.

Jenkins, J. R., and W. F. Mayhall: "Development and Evaluation of a Resource Teacher," *Exceptional Children*, **43**, pp. 21–29, 1976.

Johnson, M., and J. S. Bailey: "Cross-age Tutoring: Fifth Graders as Arithmetic Tutors for Kindergarten Children," *Journal of Applied Behavior Analysis*, **7**, pp. 223–232, 1974.

Kazdin, A. E.: *Behavior Modification in Applied Settings* (Homewood, Ill.: Dorsey Press, 1980).

Komaki, J., and K. Dore-Boyce: "Self-Recording: Its Effects on Individuals High and Low in Motivation," *Behavior Therapy*, **9**, pp. 65–72, 1978.

Krantz, P. J., and T. R. Risley: "Behavioral Ecology in the Classroom," in K. D. O'Leary and S. G. O'Leary (eds.), *Classroom Management: The Successful Use of Behavior Modification* (New York: Pergamon Press, 1977), pp. 349–366.

Lahey, B. B., J. G. Gendrich, S. I. Gendrich, J. F. Schnelle, D. S. Gant, and M. P. McNees: "An Evaluation of Daily Report Cards with Minimal Teacher and Parent Contacts as an Efficient Method of Classroom Intervention," *Behavior Modification*, **1**, pp. 381–394, 1977.

LeLaurin, K., and T. R. Risley: "The Organization of Day-Care Environments: 'Zone' *versus* 'Man to Man' Staff Assignments," *Journal of Applied Behavior Analysis*, **5**, pp. 225–232, 1972.

Litow, L., and D. K. Pumroy: "A Brief Review of Classroom Group Oriented Contingencies," *Journal of Applied Behavior Analysis*, **8**, pp. 341–347, 1975.

Long, J., and C. H. Madsen: "Five-Year-Olds as Behavioral Engineers for Younger Students in a Day-Care Center," in E. Ramp and G. Semb (eds.), *Behavior Analysis: Areas of Research and Application* (Englewood Cliffs, N.J.: Prentice-Hall, 1975), pp. 341–356.

McCarty, T., S. Griffin, T. Apolloni, and R. E. Shores: "Increased Peer-Teaching with Group-Oriented Contingencies for Arithmetic Performance in Behavior-Disordered Adolescents," *Journal of Applied Behavior Analysis*, **10**, 313, 1977.

McLaughlin, T. F., and J. E. Malaby: "Elementary School Children as Behavioral Engineers," in E. Ramp and G. Semb (eds.) *Behavior Analysis: Areas of Research and Application* (Englewood Cliffs, N.J.: Prentice-Hall, 1975), pp. 319–328.

Maletsky, B. M.: "Behavior Recording as a Treatment: A Brief Note," *Behavior Therapy*, **5**, pp. 107–111, 1974.

Millman, H. L., C. S. Schaeffer, and J. L. Cohen: *Therapies for School Behavior Problems* (San Francisco: Jossey-Bass, 1980).

Mosier, D., and J. J. Vaal: "The Manipulation of One Child's Behavior by Another in a School Adjustment Classroom," *School Applications of Learning Theory*, **2**, pp. 25–27, 1970.

Neumann, J. K.: "The Analysis of Group Contingency Data," *Journal of Applied Behavior Analysis*, **10**, pp. 755–758, 1977.

O'Leary, S. G., and D. R. Dubey: "Applications of Self-Control Procedures by Children: A Review," *Journal of Applied Behavior Analysis*, **12**, pp. 449–465, 1979.

Polirstok, S. R., and R. D. Greer: "Remediation of Mutually Aversive Interactions between a Problem Student and Four Teachers by Training the Student in Reinforcement Techniques," *Journal of Applied Behavior Analysis*, **10**, pp. 707–716, 1977.

Robertson, S. J., D. M. DeReus, and R. S. Drabman: "Peer and College-Student Tutoring as Reinforcement in a Token Economy," *Journal of Applied Behavior Analysis*, **9**, pp. 169–177, 1976.

Saudargas, R. W., C. H. Madsen, and J. W. Scott: "Differential Effects of Fixed and Variable-Time Feedback on Production Rates of Elementary School Children," *Journal of Applied Behavior Analysis*, **10**, pp. 673–678, 1977.

Schumaker, J. B., M. F. Hovell, and J. F. Sherman: "An Analysis of the Effect of Teacher Aides in an 'Open'-Style Classroom," *Journal of Applied Behavior Analysis*, **10**, pp. 449–464, 1977.

Sloane, H. N.: *Classroom Management: Remediation and Prevention* (New York: John Wiley & Sons, 1976).

Sloane, H. N., D. R. Buckholdt, W. R. Jenson, and J. A. Crandall: *Structured Teaching: A Design for Classroom Management and Instruction* (Champaign, Ill.: Research Press, 1979).

Sulzer-Azaroff, B., and G. R. Mayer: *Applying Behavior-Analysis Procedures with Children and Youth* (New York: Holt, Rinehart, and Winston, 1977).

Switzer, E. B., T. E. Deal, and J. S. Bailey: "The Reduction of Stealing in Second Graders Using a Group Contingency," *Journal of Applied Behavior Analysis*, **10**, pp. 267–272, 1977.

Tribble, A., and R. V. Hall: "Effects of Peer Approval on Completion of Arithmetic Assignments," in F. W. Clark, D. R. Evans, and L. A. Hamerlynck (eds.), *Implementing Behavioral Programs for Schools and Clinics: Third Banff International Conference* (Champaign, Ill.: Research Press, 1972), pp. 139–140.

Wilson, S. H., and R. L. Williams: "The Effects of Group Contingencies on First Graders' Academic and Social Behaviors," *Journal of School Psychology*, **11**, pp. 110–117, 1973.

3

Measurement and Research Design

Although the chapter on measurement follows those which discuss the various principles and techniques of behavior modification, its importance is second to none. The purposes of measurement are to determine the present level of a student's behavior and whether the teacher's procedures favorably or adversely affect the student's behavior (Givner and Graubard, 1974). Without carefully measuring a student's behavior, a teacher might grossly underestimate or overestimate the rate of a behavior. In a case where a student's behavior is irritating, for example, it is not unusual for the teacher to claim the problem is occurring all, or nearly all the time. In fact, most disruptive students do behave appropriately much of the time (Walker, 1979). By measuring behavior, teachers do not have to rely on tradition, guesswork, or advice to determine the best means of teaching their students (Hawkins, Axelrod, and Hall, 1976). With accurate data, a teacher has before him evidence as to whether his procedures are working, and can adjust his teaching techniques accordingly.

Hawkins et al. (1976) point out several advantages of measuring behavior. First, by forcing a teacher to carefully define behavior, the teacher will find herself focussing efforts on a specific behavior and is, therefore, more likely to be successful. Second, by measuring a behavior, a teacher is more likely to apply a planned technique consistently and exclusively. When teachers do not measure behavior, they often vacillate between different techniques and are therefore ineffective, or uncertain of the value of their techniques. Third, with frequent measurement, a teacher is more likely to make small changes in her technique and to note its effects; the final form of the procedure may be much more effective than the original. Fourth, the measurement process often helps a teacher to diagnose a student's difficulties. In one case, I observed a data record indicating that a student was well behaved at the beginning of a math assignment, but disruptive at the end of the period. Closer inspection of the youngster's behavior indicated that he completed his assignment in a short period of time and became disruptive in the absence of assigned work. When the student was relieved of his boredom he became less disruptive. Consider another case in which inappropriate behavior occurs only during language arts. In this situation, the student may be communicating that the work is too easy or too difficult (Givner and Graubard, 1974). Fifth, education has always been subject to passing fads. Some are beneficial; others are not. By measuring behavior teachers can make the appropriate discrimination. Sixth, there is now a trend toward accountability in education. The public wants students to receive the best education possible for its tax dollars. By measuring behavior one can distinguish between the teaching techniques that promote student learning and those that do not. Finally, Gelfand and Hartman (1975) point out that a prominently displayed record of a pupil's progress can reinforce both the pupil and the teacher.

My plea for teachers to measure behavior should not scare them away. Measurement in behavior modification is usually simple. It does not involve complicated statistical analyses, nor does it involve giving intelligence, achievement, or personality tests. Many times, it involves nothing more than counting behavior. In other cases, a teacher will have only to note five times in a morning whether a child is performing a certain behavior. At still other times, a teacher will merely have to look at a wall clock to find out how long it took the youngsters to complete a task or how tardy a particular student is.

In the first half of this chapter I will discuss means of defining behavior and the procedures by which behavior can be measured. There will also be a discussion of the advantages of obtaining data on a daily basis and the means by which a teacher can check the accuracy of her data. The latter portion of the chapter describes the research designs characteristic of behavior modification studies and data-based decision making.

MEASUREMENT OF BEHAVIOR

SELECTING AND DEFINING BEHAVIOR

The first step in the measurement process is to select the behaviors to be modified. In order to reduce confusion, it is best to concentrate on only one or two behaviors at the outset of a program. As progress is made, additional behaviors can become targets for change. Teachers sometimes have difficulty deciding on which behavior(s) to concentrate at the beginning of a program. One approach is to select the behavior causing the most problems. Modifying this behavior will maximally reinforce the teachers. In working with disruptive students exhibiting a variety of problems, I have often found, for example, that it is helpful to reduce out-of-seat behavior. When a student is in her seat, the amount of disruption she can cause is greatly reduced.

The second step in measurement is to define the behavior in an unambiguous manner. This means that the final definition must involve terms that are precise and concrete (Walker, 1979). Thus a term such as "hitting other students" is preferred to the term "aggressive." Similarly, the term "out-of-seat" is superior to "restless."

In order to make a term meaningful, a teacher often must break the expression down into smaller, observable units. After observing the behavior for a period of time, a teacher might define a behavior such as "disturbing others" as incidents of hitting another student and grabbing another student's possessions. If the teacher wishes to include talking out in class, this also is permissible. The decision as to what the term denotes, however, must be made in advance, not as the behavior modification program proceeds and conditions change. One adequate definition of "disturbing others" was provided by Kuypers, Becker, and O'Leary (1968): "Grabbing another's objects or work, knocking neighbor's books off desk, destroying another's property, throwing objects at another without hitting, pushing with desk" (p. 102).

It is also important that the definition specify the conditions under which the behavior must occur. An instance of yelling behavior may be considered inappropriate if it occurs during a spelling test, but not during a dodgeball game.

There are two general approaches to defining behavior (Gelfand and Hartmann, 1975; Hutt and Hutt, 1970). One is to describe the topography of the behavior, such as the movements the individual actually makes. Thus, self-abuse might be topographically described as biting, scratching, and pinching oneself. An alternative approach is to describe the behavior in functional terms; that is, terms that describe the effects on the environment or individual. A functional definition of self-abuse might refer to the number of self-inflicted sores on an individual's body. Either approach to defining behavior may be acceptable given the nature of the target behavior (Gelfand and Hartmann, 1975).

MEASUREMENT PROCEDURES

Once the behavior of interest has been defined, it is necessary to measure its occurrence quantitatively. The measurement procedures fall into two general categories: measurement of lasting products and observational recording. The decision as to which category of techniques to use depends on the nature of the behavior. Observational recording, in turn, is of four types: frequency or event recording, duration recording, interval recording, and momentary time-sampling.

Measurement of Lasting Products   The "measurement of lasting products" is presented first because it is the measurement technique closest to a teacher's experience. Many academic behaviors such as spelling words, writing book reports, computing arithmetic problems, and painting pictures result in lasting products that can be measured either right after a student completes them or at a later point in time. In addition various nonacademic products, such as pieces of litter on the playground and broken windows leave lasting changes in the environment. The main advantage of measuring lasting products is that the teacher can measure them at a convenient time, rather than at the time they occur (Hawkins et al., 1976). Thus a teacher may take a student's papers home and grade them as 60 percent correct or 95 percent complete, and return them to the student the following day. (Still, the sooner a teacher can grade a paper the better it is.)

In dealing with academic behaviors, teachers frequently determine the accuracy of a student's output. As such, a teacher may grade a student's answers to a spelling or history test as 80 percent accurate. It is important, of course, to know a student's accuracy. In some cases, however, it is not a sufficient measure of a student's work output. What is also important is measuring the individual's proficiency or productivity (Van Houten, 1980). Two typists cannot be considered equally valuable if they are equally accurate, but one types at twice the rate of the other. Similarly, it is important to know how many math problems a student can complete during a period of time, not just how accurate she is.

A good measure of a student's proficiency is the *correct rate*, that is, the number of problems completed correctly per unit of time (Van Houten, 1980). If a student does 100 math problems correctly in two minutes, the correct rate is fifty problems per minute. To obtain a more complete picture of a student's performance, it is also helpful to have a measure of *error rate*—the number of problems completed incorrectly per unit of time. By measuring both correct and error rates, a student's work rate and accuracy are apparent (Van Houten, 1980). A graph representing students' correct and error rates in math appears in Figure 3-1.

Observational Recording   Some behaviors are transitory. They occur at one point in time but not at another. Examples of such behaviors include talking out, hand raising, smiling, and striking another student. Since these behaviors leave no product, they must be measured at the time, or soon

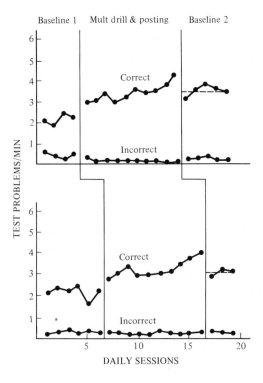

FIGURE 3-1 The mean number of test problems junior high school students in two classrooms worked correctly during each session. (*Adapted from R. Van Houten, "Learning through Feedback," New York, 1980, p. 25. By permission of the publishers.*)

after they occur. Four measurement procedures are described below. For a given behavior, the measurement procedure of choice depends on the amount of time and attention the teacher can devote to measuring the behavior, how obvious the behavior is, the duration of the behavior, how frequently it occurs, and the amount of precision which is necessary (Hawkins et al., 1976).

Frequency Recording   Perhaps the best-known type of observational measurement is *frequency* or *event* recording. With this measurement procedure, the teacher simply keeps a count of the number of times a particular behavior occurs over a certain period of time (for example, per hour, per day, and so on). For many years teachers have been recording the frequency of students' absences and tardiness by placing marks in their student record books and reporting the totals at the end of the report-card period.

Frequency recording can be used for a variety of behaviors involving classroom deportment. Teachers may obtain a record of the number of times a student blurts out answers, throws spitballs, hits classmates, or taps on the desk. It is sometimes also necessary to obtain a frequency tally using observational recording for academic behaviors that do not leave a lasting product. Thus, a teacher may count the number of errors a student makes in reciting a poem, the number of words a child omits during oral reading, and the number of math answers a student reverses when presented with flash cards on multiplication facts.

There are a variety of means for obtaining frequency records of student behaviors. Teachers may put tallies on a pad of paper on their desk, place marks on a chalkboard, or carry a clipboard containing a piece of paper. Since each of these procedures may require the teacher to move to inconvenient locations or be otherwise burdensome, teachers may consider using a variety of measurement devices. One convenient instrument is a wrist counter[1] (depicted in Figure 3-2) which golfers use to keep a record of the number of strokes they take on a certain day. The counter is attached to the wrist in a manner similar to a wristwatch. Each time the target behavior occurs, the teacher presses the counter and advances the total by one. She thus avoids carrying paper or walking to the chalkboard to make a tally. Other counters which teachers may find useful are handheld digital counters (Mattos, 1968) and counters used for grocery shopping. Still other types of recording devices are those which may be worn on the person and marked upon. Included is "Magic Mending Tape" which is nearly invisible but accepts ink marks and can be worn on the wrist or hand (Hawkins et al., 1976) and the wrist tally board[2] depicted in Figure 3-3 (Cooper, 1981). In both cases the teacher need only carry a writing instrument to make the tallies.

Frequency recording is most appropriate for behaviors that take about the same amount of time to perform on each occurrence. Typically these are short-duration behaviors, such as slapping other students and reading words. Frequency recording would *not* be an appropriate measurement procedure for behaviors of varying duration, such as out-of-seat behavior, since a student may leave her seat and remain out of her seat for a long

[1]The wrist counter may be purchased from Behavior Research Co., Box 3351, Kansas City, Kansas 66103.

[2]The wrist tally board may be purchased from Behavior Research Co., Box 3351, Kansas City, Kansas 66103.

FIGURE 3-2   Golf wrist counter, useful for classroom frequency tallies.

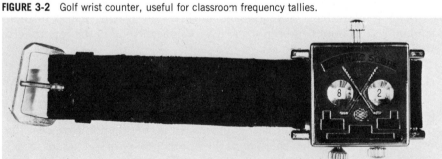

FIGURE 3-3 Wrist tally board.

period of time. A record showing that the child was out of her seat only one time in the morning would give a poor idea of the student's behavior. Similarly, it doesn't make much sense to indicate how many times a student slouched or was inattentive.

Duration Recording A second kind of measurement procedure, known as *duration* recording, would be more appropriate than frequency recording for behaviors such as out-of-seat behavior, pencil sharpening, and daydreaming. Duration recording gives a measure of how long a student engages in a certain behavior. For some behaviors a duration record is easy to obtain. If a teacher wished to know how tardy a student was, for example, she would merely have to subtract the time at which the youngster was due from the time she arrived in class. Thus, if Mia was due at 9:00 A.M. and appeared in class at 9:22 A.M., the duration of her lateness is twenty-two minutes. Similarly, if a teacher was interested in the amount of time it took a student to complete an assignment, she would subtract the time at which he began the assignment from the time at which he completed the task. In these cases the duration record can be obtained with a wristwatch or wall clock.

There are other behaviors for which it is more difficult to obtain a duration record. In these cases it is usually necessary to use a stopwatch. Consider the teacher who wishes to determine the amount of time Mike is out of his seat during the reading period. The teacher would start her stopwatch when Mike leaves his seat. When the youngster returns to his seat, she would stop her stopwatch and record the amount of time that had elapsed. When Mike again leaves his seat, she would repeat the process. At the end of the reading period, the teacher would add up the times to determine the duration of Mike's out-of-seat behavior. Instead of using a conventional stopwatch, the teacher could save herself some time and effort by using a repeater stopwatch. With this type of watch the user can stop the watch and start it again where she left off without setting the watch back to the zero point. Thus, the teacher could save herself the trouble of recording various durations and adding them up at the end of the period.

A problem with duration recording is that, in measuring certain behaviors, a teacher must continuously attend to the child of concern. This would not be a major problem for an outside observer, but it has obvious limitations for a teacher who is confronted with a variety of other tasks. As a result, duration recording tends *not* to be used by teachers who are conducting behavior modification studies. The time-sampling measurement procedure, to be discussed later, avoids most of the difficulties associated with duration recording.

Interval Recording   A third measurement technique, known as *interval recording*, is also useful for behaviors such as out-of-seat behavior and daydreaming. Interval recording is sensitive to both the frequency and the duration of a behavior. A data sheet for an interval record of out-of-seat behavior might appear as follows:

Seconds

Minutes	0	10	20	30	40	50	60
1	+	+	+	−	−	+
2	−	−	+	+	+	−
.						
.						
.						
60	+	+	−	−	−	−

The data sheet is divided into ten-second intervals for a sixty-minute period (other data sheets could use different intervals). During each consecutive interval the teacher (or another observer) records whether or not the target behavior occurs. Suppose one is concerned with out-of-seat behavior, and "+" represents in-seat behavior while "−" means out-of-seat behavior. The observer watches the child for the ten-second interval. If the child remains seated for the entire ten-second interval, the interval is scored "+". *If at any time during the ten-second interval the student leaves his seat without permission, the entire interval is scored "−".* On the data sheet above the record for the first minute would be interpreted as follows: The child was in his seat for the first thirty seconds. At some time between thirty and forty seconds the child was out of his seat, as was the case between forty and fifty seconds. During the last ten-second interval the student was always in his seat. A long string of pluses would indicate that a student was staying in his seat for lengthy periods of time. Frequent alternation of pluses and minuses would mean that the student often left and reoccupied his seat.

An advantage of interval recording over frequency recording is that it does not force the observer to decide on what constitutes one instance of the behavior. If two children hit each other, stop for a few seconds, hit each other again, call each other names, and then start hitting each other again, have one, two, or three fights occurred? The answer to this question is important in frequency recording, but irrelevant in interval recording. In interval recording the observer must only note whether or not fighting occurred during each of the measurement intervals.

Hooper (1970) provided an example of how a teacher could use interval recording for measuring talking-out behavior. The data sheet was divided into one-minute intervals from 9:00 A.M. to 9:20 A.M. daily and appeared (in adapted form) as follows:

9:01	02	03	04	05	06	07	08	09	10	11	12	13	14	15	16	17	18	19	20
		–				–									–				

Each time the teacher heard the student talk out, she looked at the desk clock and recorded a "–" in the appropriate box. Thus, if the talking-out behavior occurred after 9:03 but before 9:04, she placed a "–" in the third box. The data above indicate that the child talked out between 9:03 and 9:04, between 9:07 and 9:08, and between 9:16 and 9:17. The rest of the time, he was quiet: The reader should note that if there had been more than one talking-out instance during an interval, there would still be only one "–" for the interval.

In the Hooper study, the teacher had only to attend to the problem behavior auditorally, and she was, therefore, able to engage in her usual teaching activities. When the target behavior is one that must be attended to visually, the undivided scrutiny of the teacher is required, and the task usually becomes too burdensome for her. As a result, teachers who must conduct observations without assistance will usually find interval recording almost as impractical as duration recording. Also it is somewhat difficult to interpret data recorded with interval measurement. If a five-minute interval is "–" with respect to calling out, one cannot determine whether one, two, three, or more instances of talk outs occurred.

Momentary-Time Sampling A measurement technique that is more convenient than duration and interval recording and which provides an accurate record of student performance is called *momentary-time sampling*. With such a procedure the teacher notes only what a youngster is doing at the end of the time interval. Suppose a teacher is interested in determining the level of social interaction of a certain student. She might choose to record the behavior at two-minute intervals for a twenty-minute period, using the following data sheet:

Minute	2	4	6	8	10	12	14	16	18	20
Behavior	+	–	–	+	+	–	–	+	+	+

At exactly the two-minute mark, the four-minute mark, the six-minute mark, and so on, the teacher would rate the student's behavior. If the youngster was interacting, he would receive a "+." If he was isolated, he would receive a "–." The present record shows that the student was interacting at the 2, 8, 10, 16, 18, and 20 minute marks, and that he was not interacting at the 4, 6, 12, and 14 minute marks. Thus, it would be estimated that the student was interacting 60 percent of the time during the twenty-minute measurement period.

In momentary-time sampling it doesn't matter what a child is doing immediately before or after a measurement is due. All that matters is what the individual is doing at the measurement point. The measurement procedure is analogous to taking a snapshot and examining the product for the existence of a behavior.

As may be obvious to the reader, an advantage in time-sampling measurement is that the teacher need attend to the student's behavior only when a measurement is due. At other times she can engage in her usual teaching duties. Nevertheless, some teachers will still find it annoying to constantly check their timepieces to determine whether a measurement is due, and still other teachers will forget to make the checks. A solution to this problem was offered by O'Gorman, Schneider, and McKenzie (1970) in a study involving the finger-sucking behavior of an eleven-year-old boy. The teacher made use of an oven timer set to go off at certain intervals. Since the oven timer would ring when a measurement was due, the teacher did not have to continually check a timepiece. If the youngster did not have his fingers in his mouth when the timer went off, the teacher put a "+" on the data sheet. If his fingers were in his mouth when the timer rang, he received a "−." In addition to rating the youngster's behavior, the teacher gave the student a reward if his fingers were out of his mouth when the timer went off (providing an example of how the administering of consequences can be combined with the measurement procedure).

The reader might wonder whether a student who is exposed to a procedure such as that employed by O'Gorman et al. might learn to remove his fingers from his mouth just before the bell is scheduled to ring and then resume finger sucking after the bell goes off. The answer to the question is "yes" as long as the rings occur at standard intervals. In order to avoid this difficulty, the teacher should vary the amount of time between bell rings. Hence, the first ring might occur at five minutes, the next one two minutes later, the third one twenty-five minutes later, the fourth one three minutes later, and so on. When the amount of time between rings varies, the student must keep his fingers out of his mouth at all times in order to be certain that he will receive the reinforcer.

When using an oven timer for time-sampling measurement, the teacher is relieved of the burden of constantly having to check the student or a timepiece. An even more convenient device is a memo timer.[3] The memo timer, which is essentially a portable oven timer, is a small (1.5 inches in diameter), inexpensive timing device which people sometimes use to remind themselves that their time on a car parking meter is about to expire. (See Figure 3-4). The memo timer can be set for intervals varying

---

[3]The memo timer may be purchased from Behavior Research Co., Box 3351, Kansas City, Kansas 66103.

FIGURE 3-4 Memo timer. Diameter is 1.5 inches (3.8 centimeters).

from a few minutes up to an hour or more. When the time expires, a buzzing sound occurs which is usually audible to the entire class. The memo timer is more convenient that an oven timer because it is less bulky and because it can even be removed from the chain to which it is affixed and glued to a watch band. If teachers find the noise of the memo timer disruptive, they can keep it in a pocket or place clay around the perimeter. Another means to signal measurement is to use a tape recorder that periodically emits a sound.

Momentary-time sampling should *not* be used for behaviors that occur for very small portions of the measurement period. A youngster, for example, may pull a classmate's hair twice a morning for a total of two seconds. Momentary-time sampling is likely to miss such occurrences even though the behavior did indeed occur. (Just ask the victim.) In such cases frequency or interval recording would be superior.

Given that a behavior is occurring for a long enough period of time, the reader may wonder how many times a teacher using time sampling must rate behavior in order to obtain an accurate measure of student performance for that session. Kubany and Sloggett (1973) compared the results that were obtained when student behavior was rated eighty times per session with those obtained when the behavior was rated five times per session, and found remarkably similar results. Thus, rating the behavior only five times a session appears sufficient for valid measurement and is probably adequate for most classroom studies.

In addition to the convenience, a further advantage of momentary-time sampling is that it allows a teacher to know when during a period a problem is occurring. Thus, if "+" stands for on-task behavior, a series of pluses at the beginning of a period, followed by a series of minuses at the end of the period, indicates that the student was initially well behaved and then became disorderly. Further examination of the situation may give clues as to why the pattern is occurring. Interval recording offers the same advantage.

Devices such as "Magic Mending Tape" and the wrist tally board that are useful in frequency recording might also be helpful in momentary-time sampling.

Additional Observational Measurement Considerations   Teachers are frequently concerned that observational recording will interfere with their other teaching activities. The question then arises as to how a teacher may conveniently obtain accurate data on student behavior. One critical matter is deciding during which portion of the day to measure behavior. If a behavior is occurring at a high and uniform rate throughout the day, fifteen or twenty minutes of observation may be sufficient. Also, if the behavior is most problematic during a given period then it may be satisfactory to record behavior during that period alone. If a behavior rarely occurs, it will be necessary to record behavior continually, which is a minor problem due to the infrequent occurrence of the behavior.

Another issue is the degree of accuracy that a teacher must attain. Indications are that complete accuracy is unnecessary. In a study conducted by Packard (1970), teachers kept records of how much time students were attending to assigned tasks. The author admitted that due to conflicting activities the teacher's records were not completely precise. Nevertheless, large improvements resulted. Similarly, in a study involving lasting products, Salzberg, Wheeler, Devar, and Hopkins (1971) found that if students did not know when their papers would be graded, teachers could produce great improvement in student academic performance by grading only half the papers. It is important to note that in many behavior modification programs, the goal is to produce a large amount of change. In these cases a small degree of inaccuracy should make little difference.

In order to reduce the teacher's burden, it might be worthwhile to train teaching aides, volunteer parents, classmates, students from higher grades, guidance counselors, and college students to collect data. In some cases teachers have students keep data on themselves. To reduce the problem of cheating the teachers make periodic checks and reward the students if their data agree (Meacham and Wiesen, 1974).

For more information on observational recording the reader may consult a book by Cooper (1981) or a flowchart by Alevizos, Campbell, Callahan, and Berck (1974).[4]

---

[4]The flowchart may be obtained from Peter Alevizos, Camarillo—U.C.L.A. Neuropsychiatric Research Program, Box A, Camarillo, California 93010 or Philip L. Berck, University of Illinois, Urbana, Illinois. It has also been reprinted in Gelfand and Hartmann (1975, p. 61).

CONTINUOUS AND DIRECT MEASUREMENT

In traditional educational research, measurement of student performance occurs infrequently and indirectly. In a study involving a comparison of techniques for teaching reading, for example, students may take a standardized reading test at the beginning of the school year and retake the same test, or a similar one, at the end of the term. Judgments of the effectiveness of the techniques in question will be drawn by comparing the pretest and posttest scores of students exposed to each of the techniques. Eaton and Lovitt (1972) point out that difficulties with the practice of infrequent measurement include the possibilities that a student might guess well on the day of the test, or conversely, that he might be upset or ill on the testing day. Such problems might not be critical for the evaluation of groups of students but are of great importance when judging the progress of individual youngsters.

Behavior modifiers prefer to measure the behavior of interest *continuously*. It is likely that a teacher who is using a behavior modification technique to teach reading, for example, will obtain a daily measure of the number of words a child reads correctly. When daily measurement is used, the problem of a child guessing correctly or his having a "bad" day is greatly reduced, since it is unlikely that a child can guess correctly every day, or that each day will be a "bad" one. An additional advantage of continuous measurement is that it provides a teacher with frequent feedback on the effectiveness of her techniques. If her procedures are effective, she will receive the information early in the school term and can continue to use beneficial procedures. Conversely, if her techniques are ineffective, a teacher who measures continuously will also receive such information early in the year and can attempt alternative procedures. Teachers who depend on pre- and posttests to evaluate the effectiveness of their procedures are hampered by a lack of relevant information and might make the wrong decision as to whether they should continue or abandon the use of a certain technique. Inspection of the vast majority of graphs in this book will reveal the measurement of behavior on a daily or weekly basis.

Behavior modifiers also prefer to measure behavior *directly*. This means that if information is desired on how well a student can read from a fourth-grade reader, the teacher would test the child on a fourth-grade reader. The teacher would *not* give the student a reading achievement test. Similarly, if a student frequently had temper tantrums in class, the teacher would count the number of tantrums the youngster had, rather than give her a personality test. It is felt that when direct measurement is used, more appropriate educational decisions can be made. Achievement-test results are usually not sensitive enough to allow for appropriate recommendations on placement or instruction (Bushell, 1973). Thus, if direct measurement indicates that a student can read at fourth-grade level and an achievement test indicates that the child is at an eighth-grade level, it is probably better to trust the direct measurement. This is due to the identical correspondence between the test material and the material the student will be learning from. A study by Eaton and Lovitt (1972) showed the poor relationship between direct measurement and achievement tests, and even between different achievement tests.

RELIABILITY OF MEASUREMENT

Whenever behavior cannot be recorded with automated equipment, the judgment as to whether it occurred is made by human beings. With only one person making the observations, there is a risk that the measurements will be inaccurate in some manner. It is possible, for example, that an observer will mistakenly record an increase in behavior after being informed that a reinforcement condition is in effect. One way to reduce such risks is to have a second person periodically record the behavior independently of the first observer. The individual who is present at all sessions is called the *primary* observer, whereas the individual making the periodic checks is known as the *reliability* observer. The teacher can serve as either the primary or reliability observer, or the entire process can be conducted by outside personnel.

"Reliability" is the degree to which the independent observers agree on the occurrence or nonoccurrence of the behavior of interest. Kazdin (1980) gave three reasons for conducting reliability checks. First, high reliability probably means that scores reflect the subject's performance, rather than biased or mistaken recordings of the observer. Second, high reliability reduces the likelihood that the observer has become more lenient or stringent as sessions proceed. Finally, agreement between observers indicates whether a behavior has been precisely defined. It is unlikely that two observers will consistently agree on the occurrence of a behavior that is vaguely or imprecisely defined.

The method of calculating the degree of agreement between the observers (that is, reliability) depends on the measurement technique which is employed. If event recording is used, reliability is determined by dividing the record of the observer with the smaller number by the record of the observer with the larger number, according to the following formula:

$$\frac{\text{Smaller recorded frequency}}{\text{Larger recorded frequency}} \times 100 = \text{percent agreement}$$

Thus, if one observer records eighty instances of talking out in a day and a second observer records 100, the reliability would be $^{80}/_{100} \times 100 = 80$

percent. A similar formula would be used to determine the reliability of duration recordings. If, for example, one observer's records indicated that a student was out of her seat for fifty minutes whereas the figure for the second observer is forty-five minutes, the reliability would be $^{45}/_{50} \times 100 =$ 90 percent.

For interval and time-sampling measurements, a different formula for reliability must be employed. Suppose the records of two observers on a child's rate of study behavior over a ten-minute period are as follows:

Observer 1:	+	−	−	−	+	+	−	−	+	+
Minute	1	2	3	4	5	6	7	8	9	10

Observer 2:	+	−	−	+	−	+	−	−	+	+
Minute	1	2	3	4	5	6	7	8	9	10

It can be seen that there was agreement between the two observers on all but minutes four and five. Reliability can be calculated with the following formula:

$$\frac{\text{Number of agreements}}{\text{Total number of measurements}} \times 100 = \text{percent agreement}$$

In this case there were eight agreements out of ten measurements. Therefore, the reliability would be $^{8}/_{10} \times 100 = 80$ percent.

The formula cited above will sometimes yield inflated scores when a large number of intervals are scored "+" or "−." Although a description of a more appropriate formula is beyond the scope of this book, the interested reader should see work by Hawkins and Dotson (1975), Sulzer-Azaroff and Mayer (1977, pp. 64-65), and an issue of *Journal of Applied Behavior Analysis* (Winter, 1979).

The formula for the reliability of lasting-products measurement also depends on the type of behavior being studied. For an exercise such as listing words which rhyme with "book," reliability would be determined by employing the same formula as was used for event and duration recording. Thus, if one grader found twenty correct words whereas the second grader indicated that there were nineteen correct words, reliability would be $^{19}/_{20} \times$ 100, or 95 percent. For a spelling or arithmetic assignment, the graders would score each answer independently. Their grading would then be compared score by score to determine the percentage of times they were in agreement. Suppose a child were asked to spell the words "some," "duck," "find," "seven," and "break." Listed below is the way the student spelled the words and the manner in which each of the graders scored them ("+" means correct and "−" means incorrect).

	Grader 1	Grader 2
1. some	+	+
2. duck	+	+
3. finb	+	−
4. sevn	−	−
5. break	+	+

The graders agreed on all words except the third one. Thus, reliability would be $^4/_5 \times 100$ or 80 percent. The formula is the same as that used for interval and time-sampling measurements.

In order to be certain that reliable measurements are achieved when observational recording is employed, it is sometimes necessary to have practice sessions before experimental conditions are started. The observers should first discuss the definition of the behavior(s) of interest. If there are any disagreements or confusion as to how certain types of behavior should be rated, the observers should talk over the disparities until differences are removed. During the initial practice session(s), the observers might sit side by side (unless, of course, one of the observers is the teacher) in such a way that they can easily check each other's scoring and discuss any differences in ratings. During a later practice session, the observers should be separated from each other to determine whether independent measurements result in sufficiently high reliability for the study to be started.

When experimental sessions begin, it is imperative that the observers rate behavior independently. One way to increase the probability that the scoring will be done in an independent manner is to separate the observers from each other's view. This can be accomplished by placing some barrier, such as a portable blackboard, between the observers. Whenever possible, it is also better not to inform the observers which experimental condition is in effect. This should be done so that the expectations of the observers will not influence their ratings.

Clearly it is not always possible to assess reliability during each session. It is important, however, to have at least one or two reliability checks during each experimental condition (for example, baseline, reinforcement, and so on) and to space them during the earlier and later sessions within a condition. Also if reliability is consistently high, fewer checks are necessary (Kazdin, 1980).

There are no absolute standards as to an acceptable level of reliability. Most researchers consider reliability of less than 80 percent too low for scientific purposes. If reliability is often below 80 percent, my suggestion is that the observers discuss their differences, conduct additional practice sessions, and reexamine their definitions of the target behaviors.

Finally, it should be understood that high reliability does not insure accurate measurement. It is possible that two observers will agree that the word "finb" is spelled correctly when in fact it is not. The measurement was reliable but not accurate. Similarly, in frequency recording two observers may both tally ten hitting behaviors, but have recorded different instances of behavior. Thus, although high reliability does not guarantee accurate measurement, it does increase the probability of accurate assessment.

RESEARCH DESIGN

In describing the various studies which appear in the earlier sections of this book, the reader may have noticed that the author usually omitted terms such as "experimental group," "control group," and "statistical significance level." This is neither a coincidence nor an error. The expressions are characteristic of traditional educational research but not of behavioral research. In the present section of this chapter, the components of the research designs used in traditional educational studies will be briefly reviewed and the objections that behavior modifiers have to such research strategies will be pointed out. The research methodology preferred by behavior modifiers and the advantages of the tactics for teachers who wish to do research in their classrooms will be described in some detail later.

TRADITIONAL EDUCATIONAL RESEARCH DESIGNS

Group-Comparison Design The research design most frequently used in educational studies is known as the "group-comparison" design. An educational researcher will typically use the design in order to determine which of two or more procedures is best able to produce a certain desirable outcome. A hypothetical experiment might involve an attempt to determine whether children learn sight vocabulary words best when there is no consequence following their answers, when their correct answers are reinforced, or when incorrect answers are punished. The group-comparison design might involve randomly selecting students from a larger population and then randomly assigning them to three different groups: a control group which receives no consequences (group C), and two experimental groups—group R, which receives reinforcement, and group P, which receives the punishment procedure. The investigators would try to obtain groups which were as large as was feasible. The groups would then be exposed to the respective procedures, and their sight vocabulary scores would be compared with an appropriate statistical test. If it were found, for example, that the scores of group R students were significantly better than those achieved by groups C and P, the reinforcement procedure would be considered the best of the three techniques.

Although there is some merit to the approach, behavioral researchers have generally rejected the use of the group-comparison design. First, most studies do not draw a truly random sample (Hersen and Barlow, 1976). Instead students are selected on the basis of availability (for example, the willingness of a principal to have research done in her school). Second, practical realities also make it difficult to randomly assign students to different groups (that is, conditions). Third, it is often difficult to obtain groups of children exhibiting the same problems (Risley, 1970). Fourth, the group design does not give information as to which technique is best for each individual student. Although a particular procedure might be the best one for most students, there may be some students for whom one of the alternative techniques would be superior. Children in group R, for example, receive the reinforcement condition but not the punishment condition. Thus, if a particular child in group R would respond better to punishment than he would to reinforcement, this fact would not be known. Fifth, there is an ethical objection to having some students receiving nothing more beneficial than the control condition.

Correlational Research   A second kind of research population in education involves finding correlations between certain environmental conditions and important behaviors of students. A *correlation* between two variables is a measure of the degree to which they vary together. A *positive* correlation is one in which as one variable increases, the other variable also increases. A *negative* correlation is one in which as one variable increases, the other decreases. It is therefore likely that there is a positive correlation between the number of hours a student studies and scholastic success, since it would be expected that as the hours of studying increased, scholastic success would also increase. Likewise, one would expect to find a negative correlation between student absences and academic achievement, since as absences increased, one would expect academic success to decrease. Although correlational studies indicate many interesting relationships, behavior modifiers generally consider such investigations to be of limited value. This is so because although two variables may be highly correlated with each other, one variable does not necessarily cause the other to occur.

As an example of this notion, suppose a high positive correlation was found between the quality of students' shoes and the students' achievement levels in school. This would not mean that if society were to supply high-quality shoes to all low-achieving pupils they would suddenly do well in school. It is more likely that the pupils would continue to be low achievers, but with good shoes.

To make matters worse, correlations do not always predict the *direction* of causality. It might be noticed, for example, that there is a negative correlation between the amount of individual instruction a teacher gives to his students and the students' grades. This does not mean that individual instruction is causing poor grades. What is more likely is that the teacher is giving most of the individual instruction to the students who are doing poorly. This instruction may be helpful to the students, but not enough to bring them up to the level of classmates not requiring the extra help.

Unquestionably, researchers doing correlational studies have not even implied that, if one variable is highly correlated with a second variable, it is causing the second variable to occur. The important point, however, is that educators are interested in the conditions that will cause student performance to improve, and correlational research is suggestive but not definitive.

BEHAVIORAL RESEARCH DESIGNS

Behavior modifiers use research designs that eliminate the problems of random selection and assignment, of obtaining large groups of children, and that clearly demonstrate which factors cause an improvement in the performance of individual students. Also, as was the case with the measurement procedures, the behavioral research designs are easy for teachers to carry out. Thus, teachers can participate in the development of their field by conducting research in their own classrooms and, desirably, publishing the results in various journals. This is in marked contrast to the realities surrounding the group-comparison design, which few teachers will ever be able to engage in.

The remainder of the present section will describe the three research designs most often employed in behavior modification studies. The most commonly used design is the *reversal* design. The alternative designs to be described are the *multiple-baseline* and the *multi-element* designs.

Reversal Design In order to point out how a teacher makes use of the reversal design, I will make reference to a study by Alley and Cox (1971). The classroom for the Alley and Cox study was the home of a newlywed couple, the teacher was a recent bride, and the student was the new groom. The behavior of concern was the husband's tendency to leave items of clothing in the living room.

The first stage of almost every reversal-design study is called the *Baseline₁* stage. (See Baseline₁, Figure 3-5.) Baseline₁ is a measure of the behavior interest under normal classroom conditions. During this phase the teacher should be acting in her usual manner and should give no special attention to the problem of concern. The reason for taking baseline measurements is to provide a basis for comparing the behavior under normal conditions with behavior under conditions in which a special procedure is being applied. Without a baseline phase there would be no way of determining whether or not improvement later took place. During the seven-day Baseline₁ phase of the Alley and Cox study, it was observed that the husband left between one and three articles of clothing in the living room each day.

After the teacher conducts Baseline₁ measurements, *Experimental*

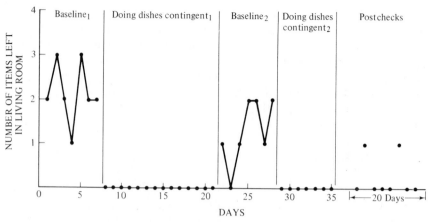

FIGURE 3-5 The number of articles of clothing left in the living room by a newlywed man. *From S. J. Alley and L. Cox, "Doing Dishes as a Contingency for Reducing a Husband's Rate of Leaving Clothes in the Living Room," in R. V. Hall (ed.),* Managing Behavior, Part III, *Lawrence, Kan., 1971, p. 42. By permission of the publishers.)*

*Phase*₁ is begun. During this period the teacher applies the procedure which is intended to improve student performance and evaluates the effect. Data are collected in the same manner as was done during Baseline₁. The technique which is used can be reinforcement, extinction, punishment, changing seating arrangements, or any other tactic which a teacher might feel would be effective. Experimental Phase₁ in the Alley and Cox study (labeled "Doing Dishes Contingent₁" in Figure 3-5) consisted of an agreement that whoever left the greater number of articles of clothing in the living room for a given week would do the dishes the following week. In case of a tie, the wife would do the dishes the new week. For the fourteen days in which the dishes contingency was in effect, the husband never left any items of clothing in the living room.

When student performance improves during Experimental Phase₁, teachers often wonder whether it actually was the procedure which they employed during this period which accounted for the change or whether other factors may have been responsible. A teacher might consider it possible that the change took place because she now knows her students better, because the weather changed, because the students had matured, or because certain youngsters had moved from her classroom. All such explanations could account for the change in behavior. To eliminate the possibility that these uncontrolled factors accounted for the improvement in behavior, a third experimental condition, known as *reversal* or *Baseline₂* phase, is necessary. (See Baseline₂, Figure 3-5.) During this stage the teacher ceases using the procedure employed during Experimental Phase₁. If students received reinforcement for correct arithmetic answers during Experimental Phase₁, for example, they will no longer receive such reinforcement during Baseline$_2$. If the behavior changes to a level similar to that which occurred during Baseline$_1$, the teacher can have confidence that the procedures she used during Experimental Phase$_1$ caused the improvement in behavior. If the rate of the behavior does not change, it is possible that uncontrolled factors were responsible for the improvement which occurred during Experimental Phase$_1$, or that the behavior modification procedure is no longer necessary.

Returning to the newlywed couple, Figure 3-5 indicates that when the husband was no longer required to do the dishes after leaving items of clothing in the living room, he quickly returned to his old ways. During the seven-day Baseline$_2$ phase, he left an article of clothing out every day but one. This provided convincing evidence that the contingency of doing dishes really did account for the improvement which occurred during the Doing Dishes Contingent$_1$ stage of the study.

For educational purposes it is usually undesirable to terminate a study when students are in the Baseline$_2$ phase. Thus, a fourth condition involves returning the children to the procedure used during Experimental Phase$_2$. This stage is known as *Experimental Phase$_2$* and is labeled "Doing Dishes Contingent$_2$" in Figure 3-5. It can be seen that when the "doing dishes" agreement was again employed, the husband's performance was consistently perfect. When behavior again improves during Experimental Phase$_2$, there is additional evidence that the procedure which the teacher used really was the cause for the change in performance.

The final stage of a behavior modification study is an extension of Experimental Phase$_2$. This phase, known as the *Postchecks* period, involves a continuation of the procedures of Experimental Phase$_2$. Measurements, however, are taken less frequently. If measurements were taken daily during Experimental Phase$_2$, they may be taken an average of only once a week during the Postchecks phase. This stage is important for determining whether the procedures have a long-lasting effect on the behavior of concern. Eight postchecks over a twenty-day period in the Alley and Cox (1971) study indicated that a total of only two items of clothing were left in the living room. (The reader should note that, although it is ideal that behavior modification studies employ all of the above phases, in practice many experiments do not include one or more of the stages. For scientific purposes, however, there should at least be Baseline$_1$, Experimental Phase, and Baseline$_2$ conditions.)

In the Alley and Cox (1971) study, the experimenters were interested only in comparing the "doing dishes" contingency with baseline conditions. Sometimes a teacher wishes to compare more than two conditions. In the hypothetical study involving sight vocabulary (see p. 107), the investigators were concerned with comparing three conditions—no consequence, reinforcment, and punishment. Unlike the group design, the experimental design using reversal procedures might involve exposing an entire class of students to Baseline$_1$ (no consequence) conditions, followed by Reinforcement₁, Punishment, Reinforcement₂, and Baseline₂. Notice that all students experience all conditions. With such a design one could compare each student's performance under each of the conditions. Thus, it might be found that fifteen students did best with reinforcement, three did best with punishment, and two did best with no consequence on their answers. With this information a teacher could individualize a child's program in accordance with the conditions under which he or she worked best. This would not be possible with the group design, since each student would receive only one condition—no consequence, reinforcement, or punishment. The group design tells educators something about groups of students but little about individuals. The reversal design can give information on both groups and individuals.

The reversal design has been more responsible for the development of behavior modification procedures than any other research design. One advantage is that the design can be used with anywhere from one student to a group of students of any size. Another advantage is that it allows a researcher to introduce a new experimental procedure with little difficulty. Thus, if Procedure A proves ineffective, one can readily determine the effect of Procedure B, and so forth.

Nevertheless, there are some circumstances in which it is not advisable to use a reversal design. One is the situation where it might be dangerous to allow a behavior to return to Baseline₁ levels. Suppose a teacher attained a Baseline₁ record of the number of times a child poked classmates in the eyes. Next, suppose a behavior modification procedure was employed and the youngster's eye-poking ceased. Although it might be scientifically interesting to determine the effect of halting the procedure and returning to Baseline₁ conditions, it would be perilous and unethical to do so, since the child could harm her neighbors during the reversal period. Even when it is not dangerous to return to Baseline₁ conditions, some teachers will refuse to do so because they see no educational benefit to the student or because they fear that the behavior may not improve again even when the behavior modification procedure is reintroduced. (In fact the latter problem rarely occurs).

Another situation in which a reversal design should not be used is one in which the behavior of interest is unlikely to return to its Baseline₁ level following the cessation of a behavior modification procedure. Axelrod and Piper (1975) found, for example, that after a behavior modification procedure improved the reading performance of several students, removal of the procedure did not lead to a deterioration of the behavior. The authors proposed that a child's environment provides so much reinforcement for reading that even when the original procedure is discontinued, reading behavior may persist. Other situations in which a behavior may not reverse are when a behavior has been reinforced on a partial-reinforcement schedule, and when there have been long experimental phases (Kazdin, 1973).

Multiple-Baseline Designs   When it is dangerous to use the reversal design, or when it appears unlikely that the behavior of interest will reverse, teachers should consider the use of a *multiple-baseline* design (Baer, Wolf, and Risley, 1968; Hersen and Barlow, 1976).

Different-Behaviors Multiple-Baseline Design   The first type of multiple-baseline design involves taking baseline measurements of several different behaviors for a period of time (for example, sight vocabulary, spelling, and arithmetic). The behaviors could be those of an individual student or of a group of students. Once the baseline level is well established for all behaviors, a behavior modification procedure is applied to only one of the behaviors. If the behavior changes in the desired direction, the procedure is continued with the first behavior but is also applied to the second behavior. If the second behavior improves when the procedure is applied to it, the procedure is then applied to the first, second, and third behaviors, and so on. If each of the behaviors improves when the procedure is applied to it, the teacher has provided strong evidence that the procedure he is using is causing the desired change in the behaviors.

Leonardi, Duggan, Hoffheins, and Axelrod (1972) employed this type of multiple-baseline design with a classroom of second graders. During a ten-day period a teacher trainee kept a record of the number of out-of-seat, disturbing-others, and talking-out behaviors the four most disruptive students engaged in during a one-hour period each day. Figure 3-6 indicates that the youngsters averaged twelve out-of-seat, sixteen disturbing-others, and twelve talking-out behaviors per hour during the ten-day period. From days 11 to 16, a group contingency procedure similar to that used by Gallagher, Sulzbacher, and Shores (1967) was applied to out-of-seat behaviors but not to disturbing-others and talking-out behaviors. The procedure was in effect for all students, but the measurements were still restricted to the four most disruptive students. The teacher listed the numbers "24, 23, 22, . . . , 0" on the board. The figures represented the number of minutes of free play which the class could receive at the end of the morning. Each time a student left his seat without permission, the teacher crossed the highest intact number off the blackboard. Whenever a number was crossed off, the entire class lost a minute of free play. Figure 3-6 indicates that out-of-seat behaviors decreased from a mean of twelve during baseline to a mean of two during the "Group-Contingency" phase for the four students. Disturbing-others and talking-out behavior, to which the contingency was not applied during days 11 to 16, changed little from the level of the first ten days.

Even though out-of-seat behaviors decreased when the group contingency was used, the possibility that uncontrolled factors were responsible for the improvement could not be ruled out. During days 16 to 25 more evidence of the effectiveness of the group-contingency procedure was provided. During this period the students lost a minute of free play for out-of-seat behaviors and for disturbing others but *not* for talking-out

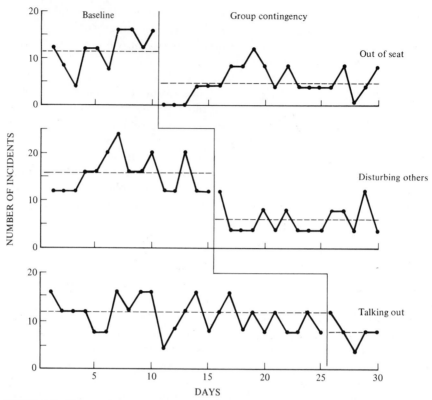

FIGURE 3-6 The number of out-of-seat, disturbing-others, and talking-out incidents in a second-grade classroom. (*From A. Leonardi, T. Duggan, J. Hoffheins, and S. Axelrod, "Use of Group Contingencies to Reduce Three Types of Classroom Behaviors." Paper presented at the meeting of the Council for Exceptional Children, Washington, D.C., March, 1972. By permission of the authors.*)

behaviors. It can be seen that out-of-seat behaviors stayed below the baseline level, disturbing-others behaviors decreased to six a day, but talking-out behavior stayed at about the same level during this period. Thus, the group contingency was effective with the behaviors to which it was applied, but not to other behaviors. From days 26 to 30 the students lost free-play time for out-of-seat, disturbing-others, *and* talking-out behaviors. Figure 3-6 indicates that out-of-seat and disturbing-others behavior remained at low levels and that instances of talking out decreased somewhat from a baseline mean of twelve to a mean of eight. The fact that each behavior improved only when the procedure was applied to it provides a strong argument for believing that the group-contingency procedure caused the change in behavior.

Different-Settings Multiple-Baseline Design The first multiple-baseline design involved measuring several *different behaviors* of an individual or group and then initiating a procedure with each of the behaviors at different points in time. The second type of multiple-baseline design involves measuring the *same behavior* of an individual or group but in *different situations*. After baseline measurements are taken in all of the situations, the experimental procedure is applied to the behavior of concern in only one of the situations. If the behavior improves in the first situation, it is also applied in the second situation. If improvement is again noted, the procedure is applied in the third situation, and so on. If improvement consistently occurs when the behavior modification tactic is applied in each of the different situations, the teacher has furnished satisfactory evidence that the technique improved the behavior of the child or group of children. The different situations to which this design could be applied might involve the same behavior during different periods of time each day (for example, classroom and home), or with different playmates, and so forth.

Hall, Cristler, Cranston, and Tucker (1970) made use of the second type of multiple-baseline design. The problem behavior was the tardiness of twenty-five fifth-grade students following the noon, morning, and afternoon recesses. A baseline of the number of students who were tardy after each of the recesses was established for thirteen days. (See Figure 3-7.) On day 14 the teacher informed the students that each child who was in his or her seat within four minutes of the end of the *noon* recess would have his or her name listed under a chart entitled "Today's Patriots." Figure 3-7 indicates that beginning with day 14 the procedure led to an immediate decrease in tardiness following the noon recess, but that tardiness following the morning and afternoon recesses stayed about the same. On day 22 the teacher told the children that it was necessary to be on time following both the *noon* and *morning* recesses in order to be a "patriot." Figure 3-7 shows that under these conditions tardiness was eliminated following the noon and morning recesses but was unchanged in the afternoon. On day 28 the teacher announced that in order to have his or her name placed on the patriots chart a student had to be punctual follwing *all three of the daily recesses*. Under these conditions there were no incidents of tardiness following any of the recesses. The type of multiple-baseline design used by Hall, Cristler et al. (1970) clearly indicated that the "Today's Patriots" procedure was an effective one, since improvement occurred in a given situation (that is, following noon, morning, afternoon recess) only when the tactic was applied in that situation.

Different-Students Multiple-Baseline Design   The third type of multiple-baseline design involves applying a procedure to the same behavior of *different students*. First, a baseline on a particular behavior is established with each student. Next, a procedure is applied to one student but not to the others. If the behavior of the first student improves, the procedure is applied to both the first and the second students. If the behavior of the second student improves, the procedure is applied to the next student, and

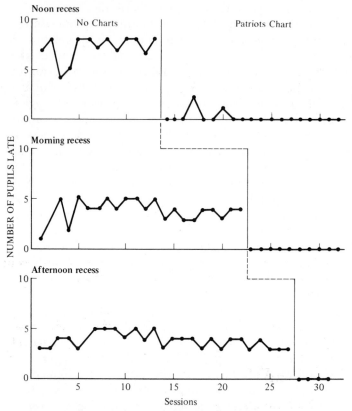

FIGURE 3-7 The number of tardy students following the noon, morning, and afternoon recesses. (*Adapted from R. V. Hall, C. Cristler, S. S. Cranston, and B. Tucker, "Teachers and Parents as Researchers Using Multiple-Baseline Designs,* Journal of Applied Behavior Analysis, 3, *p. 249, 1970. By permission of the publishers.*)

so forth, until all students have been exposed to the procedure. If the behavior of each individual improves when the procedure is applied to him or her, it has been demonstrated that the procedure caused the improvement in behavior. This type of multiple-baseline design can also be applied to different *groups,* by first applying the procedure to one group, then to a second group, then to a third group, and so on.

Another study reported in the Hall, Cristler et al. (1970) article gave an example of the third type of multiple-baseline design. The subjects for the investigation were three high school students, Dave, Roy, and Debbie, who were consistently receiving D's and F's on French quizzes. Figure 3-8 indicates that during the first ten days of baseline the median grade for all three students was F. After the tenth quiz, the teacher informed Dave that she would "help" him with after-school tutoring following each instance in which he received a D or F on a quiz. Apparently, this was the type of help

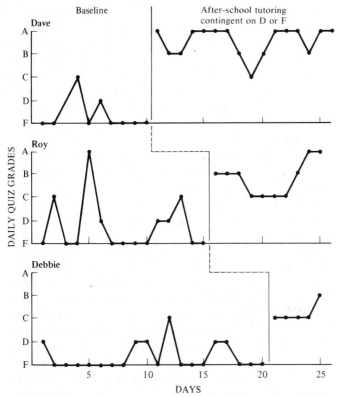

FIGURE 3-8 Daily French quiz grades for Dave, Roy, and Debbie. (*From R. V. Hall, C. Cristler, S. S. Cranston, and B. Tucker, "Teachers and Parents as Researchers Using Multiple-Baseline Designs,"* Journal of Applied Behavior Analysis, 3, *p. 251, 1970. By permission of the publishers.*)

which Dave preferred to do without. His quiz grades improved immediately. At no time during the remainder of the study did he receive a grade of less than C, and, in fact, his median grade increased to A.

Meanwhile, between days 11 and 14, baseline conditions were in effect for Roy and Debbie. Figure 3-8 indicates that their performance did not improve during this period. Following day 15, Roy was told that he would be given after-school tutoring whenever he received a D or F on a French quiz. From session 16 to the end of the study, he received no grade below a C, with his median grade increasing to B. From the sixteenth to the twentieth sessions, baseline conditions were in effect for Debbie, and her performance remained unchanged. When after-school tutoring for D's and F's was applied to her performance, following session 20, Debbie improved to the point that she never received a D or F and her median quiz score increased to C, as compared with a baseline level of F. The consequence of after-school tutoring can therefore be considered the factor causing the improvement in grades, since each student's scores increased at the point at which the contingency was applied to him or her.

Comments on Multiple-Baseline Designs Positive aspects of multiple-baseline designs are that they avoid the danger of returning behavior to baseline conditions, and that one need not be concerned about the reversibility of behavior. Also, in the multiple-baseline design involving different behaviors, a teacher attains information on several student behaviors, which may be important in evaluating the overall effects of a program.

There are some disadvantages also. Consider the case of a multiple baseline involving three different students. If a procedure effectively changed the behavior of the first two students and not the third, one cannot necessarily conclude that the procedure caused the change in behavior observed in the first two students. Second, in the multiple-baseline design involving different behaviors, it is *not* unusual to find that changing one behavior (for example, out-of-seat), changes another (such as hitting other students), even before the procedure is applied to the second behavior. In this case also, it becomes difficult to make claims on what caused the behavior to change. Finally, it is difficult to introduce new procedures in the multiple-baseline design. In a case where a teacher is using a multiple-baseline design with three different students, she may find the first procedure she attempts fails. Keeping track of three students while she attempts a second or third procedure can become cumbersome, and minimally means that one or more students will experience baseline conditions for too long a period of time.

Multi-element Design A third type of design coming into increasing usage in behavior modification research is known as the *multi-element* or *alternating-treatments* design (Barlow and Hayes, 1979; Ulman and Sulzer-Azaroff, 1975). With this design one does *not* have a condition such as baseline conducted for several consecutive sessions, followed by several consecutive sessions of another condition such as reinforcement, followed perhaps by several sessions of a third condition (for example, punishment). Instead, the student experiences one condition one session, followed by a second condition the next session, and so forth. The order of conditions is usually random and may appear as follows:

Session 1	Reinforcement
Session 2	Baseline
Session 3	Reinforcement
Session 4	Punishment
Session 5	Punishment
Session 6	Baseline

It should be noted that sessions may occur on separate days or there may be more than one session in a day. In the example above sessions 1, 2, and 3 may have occurred on day 1 and sessions 4, 5 and 6 could have occurred on day 2.

Kennedy (1980) used a multi-element design to compare three different reinforcers and baseline with a thirty-two-year-old, blind, mentally-retarded woman. At four different times each day, the researcher would ask the woman to walk between two points that were twenty feet apart. Depending on which condition was in effect, the woman would receive either touch, praise, vibration to the back, or no reinforcer when she completed the task. Inspection of Figure 3-9 clearly indicates that it took the woman the least amount of time when vibration was used as the reinforcer. The touch and praise conditions were about equal to each other and superior to the baseline condition.

There are several advantages of the multi-element design compared to other designs. First, since there is no reversal phase, one need not be concerned about behaviors that do not reverse following several sessions of exposure to a procedure. This is particularly important in studies involving academic behaviors which often do not return to baseline levels during a reversal phase. Second, a researcher is able to compare the effects of different conditions in a few sessions, since the design does not involve a long period of one condition, followed by a long period of a second condition, and so on. Note in the Kennedy study, after only four or five

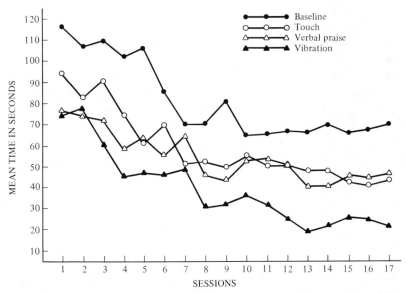

FIGURE 3-9 The amount of time it took a blind mentally retarded woman to walk twenty feet under baseline conditions and for three different reinforcers—touch, praise, and vibration. (*From A. Kennedy, "Effects of Three Reinforcers on the Mobility of a Severely Retarded Blind Woman." Unpublished manuscript, Temple University, 1980.*)

sessions it was becoming clear that vibration was the best consequence (that is, in this condition it took the woman the least amount of time to traverse the required distance). In studies involving the reversal or multiple-baseline design, baseline alone might last five or more sessions. Third, it is easy to interpret graphs in the multi-element design, since the data points are intermingled with each other. A fourth advantage is that unlike the reversal and multiple-baseline designs, it is not necessary to have stable baseline data. Again, this is important in working with academic behaviors which often produce rising baselines, as the students learn the materials. (There will be more discussion of this last point in the final section of the chapter.)

There are at least two important considerations in using the multi-element design. First, the students must be able to discriminate one procedure from another. Otherwise, they could not be expected to respond differently to different procedures. This can be accomplished with different cues signaling the different conditions. In a study comparing baseline with individual consequences and group consequences this can be achieved with signs stating the following:

Baseline—"You are not working for reward today."

Individual consequence—"You are working for your own reward today."

Group consequence—"You are working for the whole class's reward today."

Second, the procedures being compared must *not* be ones which take several consecutive days to show their effect (Kazdin and Hartmann, 1978). For example, if it typically takes five successive sessions for a phonics procedure to improve a student's reading performance, it would not be wise to use a multi-element design. The multi-element design is such that there will *not* be several *consecutive* sessions of any condition.

GRAPHING DATA

Following each session in which data have been collected, it is wise for a teacher to graph the results. With a visual representation of the data, the teacher can determine whether or not the procedure he has been using has improved his students' behavior. If student performance has improved, the teacher will be reinforced for his efforts and is more likely to continue to use the procedure. If performance has not improved, the teacher will have this knowledge available to him and can devise an alternative strategy. It has been found that graphing data can also reinforce a student's behavior. On several occasions the author has observed students reacting enthusiastically as their graph showed an improving trend, or bragging to their classmates that their performance during a given session has reached the 100 percent level. Further, a study by Jenkins, Mayhall, Peschka, and Townsend (1974) showed that when students and teachers were allowed to observe their data each day, the youngsters' reading scores improved.

A conventional graph consists of a vertical and a horizontal axis. The vertical axis consists of a series of points (each of which is known as an "ordinate") giving a measure of the behavior of interest. The vertical axis might be labeled "Frequency of temper tantrums," "Number of words spelled correctly," "Percentage of time studying," "Duration of out-of-seat behavior," and so on. In the hypothetical data of Figure 3-10 the vertical

FIGURE 3-10 Hypothetical data on the number of times a student raised his hand each day.

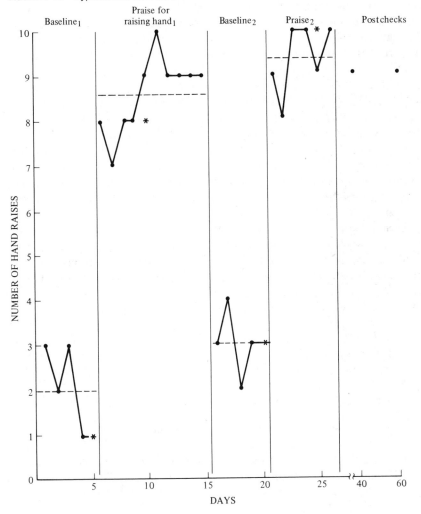

axis has been labeled "Number of hand raises." The horizontal axis consists of a series of points (each known as an "abscissa") representing the element of time. Thus, the horizontal axis might be labeled "Days," "Hours," "Sessions," and so on. In Figure 3-10 the horizontal axis has been labeled "Days." In order to determine the level of a behavior on a given day, one must find where the appropriate point falls on the vertical and horizontal axes (that is, determine the ordinate and the abscissa). In Figure 3-10, for example, there was one hand raise on day 5 and there were nine on day 14.

In reading a graph it is sometimes helpful if the *mean* (that is, average) level of the behavior during an experimental condition is indicated. The mean can be noted with a horizontal dashed line. In Figure 3-10 the mean number of hand raises during Baseline$_1$ was 2.0. During the praise for raising hand$_1$ stage, the mean was 8.6. The average for a given phase is attained by taking the sum of the data points and dividing by the number of data points. During Baseline$_1$ in Figure 3-10, the sum is $3 + 2 + 3 + 1 + 1 = 10$. The number of data points is five. Therefore, the mean is $^{10}/_5 = 2$.

Rather than showing the mean score, some people prefer to indicate the *median* score. The median is the middle point from a series of scores which have been arranged in order of magnitude. To find the median of the Baseline$_1$ scores in Figure 3-10 the points 3, 2, 3, 1, 1 are arranged in the order 1, 1, 2, 3, 3. The middle point of the five scores is 2. Therefore, the median is 2. If there is an even number of scores, calculating the median is somewhat different. Suppose the data are 5, 2, 5, 4, 2, 3. When arranged in order of magnitude, the series becomes 2, 2, 3, 4, 5, 5. In this case there would be two middle scores: 3 and 4. The median is then found by adding $3 + 4$ and dividing by 2. Therefore, the median would be 3.5. The median can also be represented on a graph with a horizontal dashed line.

The results of reliability checks are sometimes indicated on the graph. This can be done by using an asterisk to represent the data point of the reliability observer. Thus, in Figure 3-10 both observers recorded one hand raise on day 5, whereas on day 10 the primary observer recorded nine hand raises and the reliability observer recorded eight.

Hall (1971) made some suggestions for graphing data:

1 Experimental conditions should be separated by dark, vertical lines.

2 Experimental conditions should be labeled as descriptively as possible. The label "Praise for raising hand" is, therefore, preferable to the title "Reinforcement" or "Praise."

3 Data points between different experimental conditions should not be connected.

4 Data points between postchecks should not be connected.

Although the conventional graph is suitable for most purposes, there are investigators who sometimes use a *cumulative graph*. With a cumulative graph the vertical axis indicates the total number of behaviors which have occurred since the beginning of the study. In other words, the number of behaviors observed during day 1 is added to the number of behaviors recorded on the second day. This sum is then added to the number of behaviors occurring during the third session (Cooper, 1981). The cumulative graph differs from the conventional graph, in which the vertical axis indicates only the number of behaviors which occurred during each session. The horizontal axis will still represent the dimension of time (such as "Days"). An example of each type of graph should make the distinction clear. Suppose Randy's record of instances of talking out during a ten-day baseline period was: 6, 2, 0, 5, 3, 0, 4, 1, 3, and 5. The conventional graph of the data is represented in the top portion of Figure 3-11. The lower portion of Figure 3-11 is the cumulative graph of the same data. On day 1 Randy had six instances of talking out. On day 2 there were two more occasions of talking out, for a total of eight since the beginning of the study. On day 3 there was no talking out. Therefore, the total number of instances of talking out remained at eight. On day 4 there were five more instances of talking out, for a total of thirteen. After ten sessions a total of twenty-nine occasions of talking out was recorded. The same information can be derived from either graph, but the conventional graph gives a more convenient representation of daily performance whereas the cumulative graph gives a more convenient picture of the total number of behaviors since the beginning of study. It is my opinion that the cumulative graph is of limited use for most classroom studies, and that the conventional graph is usually to be preferred.

DATA BASED TEACHING DECISIONS

A purpose of collecting and graphing data is to help teachers make appropriate instructional decisions. The process can best be brought about by graphing and inspecting the data after each session. All too often I have seen teachers collect large amounts of data, store them for several weeks, and then plot the data in time for a course requirement or a parent-teacher conference. This process may help a teacher get through an assignment, but it cannot maximally benefit her students.

Plotting and inspecting data can help a teacher to determine whether to continue with or change a teaching procedure. If a student's reading performance does not increase after seven or eight days of using a procedure, it is probably time to modify or abandon the procedure. If a student's performance increases for several days with a given reinforcement program and then levels off, the student might be satiating on the reinforcers.

By examining a graph of the data, the teacher can answer the common

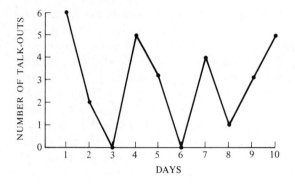

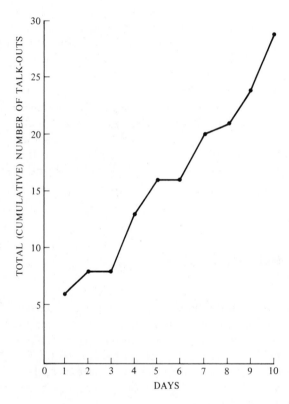

FIGURE 3-11 The top portion of the figure is a hypothetical conventional graph of the number of times Randy talked out each day. The bottom portion of the figure is a cumulative graph of the same data.

question as to how long an experimental condition (particularly Baseline₁) should be conducted. Aside from recommending that the Baseline₁ stage be carried out for a minimum of five sessions, my main suggestion is that the decision as to the length of each condition be based on an inspection of a graph of the data. With the reversal and multiple-baseline designs, the more stable the data, the shorter the Baseline₁ phase can be. Broden (1968) pointed out that:

Five sessions indicating a behavior occurred 30%, 40%, 25%, 35%, and 30% of the time respectively might be all that is needed to substantially indicate a stable rate. More time might be needed if the percentages read 10%, 90%, 50%, 30%, and 60% simply because of the wide variability of the scores (p. 31).

In using the reversal and multiple-baseline designs, another important factor determining the length of the Baseline$_1$ phase is the trend of the data. Suppose the data representing the rate with which a student hits his classmates during a five-day Baseline$_1$ phase are those presented in Figure 3-12. Since it is desirable that the frequency of the hitting behavior decrease, and the rate is already decreasing, it would be unwise to discontinue Baseline$_1$ measurements after day 5. If improvement was noted when an experimental procedure was employed, it would be difficult to determine whether the change was due to the technique the teacher was using, or whether the improvement would have occurred without any special procedures. In such a case Baseline$_1$ measurements should be continued for more sessions. Similar considerations should be taken into account if it is desirable to increase the level of a behavior and the data already show an increasing trend during Baseline$_1$.

Broden (1968) pointed out that the length of Experimental Phase$_1$ also depends on the stability and trend of the data. Perhaps the best rule to

FIGURE 3-12 Hypothetical data of the number of times a student hit his classmates during a seven-day Baseline$_1$ period.

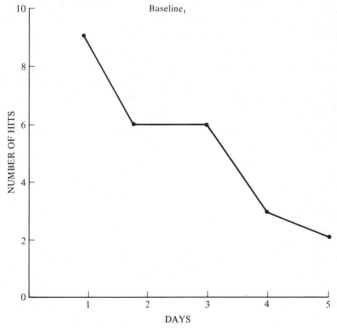

follow is that Experimental Phase$_1$ should be carried on until the data demonstrate a clear improvement in the behavior. The Baseline$_2$ (or Reversal) phase should be conducted until it is demonstrated that the behavior has deteriorated from the Experimental Phase$_1$ level. It is often possible to have fewer Baseline$_2$ sessions than Baseline$_1$ sessions. Also, there is no reason why each experimental condition should be conducted for the same number of sessions.

It should be noted in using the multi-element design, the stability and trend of the data are matters of less importance than is the case for the reversal and multiple-baseline designs. Since the data points from each condition are intermingled with each other, one must only inspect the graph to determine under which condition the data are changing most favorably. Examining the data in Figure 3-9, one would conclude that even though the data are decreasing in all conditions, vibration, praise, and touch are superior conditions to baseline, and that vibration is superior to praise and touch.

Another question a teacher may raise is whether she has modified student behavior sufficiently that her efforts may be considered successful. A teacher may wonder, for example, whether a 20 percent improvement in behavior is too small or whether she must strive for a higher figure, such as 50 percent. The question can be answered only be examining the student's problem and determining what level of performance is necessary for adequate functioning (Risley, 1970). If it is desired to bring a child up to grade level in reading and a 20 percent improvement will achieve this end, then a procedure producing this amount of change is a useful one. On the other hand, if a 50 percent improvement is insufficient to achieve the desired goal, the teacher must attempt to find an even better technique.

Behavior modifiers strive for educational significance rather than statistical significance. To illustrate the difference, it may be the case that a response-cost procedure reduces talking-out behavior from 1000 to 800 per day. This result may be statistically significant, but will matter little to the teacher who is still confronted with daily chaos. To be educationally significant, it may be necessary to reduce talk outs to twenty-five per day.

SUMMARY

Behavior modifiers are committed to the practice of obtaining an ongoing record of student performance. By measuring a child's behavior, a teacher can objectively determine whether the behavior should be modified and whether the procedures she is using are effective or not. Measurement helps a teacher to be consistent, to improve her procedures, to diagnose students' problems, and to be accountable. In most cases measurement can be carried out without interfering with the other chores facing a teacher.

After deciding on which behavior to modify, the next step is to define the behavior in precise and concrete terms. The choice of a measurement procedure will depend on the type of behavior the teacher is measuring. If the student's behavior leaves a tangible product, the teacher will use measurement of lasting products and may measure the correct rate, the error rate, accuracy, or percentage complete of an assignment.

If the behavior does not leave a tangible product, a teacher must make an observational record of the behavior soon after it occurs. There are four types of observational recording. One type is known as frequency recording and consists of noting the number of times a certain behavior occurs. Thus, a frequency record might indicate that a student talked out thirteen times during a morning session. Frequency recording is appropriate for behaviors that take about the same amount of time to perform on each occurrence. When the amount of time a behavior lasts varies, duration recording can be used.

A duration record might show that a student was twenty minutes tardy or that he gazed out a window for an hour. For some behaviors teachers will find duration recording too time-consuming, and alternative procedures must be sought.

Another measurement operation that can be used when the duration of the behavior is important, is known as interval recording. The data sheet for such recording might appear as follows:

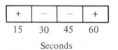

The sheet is divided into fifteen-second intervals for a one-minute period. The observer records whether or not the behavior occurs during each interval. If "+" means in-seat behavior and "−" denotes out-of-seat behavior, the recorder places a "+" in the interval if the student refrains from out-of-seat behavior for the entire interval. If he leaves his seat at any time during the interval, he receives a "−." An advantage in interval recording is that it doesn't force the observer to decide on what constitutes one instance of a behavior. As was the case with duration recording, however, interval recording often requires too much of a teacher's attention. A fourth procedure, which is usually easy to implement, is known as momentary-time sampling. Using the same data sheet as for interval recording, a teacher employing time-sampling measurement notes only what the student is doing at the end of the interval. Thus, if a student were in his seat at the fifteen-second mark, he would receive a "+"; if he were not in his seat at this moment, he would receive a "−." With as few as five measurements a day, time sampling can give an accurate measure of a student's behavior. The measurement process can be facilitated by having a timer sound when a measurement is due.

Behavior modifiers attempt to measure behavior as often as possible—usually on a daily basis. Continuous measurement gives a more accurate record of a student's performance because it eliminates problems such as the student being ill or guessing well on the testing day. Direct measurement, as opposed to the use of achievement tests, is also employed. In order to increase the probability of accurate measurement, many behavior modification studies employ reliability checks. The process consists of having a second observer independently rate the behavior of the student, and then determine the degree to which the observers' records agree with each other. Reliability checks usually occur on about one out of every five sessions.

Measurement allows a teacher to know whether or not a behavior has changed. The purpose of research design is to allow the teacher to determine the reason for the change. Behavior modifiers reject the use of the group-comparison design because it is difficult to randomly select and assign students, and because the design does not provide information on individuals.

Behavioral researchers have most often used the reversal design. Typically, the student's behavior is measured under baseline conditions. Next the student receives a procedure which is intended to improve the behavior. If the technique is ineffective, he might receive a second procedure. Once a procedure improves the student's behavior, the researcher will usually revert to baseline conditions. If the behavior deteriorates, the researcher can be certain that the previously noted improvement in behavior did not result from uncontrolled factors.

When a behavior is unlikely to reverse, or when a reversal phase might prove dangerous, the multiple-baseline design can be employed. One type of multiple-baseline design involves taking separate measurements on two or more behaviors. A procedure is applied to one behavior, and if the behavior improves, the procedure is applied to the second behavior, and so on. If each behavior improves only after receiving the procedure, one can be confident that the procedure that was used accounted for the improvement in student performance. A second type of multiple-baseline design involves applying the procedure to the same behavior in different settings, and the third type consists of applying the procedure to different students at different points in time.

A further type of research design is the multi-element design in which students alternately receive each of the experimental conditions from one session to the next. Advantages of the design are that the behavior does not have to be reversible, the baseline does not have to be stable, and the teacher obtains important information in a short period of time.

After collecting data each day, teachers should plot the results on graph paper. By inspecting the graph, a teacher can make an appropriate decision on whether certain procedures are beneficial or not, whether a slow but definite improvement or regression is occurring, and whether she should cease one phase and begin another.

QUESTIONS AND ACTIVITIES

1 Describe four advantages in measuring behavior. Can you think of two disadvantages?

2 Consider the expressions defiant, obnoxious, sullen, hostile, lazy, and uninterested. Define three of the expressions in precise and concrete terms. Ask a colleague to describe one of the expressions you have defined and note the degree of correspondence.

3 Suppose a student correctly answers 250 math problems in ten minutes. What is his correct rate?

4 Suppose a student's correct rate on long division is nine problems per minute and her incorrect rate is one problem per minute. What is her percentage accuracy?

5 Why is accuracy an insufficient measure of student performance?

6 When is it necessary to use observational recording? Describe three factors that determine the type of observational measurement procedure a teacher should use.

7 For what type of behavior is it appropriate to use frequency recording?

8 Distinguish between interval and momentary-time sampling recording. Why is it usually easier to use momentary-time sampling?

9 For a behavior such as peer interaction, which type of observational measurement procedure should you use? Why?

10 Describe factors that will determine how often and for how long a teacher should record student behavior.

11 What is continuous measurement? What are the benefits of continuous measurement for the teacher?

12 Describe how you might obtain a direct measure of a student's relationship with peers. How would you obtain an indirect measure?

13 What types of measurement problems are reduced when one conducts reliability checks? Why does high reliability *not* guarantee accurate measurement?

14 Have someone else and yourself independently record a behavior. Determine the reliability of your observations.

15 Why have behavior modification researchers generally rejected the use of the group-comparison design?

16 For the reversal, multiple-baseline, and multi-element designs, do the following:

a Describe the designs.
b Give the advantages and limitations.
c Describe a problem for which the design is appropriate.
d Describe a problem for which the design is inappropriate.

17 Conduct a study using either a reversal, multiple-baseline, or multi-element design. Indicate why you chose the design you did.

18 Draw a cumulative graph for the following data on the number of times a student raised his hand during class: 6, 1, 2, 5, 8, 6, 9.

19 What types of decisions is a teacher in a better position to make when she graphs data?

ANSWERS

3 25 problems/min.

4 90%

REFERENCES

Alevizos, P. N., M. D. Campbell, E. J. Callahan, and P. L. Berck: "Communication," *Journal of Applied Behavior Analysis*, **7**, p. 472, 1974.

Alley, S. J., and L. Cox: "Doing Dishes as a Contingency for Reducing a Husband's Rate of Leaving Clothes in the Living Room," in R.V. Hall (ed.), *Managing Behavior, Part III* (Lawrence, Kan.: H & H Enterprises, 1971), pp. 42–43.

Axelrod, S., and T. J. Piper: "Suitability of the Reversal and Multiple-Baseline Designs for Research on Reading Behaviors." Paper presented at the meeting of the Association for the Advancement of Behavior Therapy, San Francisco, December, 1975.

Baer, D. M., M. M. Wolf, and T. R. Risley: "Some Current Dimensions of Applied Behavior Analysis," *Journal of Applied Behavior Analysis*, **1**, pp. 91–97, 1968.

Barlow, D. H., and S. C. Hayes: "Alternating Treatments Design: One Strategy for Comparing the Effects of Two Treatments in a Single Subject," *Journal of Applied Behavior Analysis*, **12**, pp. 199–210, 1979.

Broden, M.: "Notes on Recording and Conducting a Basic Study." Unpublished manuscript, University of Kansas, 1968.

Bushell, D.: *Classroom Behavior: A Little Book for Teachers* (Englewood Cliffs, N.J.: Prentice-Hall, 1973).

Cooper, J. O. *Measuring Behavior* (Columbus, Ohio: Charles E. Merrill, 1981).

Eaton, M. D., and T. C. Lovitt: "Achievement Tests versus Direct and Daily Measurement," in G. Semb, D. R. Green, R. P. Hawkins, J. Michael, E. L. Phillips, J. A. Sherman, H. Sloane, and D. R. Thomas (eds.), *Behavior Analysis and Education —1972* (Lawrence, Kan.: Support and Development Center for Follow Through, Department of Human Development, University of Kansas, 1972), pp. 78–87.

Gallagher, P. A., S. I. Sulzbacher, and R. G. Shores: "A Group Contingency for Classroom Management of Emotionally Disturbed Children." Paper presented at the meeting of the Kansas Council for Exceptional Children, Wichita, March, 1967.

Gelfand, D. M., and D. P. Hartmann: *Child Behavior: Analysis and Therapy.* (New York: Pergamon Press, 1975).

Givner, A., and P. S. Graubard: *A Handbook of Behavior Modification for the Classroom* (New York: Holt, Rinehart, and Winston, 1974).

Hall, R. V.: *Behavior Management Series: Part I–The Measurement of Behavior* (Lawrence, Kan.: H & H Enterprises, 1971).

Hall, R. V., C. Cristler, S. S. Cranston, and B. Tucker: "Teachers and Parents as Researchers Using Multiple-Baseline Designs," *Journal of Applied Behavior Analysis*, **3**, pp. 247–255, 1970.

Hawkins, R. P., S. Axelrod, and R. V. Hall: "Teachers as Behavior Analysts: Precisely Monitoring Student Performance," in T. A. Brigham, R. P. Hawkins, J. W. Scott, and T. F. McLaughlin (eds.), *Behavior Analysis in Education* (Dubuque, Iowa, Kendall/Hunt Publishing, 1976).

Hawkins, R. P., and V. A. Dotson: "Reliability Scores That Delude: An Alice in Wonderland Trip Through the Misleading Characteristics of Interobserver Agreement Scores in Interval Scoring," in E. Ramp and G. Semb (eds.), *Behavior Analysis: Areas of Research and Application* (Englewood Cliffs, N.J.: Prentice Hall, 1975).

Hersen, M., and D. H. Barlow: *Single Case Experimental Designs* (New York: Pergamon Press, 1976).

Hooper, W.: "The Effects of Teacher Attention and a Token Reinforcement Program on the Classroom Behavior of a First Grade Child." Unpublished manuscript, University of Kansas, 1970.

Hutt, S. J., and C. Hutt: *Direct Observation and Measurement of Behavior* (Springfield, Ill.: C.C. Thomas, 1970).

Jenkins, J., W. Mayhall, C. Peschka, and V. Townsend: "Using Direct and Daily Measures to Increase Learning," *Journal of Learning Disabilities,* **10**, pp. 245–250, 1974.

Kazdin, A. E. *Behavior Modification in Applied Settings.* (Homewood, Ill.: Dorsey Press, 1980).

Kazdin, A. E. "Methodological and Assessment Considerations in Evaluating Reinforcement Programs in Applied Settings," *Journal of Applied Behavior Analysis,* **6**, pp. 517-531, 1973.

Kazdin, A. E., and D. P. Hartmann: "The Simultaneous-Treatment Design," *Behavior Therapy,* **9**, pp. 912–922, 1978.

Kennedy, A.: "Effects of Three Reinforcers on the Mobility of a Severely Retarded Blind Woman," Unpublished manuscript, Temple University, 1980.

Kubany, E. S., and B. B. Slogett: "Coding Procedures for Teachers," *Journal of Applied Behavior Analysis,* **6**, pp. 339–344, 1973.

Kuypers, D. S., W. C. Becker, and K. D. O'Leary: "How to Make a Token System Fail," *Exceptional Children,* **35**, pp. 101–109, 1968.

Leonardi, A., T. Duggan, J. Hoffheins, and S. Axelrod: "Use of Group Contingencies to Reduce Three Types of Inappropriate Classroom Behaviors." Paper presented at the meeting of the Council for Exceptional Children, March, 1972.

Mattos, R. L.: "A Manual Counter for Recording Multiple Behaviors," *Journal of Applied Behavior Analysis,* **1**, p. 130, 1968.

Meachem, M. L., and A. E. Wiesen: *Changing Classroom Behavior* (New York: Intext Educational Publishers, 1974).

O'Gorman, M., B. Schneider, and H. McKenzie: "P 12," in H. McKenzie (ed.), *1968-1969 Report of the Consulting Teacher Program, vol. II* (Burlington, Vt.: Consulting Teacher Program, College of Education, University of Vermont, 1970).

Packard, R. G. "The Control of 'Classroom Attention': A Group Contingency for Complex Behavior," *Journal of Applied Behavior Analysis,* **3**, pp. 13–28, 1970.

Risley, T. R.: "Behavior Modification: An Experimental-Therapeutic Endeavor," in L. A. Hamerlynck, P. O. Davidson, and L. E. Acker (eds.), *Behavior Modification and Ideal Mental Health Services* (Calgary, Alberta, Canada: University of Calgary Press, 1970), pp. 103–127.

Salzberg, B. H., A. J. Wheeler, L. J. Devar, and B. L. Hopkins: "The Effect of Intermittent Feedback and Intermittent Contingent Access to Play on Printing in Kindergarten Children," *Journal of Applied Behavior Analysis*, **4**, pp. 163–171, 1971.

Sulzer-Azaroff, B., and G. R. Mayer: *Applying Behavior Analysis Procedures with Children and Youth* (New York: Holt, Rinehart, and Winston, 1977).

Ulman, J. D., and B. Sulzer-Azaroff: "Multielement Baseline Design in Educational Research," in E. Ramp and G. Semb (eds.), *Behavior Analysis: Areas of Research and Application* (Englewood Cliffs, N.J.: Prentice-Hall, 1975), pp. 377–391.

Van Houten, R. *Learning Through Feedback* (New York: Human Sciences Press, 1980).

Walker, H. M. *The Acting-Out Child: Coping with Classroom Disruption* (Boston: Allyn and Bacon, 1979).

4

Typical School Management Problems and How Educators Have Solved Them

The information in the preceding chapters is the foundation on which teachers can build their own behavior modification programs. They should view the principles as being helpful not only to remediate problems but also to prevent difficulties. Initially, it is probably best for teachers to attempt to modify relatively minor problems than to attack major ones. (Shaping is important for adults as well as for children.) Thus, a teacher's first effort might be to increase the hand-raising rate of one child or to decrease the out-of-seat behavior of another youngster. Only after he has had a considerable amount of practical experience should he concern himself with a problem so grandiose as getting children to be less argumentative on the school playground.

Although it is a common practice for teachers to call upon outside help when they encounter problems, they should rely, as much as possible, on their own resources. Teachers have the advantage of observing students over long periods of time and, therefore, know the likes and dislikes of their students as well as the conditions under which desirable and undesirable behaviors tend to occur. Although the observations are informal, the information is worthwhile and can serve as the basis for an effective behavior modification program. If a teacher feels that the principal's or counselor's help is necessary, it is better to bring such individuals to the classroom to make recommendations, than to send problem children to the principal's or counselor's office.

Before attempting to modify a behavior, a teacher must decide whether or not the behavior should be modified. O'Keefe and Smaby (1973) suggest that teachers consider the following questions: Does the problem prevent students from learning or the teacher from teaching?

Does the behavior harm the students or others? Does the behavior prevent social acceptance? Has the problem been occurring for a long period of time or at a high frequency? If at least some of these questions can be answered in the affirmative, it is appropriate to set up a behavior modification program. It should be understood that a teacher should *not* set up a behavior modification program for every school management problem. Teachers should be able to tolerate some small level of student disruption. Teachers who have difficulty achieving this state should give priority to modifying their own behavior rather than their students'.

As indicated in Chapter 3, once the decision to modify behavior is made, the teacher's first task is to define the behavior. This job can be easy or difficult, depending on the number of behaviors that appear to be problems and the degree to which each behavior lends itself to precise analysis. When a number of behaviors is of concern, the teacher is usually better off if he initially concentrates on modifying only one or two behaviors. Often, he will find that solving one management or academic problem will lead to a corresponding improvement in other behaviors. Also, trying to modify too many behaviors at once can prove too difficult a task for both the teacher and the students.

In order to derive a definition of an apparently diffuse behavior, it is sometimes helpful for a teacher to jot down a description of each occurrence of the behavior. It may be the case, for example, that Carl consistently "annoys" his classmates. Before the teacher attempts to modify the behavior, she should specify exactly what she means by "annoy." Hence, when she sees Carl jabbing a classmate in the ribs, she should make a note of this. Later, if she notices that Carl removes some material from another student's desk and hides it from view, she should also record this information. After a few days of obtaining such information, the teacher can peruse her notes and devise an adequate definition of the behavior. A teacher cannot be too precise in defining a behavior for herself or her students. I can recall an early effort in which I attempted to modify out-of-seat behavior. The students were informed that if they left their seats without permission, they would lose free-play time. The students soon determined that they could avoid the penalty by moving the seats with them. Aghast, I watched as children propelled themselves through the classroom with seats attached to their rear ends! Clearly, I needed a better definition of out-of-seat behavior.

Once a teacher has defined the target behavior, he should decide on a measurement technique that strikes a balance between yielding representative data and feasibility, given the myriad of tasks he must accomplish. Hence, if a student is calling out during the entire school day, he might make a frequency count for only fifteen to thirty minutes a day. If the calling-out activities occur occasionally but are of an extremely hostile nature, the teacher should find it practicable to keep a record of the talking-out activities throughout the school day.

When a teacher has devised a measurement technique which he feels comfortable with, he can take Baseline$_1$ measurements. He should view the data he obtains not merely as being necessary for scientific purposes, but as providing an information base for the ensuing behavioral technique which he intends to employ. Hence, if Baseline$_1$ data indicate that students talk out 100 times a day, the criterion for reinforcement might initially be set at seventy-five instances of talking-out behavior per day. As the class improves, the criterion can gradually be lowered. Whatever the data indicate, the teacher should write a report of what he attempted and the results he attained, so that future teachers can benefit.

The technique a teacher implements in order to bring about behavioral improvement depends on such factors as the severity of the problem, the types of procedures that have been effective with the student or class in the past, and the amount of resources available to her. Teachers should not immediately turn to contingency operations to solve their problems. At times it is more profitable to determine whether children are receiving adequate nutrition at home, whether they might benefit from auditory and visual examinations, whether the heating or lighting conditions of the classroom could be improved, and whether seating arrangements should be changed. When the use of contingencies seems to be called for, teachers should first consider using positive-reinforcement and extinction techniques. The initial types of positive-reinforcement procedures might be various forms of praise for appropriate behavior. If social reinforcement does not seem reasonable, or if it proves ineffective, more complex systems, such as token-reinforcement procedures, might be attempted. In these cases teachers should first consider back-up reinforcers intrinsic to the classroom, such as the privilege of being classroom messenger, before contemplating the use of reinforcers extrinsic to the classroom, such as candy, toys, and trips. Lists of reinforcers useful in classroom management are provided by Homme (1969, p. 84); Givner and Graubard (1974, p. 159); and Sloane, Buckholdt, Jenson, and Crandall (1979, pp. 76–81).

When punishment tactics appear necessary, teachers should initially consider using techniques that are most socially acceptable. Thus, response cost involving the loss of extra minutes of free play should probably be considered long before exclusion time out. Teachers should be particularly careful to inform parents and their principal of any punishment procedure they intend to use. Informed parents and principals are more likely to be cooperative and helpful than uninformed ones.

Whether a teacher decides to use a reinforcement, extinction, or punishment procedure, she should apply it consistently and for a long enough period of time to determine its effectiveness. If the procedure proves ineffective under these conditions, she should seek alternative methods. Teachers should not always feel required to devise their own ideas for remediation. They should also make use of published studies in order to obtain ideas on effective methods. A practical, readable, and detailed source for such studies is provided by Millman, Schaefer, and Cohen (1980).

In order to familiarize the reader with the behavior modification approach to solving management problems, the present chapter has been devoted to a description of a variety of school difficulties and the remedial techniques educators have employed. The population of students ranges from preschool through elementary, junior high, and senior high school youngsters. The settings include regular and special-education classes, as well as the lunchroom and the school bus. The number of individuals in the studies varies from 1 to 455. The individuals responsible for carrying out the procedures include teachers, a principal, a counselor, and a bus driver. Although interobserver reliability was assessed in most studies, the information is not presented, in order to save space and prevent tedium.

The sources of studies consist of books, journals, and student reports. An effort was made to select studies which were carried out within the educational realities of personnel, cost, and time. The accounts which follow are my own summary of the original authors' reports. In addition to the implemented procedure, some alternative approaches that educators *might* have considered to solve the problems will be described. For one reason or another, these alternatives were unacceptable tactics but in many cases illustrate approaches that have typically been used in education. It is suggested that the reader examine the following studies for suggestions on procedures to use when problems occur, or to prevent difficulties from arising. Readers should not be put off if the population described is different from theirs, if the behavior problem is not exactly the same, or if a reinforcer or punisher is unrealistic in their situation. With small adjustments similar procedures are often effective across a wide range of situations. Of course, there is no guarantee that a procedure that works in one situation will work in another, but procedures with some history of success provide a good starting point.

SITUATION 1: KINDERGARTEN STUDENTS NOT FOLLOWING INSTRUCTIONS

BACKGROUND

When students inconsistently follow their teacher's instructions, classroom control becomes difficult to achieve. The problem is particularly common with preschool children, who have a unique ability to ignore directions which do not appeal to them. If a teacher is unable to acquire instructional control over students' behavior, she will find herself putting away materials students are responsible for, repeating the same instructions several times, and wondering why she chose teaching as a profession. Although there may be many factors which affect the degree to which students will obey their teacher's requests, one important element is whether compliance is associated with positive consequences. Thus, if students behave in accordance with a teacher's directions and receive reinforcement, they are likely to follow teacher directions in the future. If they do not receive reinforcement, it should be expected that the students will tend *not* to follow teacher directions in the future.

PROBLEM

The study involved five girls, five to six years of age, who were enrolled in a regular kindergarten classroom. The girls were generally well behaved but had a tendency not to follow many of their teacher's instructions.

REJECTED REMEDIAL ALTERNATIVES

1 The teacher could read a book on child development to determine whether it is natural for young children to ignore instructions.

2 The teacher could overlook the problem on the assumption that it will correct itself with maturity.

3 The teacher could send a note home to the parents complaining about the girls' lack of compliance with requests.

IMPLEMENTED BEHAVIORAL SOLUTION

The initial step for the teacher was to devise ten instructions which she would give the girls each day. The instructions were, "Pick up the toys," "Sit down," "Come and get a pencil and paper," "Fold your paper," and so on. The behavior of concern was defined as follows:

Definition of Instruction Following Every time a child complied with an instruction within fifteen seconds of the time the teacher spoke, she was considered to have followed the instruction.

Procedure and Results During Baseline$_1$ the teacher gave each of the girls the ten instructions every afternoon. She responded to the girls in the same manner, whether or not they followed the instructions. Figure 4-1 indicates that the five girls followed the teacher's instructions an average of 60 percent of the time during Baseline$_1$. In the second phase of the study, the

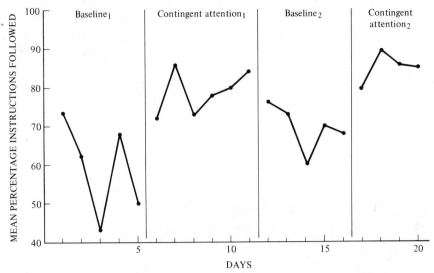

FIGURE 4-1 The mean percentage of teacher instructions five kindergarten girls followed each day during Baseline and Contingent Attention phases. *(From R.C. Schutte and B. L. Hopkins, "The Effects of Teacher Attention on Following Instructions in a Kindergarten Class,"* Journal of Applied Behavior Analysis, 3, *p. 120, 1970. By permission of the publishers.)*

teacher continued to give the girls the ten instructions each day but also complimented the girls each time they followed an instruction. She might say, "Thank you for doing what I asked, Didi," or "You are so good today, Michelle!" The effects of reinforcing the girls for complying with instructions were immediate. On the first day of Contingent Attention₁, the girls followed instructions 74 percent of the time and averaged 78 percent for the entire phase. When the teacher ceased complimenting the girls during Baseline₂, the percentage of instructions decreased to 69 percent but increased to a higher level when compliments were reinstated during the final phase.

HIGHLIGHTS

1 When a teacher makes a request and a student obeys her instruction, there is a tendency for the teacher to be pleased with the student's behavior but to fail to express her appreciation to the student. If this sequence of events occurs a sufficient number of times, it is likely that students will eventually fail to follow teacher directions. If teachers compliment students for observing their directions, they will usually find that students will comply with their requests.

2 The study involved nonhandicapped preschool youngsters who were

basically well behaved. The fact that they sometimes failed to observe the teacher's directions was hardly a cause for alarm. Nevertheless, the study indicated that a teacher who is capable-of applying reinforcement principles to mild behavioral problems is able to acquire a high degree of classroom control without resorting to aversive techniques. In so doing the teacher can achieve a more pleasant atmosphere for herself and her students.

Reference Schutte and Hopkins (1970).

SITUATION 2: IMPROVING PRESCHOOLERS' BATHROOM BEHAVIORS

BACKGROUND

Appropriate care of toilet facilities is important both for the health of the users and to minimize the consumption of natural resources (for example, paper and water). Perhaps due to the fact that many preschool children have not learned the correct means to treat toilet facilities, many preschool teachers have bathrooms in which paper towels and toilet tissues litter the floor, toilets are unflushed, and sinks are dirty. Part of the problem might also be that preschool teachers do not always require students to care for the facilities, nor do they praise students when the facilities are clean and tidy.

PROBLEM

The study involved sixty-five preschool children who used a common bathroom between 10 A.M. and 2 P.M. daily. The bathroom consisted of three sinks, four toilets, and a trash receptacle. The teachers were concerned that the children were littering the floors with large numbers of paper towels, failing to flush toilets, stopping-up sinks, and leaving water faucets on.

REJECTED REMEDIAL ALTERNATIVES

1 The teachers could speculate that the children were in the midst of their anal stage of development and leave the problem untreated.

2 The teachers or school custodian could attend to the bathroom several times a day, so the children would always have pleasant facilities to use.

IMPLEMENTED BEHAVIORAL SOLUTION

Definition and Measurement of Behaviors Each hour between 10:00 A.M. and 2:00 P.M., an observer entered the bathroom and noted the occurrence of each behavior of concern. The number of paper towels and pieces of toilet paper on the floor was counted, as was the number of unflushed toilets and dirty sinks. A flushed toilet had to consist of only clear water. A sink was considered to be dirty when material prevented the drain from operating properly. The observer also noted the number of running faucets. To be considered a running faucet, water had to be coming out in a steady stream, not merely dripping.

Procedure and Results During a thirteen-day Baseline$_1$ period, no contingency was in effect for any of the four target behaviors. Teachers instructed the students to flush the toilets, clean the sinks, and so on, but in many cases did the tasks themselves when the children neglected them. As shown in Figure 4-2 the average number of unflushed toilets was nine (during all five measurement periods combined), dirty sinks was almost two, as was the number of running faucets, and the number of misplaced towels was thirty-seven. In the second phase of the study, each of the teachers was instructed to randomly enter the bathroom five times daily and check the behavior of the students and the condition of the bathroom. If a youngster was seen placing a towel in a trash receptacle, the teachers praised her. If a teacher noted towels on the floor, he would ask a child who was present to place the towel in the receptacle and would praise her when she did. If a youngster was seen flushing a toilet, the teacher might say, "Wow! What a good helper. You really know how to keep the bathroom clean!" If the teacher noted unflushed toilets, he would direct the children to flush them. Similarly the teachers praised students for spontaneously cleaning sinks and turning off faucets and instructed them to do the tasks if they had been neglected. During the Praise$_1$ phase the average number of unflushed toilets decreased to three, dirty sinks to 0.5, faucets to 0.25, and paper towels on the floor to three. Results obtained during Baseline$_2$ and Praise$_2$ were similar to those which occurred during Baseline$_1$ and Praise$_1$, respectively.

HIGHLIGHTS

1 Sloane (1977) advises parents that if they wish to teach children to clean their rooms—"Never Clean the Child's Room." The same starting point might be advisable to achieve clean and tidy bathroom facilities from preschoolers.

2 The present study involved many students distributed over several

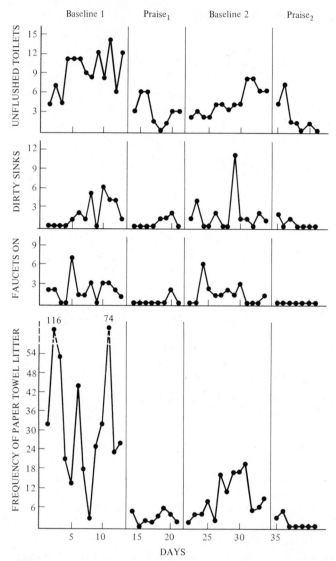

FIGURE 4-2 Frequency of unflushed toilets, dirty sinks, faucets on, and paper towel litter during Baseline and Praise conditions. *(From M. J. Taylor and T. R. Kratochwill, "Modification of Preschool Children's Bathroom Behaviors by Contingent Teacher Attention," Journal of School Psychology, 16, p. 69, 1978. By permission of the publishers.)*

classrooms, using the same bathroom. In situations where a bathroom is present in all classrooms, the present procedure may be even easier to apply.

Reference Taylor and Kratochwill (1978).

SITUATION 3: REDUCING DISCIPLINE PROBLEMS WITH A HOME-BASED REINFORCEMENT SYSTEM

BACKGROUND

An advantage of programs in which reinforcers are distributed in the school is that teachers can directly control the administration of reinforcers and need not solicit the cooperation of individuals remote from the school setting. Nevertheless, in some cases the reinforcers which schools can offer are not powerful enough to control the behavior of some students. In such cases it may prove worthwhile to have parents provide reinforcers based on their youngsters' individual preferences.

PROBLEM

The children in the study were twenty-three third graders who were approximately one year behind in reading and math. By the middle of the school year, classroom control was so poor that some children were sent daily to the principal, and on at least two occasions, approximately one-third of the students left the classroom through the windows. Not surprisingly, the teacher requested help in managing the class. Initially a program was implemented that offered students school reinforcers for academic behaviors and nondisruptiveness. The program was successful for only a short period of time.

REJECTED REMEDIAL ALTERNATIVES

1 The teacher could bolt the windows closed so that students could not escape the classroom.

2 The teacher could recommend that the most disruptive students be suspended or placed in special-education classes.

IMPLEMENTED BEHAVIORAL SOLUTION

Definition and Measurement of Behavior The authors chose out-of-seat, talking-out, and any other motor behavior that interfered with another youngster's studying as targets for modification. The exact definitions of these terms appears in Becker, Madsen, Arnold, and Thomas (1967). An outside observer monitored the students' behavior one row at a time. Each ten seconds he noted whether disruptive behavior had occurred.

Procedure and Results As indicated in Figure 4-3, students were disruptive during an average of 90 percent of the ten-second intervals. Given the failure of the previous school-based reinforcement system, the authors speculated that effective and enduring reinforcers might be provided by a home-based reinforcement system. Therefore, a meeting was set up in which parents were asked to assist in solving their youngsters' management problems with the use of home-based rewards. The authors informed the parents that they should provide rewards for their children whenever they brought home a "Good Behavior" letter. The parents were told to use their own judgment as to what the students would consider rewarding. Reports indicated that the parents used a combination of praise and special treats such as movies, extra television time, and additional allowance money. If the students did not bring home the letter, the parents were to assume that the children behaved inappropriately that day and provided no special reinforcers. In order to receive a "Good Behavior" letter, a student could behave inappropriately no more than two times in any fifteen-minute interval. For the twelve days in which the procedure was used, disruptive behavior decreased to an average of 10 percent and was at zero for the last four days. When "Good Behavior" letters were given to students regardless

FIGURE 4-3 The percentage of ten-second intervals in which twenty-three third graders were disruptive during a baseline phase, a phase in which students received a "Good Behavior" letter for appropriate behavior, and a condition in which they received the letter regardless of their behavior. *(Adapted from T. Ayllon, S. Garber, and K. Pisor, "The Elimination of Discipline Problems through a Combined School-Home Motivational System,"Behavior Therapy, 6, p. 622, 1975. By permission of the publishers.)*

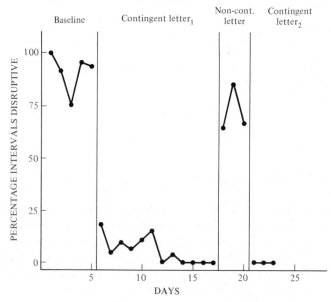

of their performance, disruptions rose to 50 percent, but again diminished to zero, when letters were used contingently.

HIGHLIGHTS

1 Although the present system involved the use of outside observers, success could probably have been achieved if the teacher marked down each student's disruptive behaviors and sent a "Good Behavior" letter home only when a student misbehaved below a specified criterion (for example, four times).

2 Remarkable success was achieved in spite of the fact that many of the parents in the study had little education and received little training. The keys appear to be simple and specific systems.

3 Unlike most studies using a reversal design, the present authors did not return to Baseline$_1$ conditions. Instead, they used a variation of the reversal design in which reinforcers are provided noncontingently.

Reference Ayllon, Garber, and Pisor (1975).

SITUATION 4: DISRUPTIVE BEHAVIOR IN THE CAFETERIA

BACKGROUND

One of the settings in which it is most difficult to control disruptive behavior is the school cafeteria at lunchtime. In classroom situations there is a limited number of children; the teacher's responsibility for the behavior of each child in the class is clearly established; and a set of rules for classroom behavior is usually well defined. In the cafeteria the above conditions usually do not exist. The students of several classrooms gather together in one large room; the number of faculty members present for lunch duty is often insufficient for the number of students present; and it is not always easy to say exactly which behaviors are appropriate and which are inappropriate (for example, talking loudly, leaving the seat, and so on). The problems which result include fighting, the throwing and stealing of food, and running through the aisles. When the situation becomes sufficiently chaotic, teachers will often find themselves ill equipped to deal with the problems.

PROBLEM

The study took place in a combination elementary and middle school consisting of 455 students in grades one through eight. The children ate lunch at various intervals between 11:45 A.M. and 12:45 P.M. every day. Problems included running, loitering, and physical aggression. The cafeteria contained fourteen large tables seating ten children each, with the youngsters permitted to choose their own seats.

REJECTED REMEDIAL ALTERNATIVES

1 The school administration could require that the students eat their lunch in a classroom.

2 The administration could hire additional personnel to monitor the cafeteria.

3 The school could suspend children who violate specified lunchroom rules.

IMPLEMENTED BEHAVIOR SOLUTION

Definition and Measurement of Behaviors "Loitering" was defined as any instance in which a student stayed in the cafeteria when he was not supposed to be there. "Physical aggression" included hitting, pushing, and kicking. Seventh- and eighth-grade students in the school were employed as observers and kept a frequency tally of each incident of running, loitering, and aggression. The students were also provided with a sound-level meter and recorded the number of times the sound in the cafeteria exceeded eighty decibels—a level considered appropriate for the cafeteria setting.

Procedure and Results The first seven days of the study constituted Baseline$_1$. The observers recorded each of the target behaviors, but no contingencies were placed on the students for performing any of the inappropriate behaviors. Figure 4-4 gives the total number of running, loitering, and aggressive behaviors that occurred each day in the cafeteria. Misbehaviors ranged from 135 to 304, with a mean of 188 for the one-hour lunch periods.

The mean number of times the sound level exceeded eighty decibels was 285, with a range of 155 to 595.

Before the initial day of Group Contingency$_1$, Mr. Adler Muller, the school principal, visited each classroom and told the students that a point system would be implemented. One point was to be awarded daily to each

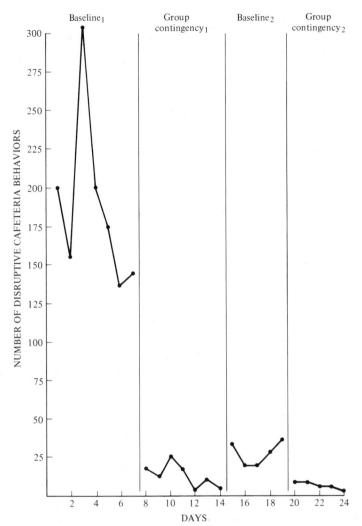

FIGURE 4-4 Total number of loitering, running in the school cafeteria, and aggressing incidents by 455 students in grades one through eight. *(From A. J. Muller, S. E. Hasazi, M. M. Pierce, and J. E. Hasazi, "Modification of Disruptive Behavior in a Large Group of Elementary School Students," in E. Ramp and G. Semb (eds.),* Behavior Analysis: Areas of Research and Application, *Englewood Cliffs, N.J.: Prentice-Hall, p. 275, 1975. By permission of the publishers.)*

class that completely refrained from running, loitering, and aggression. When the total of points for the entire school reached twenty-five, Mr. Muller examined the data of all classes and awarded the members of the class with the highest total an extra thirty minutes of recess. The points were registered each afternoon on a large chart displayed in the main hall of the school, and the results were announced to the entire school over the public address system. The point system produced immediate and large decreases in each of the target behaviors. The mean number of disruptive acts diminished to fifteen (about 8 percent of the $Baseline_1$ level).

Although there was no contingency on making noise, the number of times the sound level exceeded 80 decibels decreased to an average of thirty-five times, which is approximately 12 percent of the $Baseline_1$ rate. When the group contingency procedure was discontinued during $Baseline_2$, disruptive behaviors increased only slightly, but they were virtually eliminated during the Group $Contingency_2$ phase. The noise level increased more substantially during $Baseline_2$, but it was still well below the $Baseline_1$ level, and it decreased to low levels during Group $Contingency_2$.

HIGHLIGHTS

1   The awarding of the free time was set up in such a manner that when the total number of points for all classes reached twenty-five, the principal of the school inspected the records of all classes and gave the class with the greatest number of points extra recess time. I feel that this procedure permits too few classes to receive the reinforcers; over a long period of time, classes that improve but do not receive the extra free time might eventually become disruptive again. My preference would be for a tactic that awarded each class its free time contingent upon that class reaching some predetermined number of points (for example, five points). In that manner, classes that showed improvement but were not the most outstanding would still be rewarded. (Remember shaping principles!)

2   It is gratifying to see the principal become actively involved in the solution to an important school problem. Given the great prestige of many principals, it is unfortunate that more of them don't take advantage of their reinforcing capacity to improve the performance of students and teachers alike.

Reference   Muller, Hasazi, Pierce, and Hasazi (1975).

SITUATION 5: OUT-OF-SEAT BEHAVIOR ON THE SCHOOL BUS

BACKGROUND

The problems that occur in the school cafeteria are serious ones, but the difficulties that arise on the school bus are utterly dangerous. Greene,

Bailey, and Barber (1981) cite studies that indicate that approximately 200 deaths and 7,200 injuries occur in school bus accidents yearly (Accident Facts, 1977; 1978). They further indicate that the fatality rate on school buses is almost three times that which occurs in automobile accidents.

It is not difficult to see why serious problems occur on the bus. One contributing element is the frequent absence of any school personnel to maintain discipline. A second problem is that the driver must direct attention toward operating the vehicle safely. In any event, the driver has difficulty seeing and addressing the children, because his back is turned toward them. Finally, when the bus ride is for relatively long periods of time, students become restless, particularly at the end of a school day. Thus, given the nature of a bus driver's duties and the fact that most operators are unfamiliar with behavioral principles, any procedure designed to reduce misbehaviors on the bus must be easy to implement and should have an immediate effect on the target behaviors.

PROBLEM

The children in the study were fifty students in grades one to eight who rode the same bus to school every day. The youngsters had experienced several years of busing, changing schools, and community turbulence following court rulings on school integration. There were numerous incidents of running through aisles, climbing and standing on seats, and shouting.

REJECTED REMEDIAL ALTERNATIVES

1 Use more buses so that fewer children will be present on each bus.

2 Prohibit the most offensive children from using the bus. If this is not possible, place such children in special-education schools closer to their homes.

3 Remarkably, Greene et al. report that some drivers have driven disruptive students to jail and even assaulted them.

IMPLEMENTED BEHAVIORAL SOLUTION

Measurement of Behavior   It was surmised that the majority of the problems described above would be eliminated or reduced if the children remained in their seats. Out-of-seat behavior was, therefore, chosen as the target for modification. Each afternoon, the bus driver recorded the number of times the students left their seats during the ten-minute trip from school to the first stop. It was during this period of time that most disruptive behavior occurred. At the first stop, or shortly thereafter, most misbehaving children left the bus. The driver made use of his large rear-view mirror and a pencil and pad to count the number of children on each side of the bus who were out of their seats.

Procedure and Results During the six-day Baseline₁ phase, the bus driver recorded the out-of-seat behaviors of the fifty students and found that they left their seats an average of thirty-four times during the ten-minute period (see Figure 4-5). On day 7 the driver told the students that the bus was to be divided into two groups by the aisle. The students on each side of the bus would receive a piece of candy at the end of the trip if the group members left their seats only three or fewer times. If the members of one group exceeded three out-of-seat behaviors, the members of the other group could still receive the prize by meeting their group criterion. The candy was given out by an eighth-grade girl who also praised the students when she gave them their treats. The effect of the procedure was immediate, with out-of-seat behaviors dropping to two on the first day of the Candy for In Seat₁ phase. On eleven of the thirteen days of the phase, both groups received candy, and on six days there were no out-of-seat behaviors. The mean for the entire stage was 1.5 out-of-seat behaviors per day. In the Baseline₂ phase, the reinforcement procedure was discontinued, and out-of-seat behaviors occurred a mean number of fourteen times per day, with an increasing trend in the data. During the Candy for In Seat₂ phase,

FIGURE 4-5 Number of times fifty students left their seats on the school bus during the first ten minutes of the trip. *(From J. W. Willis, T. R. Hobbs, D. G. Kirkpatrick, and K. W. Manley, "Training Counselors as Researchers in the National Environment," in E. Ramp and G. Semb (eds.),* Behavior Analysis: Areas of Research and Application, *Englewood Cliffs, N.J.: Prentice-Hall, p. 183, 1975. By permission of the publishers.)*

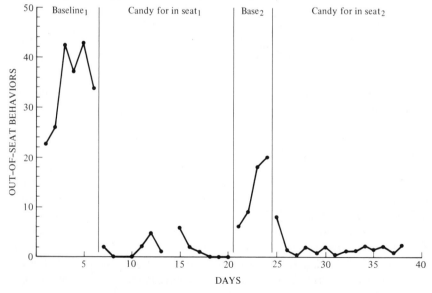

the contingency was reinstated. Beginning with day 27, however, candy was given out every other day and, ultimately, every third day, with the students not knowing on which days rewards were available. In spite of the less frequent reinforcement, out-of-seat behaviors returned to low levels, with a mean of 1.8 per day.

HIGHLIGHTS

1 The fact that the bus driver in the present study was willing and able to carry out the behavior modification procedures does not mean that such a policy should typically be employed. On routes in which there have been serious problems, it would be better to have a teacher, an aide, or a bus matron available to carry out the desired technique. (Drive your bus and leave the behavior modification to us!)

2 There have been additional reports of successful efforts to reduce school bus problems. In one case it was found that delaying the home dismissal of two preschool boys reduced their level of aggressive behavior (Whitehurst and Miller, 1973). In another case it was found that when background music was interrupted upon the occurrence of a disruptive behavior, an eight-year-old retarded girl's bus behavior improved greatly (Barmann, Croyle-Barmann, and McLain, 1980).

Reference Willis, Hobbs, Kirkpatrick, and Manley (1975, Study 2).

SITUATION 6: GETTING STUDENTS READY TO WORK

BACKGROUND

It is not unusual for a teacher to have excellent classroom control once students are in their seats and ready to work. The problem that frequently occurs is that it takes a great deal of time to get students to settle down following another activity, such as physical education or recess. The objective then is to devise procedures that will decrease transition times, without the necessity of threatening or reprimanding the students.

PROBLEM

The study involved a fourth-grade class in which the students took a considerable amount of time getting ready for the next classroom activity, after returning from an event which took place outside the classroom. The teacher had publicly posted the classroom schedule so that all students were aware of their next assignment.

REJECTED REMEDIAL ALTERNATIVES

1 The teacher could stand in front of the class with her arms folded and sullenly proclaim, "I Am Waiting!"

2 The teacher could inform the students that they will have a detention corresponding to the amount of time it took them to get ready.

3 The teacher could point out to the students that they are now in fourth grade and they should not behave in such an immature manner.

IMPLEMENTED BEHAVIORAL SOLUTION

Definition and Measurement of the Behavior   The teacher noted how long it took from the time the first student walked into the classroom until all students were seated and had the appropriate materials on their desks. Although not noted in the article, measurement could be done with either a wall clock or stopwatch.

Procedure and Results   During the nine days of Baseline$_1$ the teacher posted assignments and waited four minutes before she called the class to order and directed the students to do their work. On four of the nine days it took the students more than four minutes to get ready, and on all but one day it took more than three minutes. During the first seven days of the next phase, the teacher informed the students that they should attempt to be ready to work within 120 seconds of their return from the previous activity. When they settled down she informed each student how long it had taken him to get ready (in other words, gave him feedback) and praised him if it took less than 120 seconds. On all but one occasion all students met the criterion. Later the criterion was lowered to seventy seconds and the condition of being quiet was added. Ready time averaged about sixty seconds, thereafter.

HIGHLIGHTS

1 The teacher informed each of the students how long it had taken him to get ready. As such, students compared their progress with each other and encouraged their classmates to "beat the clock." A great deal of mutual reinforcement occurred.

2 Another procedure I have found helpful in decreasing transition times

is to set a timer for one minute after students enter the class. If all students are seated and ready to work when the timer sounds, the class receives a point that can be exchanged for a later reward (such as free time).

Reference   Struble (1971).

SITUATION 7: POOR SCHOOL ATTENDANCE

BACKGROUND

One of the most serious and pervasive school problems is poor attendance. Sheats and Dunkleberger (1979) cite research indicating that absenteeism in United States schools is about 9 percent—almost half of which is due to truancy. They also indicate that the most frequent truants are likely to be the least capable students academically. Clearly school progress is disrupted when students habitually fail to attend classes.

PROBLEM

The study involved nine elementary school students who had registered for a remedial summer-school program. Attendance through the first week of summer school was almost nonexistent. It was suspected that part of the problem was the lack of interest on the part of parents in their children's attendance.

REJECTED REMEDIAL ALTERNATIVES

1   Suspend the children for truancy. (This has actually happened.)

2   Fine the parents of the truant children.

IMPLEMENTED BEHAVIORAL SOLUTION

Procedure and Results   Students were divided into two groups. The first group consisted of four students whose attendance during baseline was near zero. In the next phase the principal telephoned the parents of each of the students and asked them to send their children to school. After two days, attendance reached 100 percent, but gradually declined to 0 percent ten days later. The principal then contacted the parents again, but attendance remained at low levels.

The second group of students never attended school during Baseline₁. As was the case with the first group, the principal called the parents and urged them to send their children to school. If the children did come to school, the principal called the parents again and praised them for their efforts. He also made a comment relevant to their child's school progress. With these procedures, attendance reached a mean of 83 percent.

HIGHLIGHTS

1 It appears that one of the keys to long-term behavior change is not simply to complain when a situation is unacceptable, but to reinforce the behavior when it improves.

2 It is encouraging to see the school principal use his prestige to praise appropriate behavior. Even so, Sheats and Dunkleberger (1979) showed that the role served by the principal could also be fulfilled by the school secretary. It would seem that truancy officers and teachers could also use the same procedure.

3 Another successful effort to increase school attendance was carried out by Barber and Kagey (1977) who offered students a party and reduced work assignments for meeting attendance criteria.

Reference   Copeland, Brown, Axelrod, and Hall (1972).

SITUATION 8: REDUCING TALK OUTS FROM SPECIAL-EDUCATION STUDENTS

BACKGROUND

Perhaps the most common problem teachers have encountered in managing their classrooms has been unauthorized talking out among their students. I once noted that 27 percent of the teachers enrolled in my courses in behavior modification chose talking-out behavior as a target for modification. Talking out, of course, is not as serious a problem as aggressive behavior or an inability to read. Nevertheless, it interferes with the work habits of more cooperative students, may be incompatible with completing academic assignments, and is distracting and annoying to teachers. When talking out is occurring at a high rate, teachers might consider using a DRL schedule.

PROBLEM

The study involved ten students in an elementary special-education class-room. The teacher described the students as extremely disruptive and wished to reduce the rate of talk outs.

REJECTED REMEDIAL ALTERNATIVES

1 The teacher could try to get the students to be quiet by yelling at them.

2 The teacher could attempt to embarrass the worst offenders by having them apologize to the entire class.

3 The teacher could ask the principal to "read the riot act" to the students.

IMPLEMENTED BEHAVIORAL SOLUTION

Definition and Measurement of Behavior   Talk outs were defined as: "talking to the teacher or classmates without the teacher's permission; talking, singing, or humming to oneself; and making statements not related to the ongoing class discussion." A frequency count was kept of the number of talk outs for the entire class during a fifty-minute period.

Procedure and Results   During Baseline$_1$ the teacher proceeded in the usual manner and applied no consequences to talking out. As shown in Figure 4-6, the youngsters averaged thirty-three instances of talking-out behavior per fifty minutes. In the second phase the teacher used a DRL schedule in which the students received two pieces of candy at the end of the day if the class's total number of talking-out behaviors was five or fewer. For the fifteen days in which the procedure was used, talking-out behavior decreased to an average of three and exceeded the limit of five on only one occasion. When the DRL procedure was discontinued in the final phase talking out increased markedly.

HIGHLIGHTS

1 The group contingent DRL schedule was successful in the present case. If it had not been, the teacher could have set up individual DRLs. For example, each student with three or fewer incidents of talking-out behavior could have received the reward.

2 Another alternative, had the present procedure failed, would have

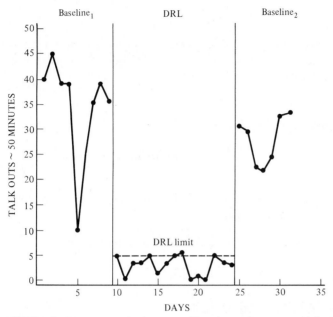

FIGURE 4-6 The number of talk outs per fifty minutes from ten special-education students during Baseline and DRL phases. *(From S. M. Dietz and A. C. Repp, "Decreasing Classroom Misbehaviors through the Use of DRL Schedules of Reinforcement,"* Journal of Applied Behavior Analysis, 6, *p. 460, 1973.* Copyright 1973 by the Society for the Experimental Analysis of Behavior, Inc.)

been to use a progressive DRL, in which the students first had to have twenty or fewer incidents of talk out, then fifteen, and ten, and so on.

Reference   Dietz and Repp (1973).

SITUATION 9: IT *CAN* HURT TO ASK

BACKGROUND

Undoubtedly it is important that students have the opportunity to ask teachers questions in order to obtain information and directions. There are times, however, when students continually ask teachers questions they can already answer, or that would be unnecessary if the youngsters had attended to teacher instructions. In such cases teachers may spend a disproportionate amount of time with a few students and become frustrated at having to repeat information that has already been provided.

PROBLEM

The study involved eight students in a classroom of twenty-nine fifth-grade students. Although they constituted only 27 percent of the class, they asked 61 percent of all questions. In addition it was noted that 85 percent of their questions were unwarranted.

IMPLEMENTED BEHAVIORAL SOLUTION

Procedure and Results   During a five-day baseline period, the eight students each asked the teacher an average of twelve questions per day. In the second phase the students were given five tokens at the beginning of each school day and were told that any time they asked the teacher a question, it would cost one token. After they used five tokens, further questions would be ignored. Using the system the average number of questions each student asked decreased to an average of 4.3 per day.

HIGHLIGHTS

1   There may be concern that when teachers use the present token system, students will refrain from asking necessary questions. As it turned out, even though the students asked fewer questions with the token system, they actually asked more warranted questions when the procedure was used (an average increase from 1.8 to 2.8 warranted questions.)

2   The twenty-one students who did not receive the token program were asking an average of less than two questions a day during baseline. It was hypothesized that these students would ask more questions when their eight classmates received the treatment, because the teacher would have more time to attend to their questions. As predicted, there was an increase in questions from the twenty-one students, 92 percent of which consisted of warranted questions.

Reference   Flowers (1974).

SITUATION 10: TEACHING A STUDENT TO BRING MATERIALS TO CLASS

BACKGROUND

There are few problems that irritate teachers as much as the tendency of some students not to bring necessary materials (for example, pencils, paper, and so on) to class. When the problem occurs teachers often reprimand the students and then request that classmates provide the youngster with the missing items. If the students are unaffected by the teachers complaints, there is little incentive for them to bring the articles to class. The question then becomes whether teachers can devise procedures to motivate the students to behave in a more responsible manner.

PROBLEM

The case involved a thirteen-year-old, eighth-grade boy who frequently neglected to bring necessary items to school.

REJECTED REMEDIAL ALTERNATIVES

1 The school counselor could send a note home to the parents requesting that their son bring the required articles to school each morning.

2 One of the teachers could give the youngster a lecture about being more responsible now that he is a teenager.

3 The teachers could require that the student do at home any work he could not complete in school because of his neglectful behavior.

IMPLEMENTED BEHAVIORAL SOLUTION

Definition and Measurement of Behavior The teachers of the student's six daily classes defined irresponsible behavior as not bringing a pencil, paper, or the appropriate textbook to class. An irresponsible behavior was scored for every class in which he neglected to bring one or more of the necessary items. Thus, he could perform a maximum of six irresponsible behaviors a day.

Procedure and Results During Baseline$_1$ the youngster averaged 4.5 irresponsible behaviors per day. In the second phase the teachers awarded him a point each time he came to class with a pencil, paper, and text. His counselor worked out an agreement with his parents that he could exchange four points for an hour of leisure time at home to listen to the radio, play records, or play his guitar. The number of irresponsible behaviors decreased to an average of 1.4 per day. In the third phase points were initially awarded every other day and later were awarded only on Fridays. In spite of less frequent reinforcement, irresponsible behaviors further decreased to an average of 0.25 per day.

HIGHLIGHTS

1 Much of the success of the present study is probably due to the precise manner in which the behavior was defined. As a result the student knew exactly what was expected of him. Responsible behavior became concrete, rather than abstract.

2 Many parents would find it difficult to restrict their child's access to leisure activities as was done in the present study. In such cases the youngster might work for another reinforcer (such as a new bike, dinner at a favorite restaurant, and so on). It is also possible that an in-school reinforcing activity could have been used.

Reference Willis, Hobbs, Kirkpatrick, and Manley (1975).

SITUATION 11: REDUCING DEROGATORY AND PESTERING COMMENTS WITH A GRADE-POINT SYSTEM

BACKGROUND

It is not unusual for high school students to make derogatory statements to each other and to have their classmates respond in kind. The ensuing series of events will sometimes escalate into physical violence. Given the great difficulty of managing severely disruptive behavior involving high school students and to avoid the distraction caused by derogatory comments, it is necessary that teachers use procedures that produce immediate and large decreases in inappropriate verbal behavior.

PROBLEM

The youngsters in the study were students in a high school class for behaviorally disordered children. They appeared interested in achieving good grades in their physical-science class, but they frequently made derogatory or pestering comments about each other. One student, Gary, was a particular source of disruption.

REJECTED REMEDIAL ALTERNATIVES

1 The teacher could give students a lecture on reasons why they should refrain from demeaning others.

2 The teacher could ridicule the most offensive students to show them "how it felt."

IMPLEMENTED BEHAVIORAL SOLUTION

Definition and Measurement of Behaviors A derogatory comment was defined as any verbal statement that detracted from the character of another person in the class. A pestering comment was one which resulted in a statement of annoyance by the recipient. For example, Gary frequently offered to buy the girls lunch or to take them to a show. Since they were not interested in dating him, they found Gary's offers annoying.

A student in the class used a pencil and paper to keep a frequency record of the number of derogatory and pestering comments of the entire class.

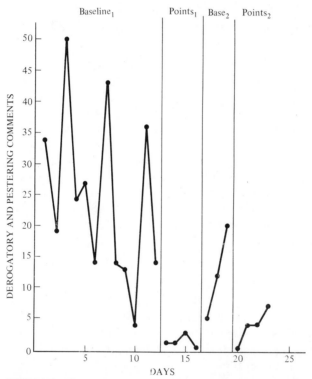

FIGURE 4-7 The number of derogatory and pestering comments from a high school behaviorally disordered class during Baseline conditions and a condition in which students lost points from their grades for inappropriate verbalizations. *(From F. Wilderman, Reducing Derogatory and Pestering Comments with a Grade-Point System, unpublished study, Temple University, 1975. By permission of the author.)*

Procedure and Results Prior to the study, the pupils had responded favorably to earning credit points for their work. They earned the points by answering questions, by completing experiments and lab reports, and by performing well on tests. Their report-card grades were determined by the number of points they had earned. During Baseline$_1$ the grade-point system was left intact and the students averaged twenty-four derogatory and pestering comments per period. (See Figure 4-7.) During Points$_1$ a student would lose a credit point for the inappropriate verbalizations. In addition whenever Gary got through an entire period without a verbal misbehavior, all students received an extra credit point. During Points$_1$ the average number of derogatory and pestering comments quickly decreased to an average of 1.2 per period. During Baseline$_2$ the point system was removed and inappropriate verbal behaviors increased to thirteen, but decreased to four during Points$_2$.

HIGHLIGHTS

1 The procedure used in the present student was effective only because the students were motivated by good grades. If this had not been the case the teacher would have had to devise a more meaningful consequence.

2 Gary's report-card grade improved from an F to a D in physical-science class. There was no evidence on whether the girls now wanted to date him.

Reference Wilderman (1975).

SITUATION 12: INCREASING STUDY BEHAVIOR IN A NINTH-GRADE ENGLISH CLASS

BACKGROUND

It is sometimes assumed that classroom disruption is caused by a failure to account for each student's individual learning styles, interests, and deficiencies. If this is the case, one would expect that individualized programs would lead to a smaller number of management problems. Yet, in the present study, it was found that students were disruptive, in spite of programs specifically devised for each of them.

PROBLEM

The students in the present study were members of a high school English class which met for fifty-four minutes daily. Each student received an assignment based on her unique deficiencies in English. Despite the individualized programs, the students spent little time attending to their work. The noise level in the class was high, some students roamed around the room to chat with their classmates, and several students failed to complete their daily assignments.

REJECTED REMEDIAL ALTERNATIVES

1 The teacher could further individualize instruction on the assumption that her initial efforts missed the mark.

2 The teacher could change her curriculum to include less academic content on the assumption that the students will probably not make use of the material anyway.

IMPLEMENTED BEHAVIORAL SOLUTION

Definition and Measurement of Behavior   The behavior being measured was the percentage of time the class as a whole was engaged in study behavior. The rules for study behavior were that a student sit in his assigned seat, that he talk only with the permission of the teacher, that he use appropriate language, and that he use all classroom materials properly. Measurements were taken with the aid of an oven timer which was set to go off ten times during the fifty-four-minute period. Intervals between rings of the timer varied from one measurement to the next. Hence, the first measurement might be taken after four minutes, the second one two minutes later, the third one ten minutes later, and so on. Whenever the timer rang the teacher recorded a "+" if *every* student was engaged in study behavior. Otherwise, she recorded a "−".

Procedure and Results   During Baseline$_1$ the teacher recorded behavior when the timer rang, but did not apply a consequence to the students' behavior. As shown in Figure 4-8, the mean level of study behavior was 10 percent for the entire class. (Remember that the behavior of all students had to be appropriate in order for the class to receive a "+." During Contingent Free Time$_1$, the teacher informed the class that if all students were engaged in study behavior when the timer went off, the class would receive one minute of free time. The time was accumulated and engaged in at the end of the period. The maximum amount of free time the students could earn was ten minutes. Under these conditions the class's study behavior increased to 79 percent. During Baseline$_2$ the class's study rate

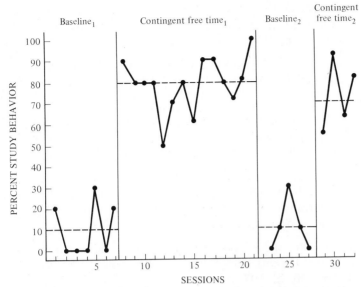

FIGURE 4-8 The percentage of time students in a high school English class engaged in study behavior each day. *(From M. Malcolm and I. Abruscato, "The Effects of Contingent Free Time on the Study Behavior of a Ninth-Grade English Class," in A. Egner (ed.),* Individualizing Junior and Senior High School Instruction to Provide Special Education within Regular Classrooms, *Burlington, Vt.: University of Vermont, p. 130, 1973. By permission of the publishers.)*

decreased to 10 percent but returned to high levels during Contingent Free Time$_2$.

HIGHLIGHTS

1   Applying behavior modification procedures in a departmentalized high school can be difficult due to the short time periods in which the class meets. An alternative to having free time occur at the end of each period is to have students accumulate time until they achieve an entire period off.

2   A student who had been particularly troublesome during Baseline$_1$ doubled his work output with the free-time consequence. Hence, earning time off benefited rather than hurt her academic program.

Reference   Malcolm and Abruscato (1973).

REFERENCES

Accident Facts (Chicago: National Safety Council, 1977).

Accident Facts (Chicago: National Safety Council, 1978).

Ayllon, T., S. Garber, and K. Pisor: "The Elimination of Discipline Problems Through a Combined School-Home Motivational System," *Behavior Therapy*, **6**, pp. 616–626, 1975.

Barber, R. M., and J. R. Kagey: "Modification of School Attendance for an Elementary Population," *Journal of Applied Behavior Analysis*, **10**, pp. 41–48, 1977.

Barmann, B. C., C. Croyle-Barmann, and B. McLain: "The Use of Contingent-Interrupted Music in the Treatment of Disruptive Bus-Riding Behavior," *Journal of Applied Behavior Analysis*, **13**, pp. 693–698, 1980.

Becker, W., C. Madsen, R. Arnold, and D. Thomas: "The Contingent Use of Teacher Attention and Praise in Reducing Classroom Behavior Problems," *Journal of Special Education*, **1**, pp. 287–307, 1967.

Copeland, R. E., R. Brown, S. Axelrod, and R. V. Hall: "Effects of a School Principal Praising Parents for Student Attendance," *Educational Technology*, **12**, pp. 56–59, 1972.

Dietz, S. M., and A. C. Repp: "Decreasing Classroom Misbehavior Through the Use of DRL Schedules of Reinforcement," *Journal of Applied Behavior Analysis*, **6**, pp. 457–463, 1973.

Flowers, J. V.: "A Behavior Modification Technique to Reduce the Frequency of Unwarranted Questions by Target Students in an Elementary Classroom," *Behavior Therapy*, **5**, pp. 665–667, 1974.

Givner, A., and P. S. Graubard: *A Handbook of Behavior Modification for the Classroom* (New York: Holt, Rinehart, and Winston, 1974).

Greene, B. F., J. S. Bailey, and F. Barber: "An Analysis and Reduction of Disruptive Behavior on School Buses," *Journal of Applied Behavior Analysis*, **14**, pp. 177–192, 1981.

Homme, L.: *How to Use Contingency Contracting in the Classroom* (Champaign, Ill.: Research Press, 1969).

Malcolm, M., and I. Abruscato: "The Effects of Contingent Free Time on the Study Behavior of a Ninth-Grade English Class," in A. Egner (ed.), *Individualizing Junior and Senior High Instruction to Provide Special Education within Regular Classrooms* (Burlington, Vt.: University of Vermont, 1973), pp. 127–133.

Millman, H. L., C. S. Schaeffer, and J. L. Cohen: *Therapies for School Behavior Problems* (San Francisco, Calif.: Jossey-Bass, 1980).

Muller, A. J., S. E. Hasazi, M. M. Pierce, and J. E. Hasazi: "Modification of Disruptive Behavior in a Large Group of Elementary School Students," in E. Ramp and G. Semb (eds.), *Behavior Analysis: Areas of*

Research and Application (Englewood Cliffs, N.J.: Prentice-Hall, 1975), pp. 269–276.

O'Keefe, M., and M. Smaby: "Seven Techniques for Solving Classroom Discipline Problems," *High School Journal*, **56**, pp. 190–199, 1973.

Schutte, R. C., and B. L. Hopkins: "The Effects of Teacher Attention on Following Instructions in a Kindergarten Class," *Journal of Applied Behavior Analysis*, **3**, 117–122, 1970.

Sheats, D. W., and G. E. Dunkleberger: "A Determination of the Principal's Effect in School-Initiated Home Contacts Concerning Attendance of Elementary School Students," *Journal of Educational Research*, **72**, pp. 310–32, 1979.

Sloane, H. N.: *Not 'Til Your Room's Clean* (Fountain Valley, Calif.: How To Publications, 1977).

Sloane, H. N., D. R. Buckholdt, W. R. Jenson, and J. R. Crandall: *Structured Teaching: A Design for Classroom Management and Instruction.* (Champaign, Ill.: Research Press, 1979).

Struble, J. B. "The Application of Positive Social Reinforcement to the Behaviors of Getting Ready to Work," *School Applications of Learning Theory*, **1**, pp. 34–39, 1971.

Taylor, M. J., and T. R. Kratochwill, "Modification of Preschool Children's Bathroom Behaviors by Contingent Teacher Attention," *Journal of School Psychology*, **16**, pp. 64–71, 1978.

Whitehurst, C., and E. Miller. "Behavior Modification of Aggressive Behavior on a Nursery School Bus: A Case Study," *Journal of School Psychology*, **11**, pp. 123–127, 1973.

Wilderman, F. "Reducing Derogatory and Pestering Comments with a Grade Point System," unpublished study, Temple University, 1975.

Willis, J. W., T. R. Hobbs, D. G. Kirkpatrick, and K. W. Manley: "Training Counselors as Researchers in the National Environment," in E. Ramp and G. Semb (eds.), *Behavior Analysis: Areas of Research and Application* (Englewood Cliffs, N.J.: Prentice-Hall, 1975), pp. 175–186.

5

Modifying Academic Behavior

Carolynn C. Hamlet
Temple University

Although it is important to establish order in the classroom and to manage student activities in a smooth manner, the ultimate measure of teaching success is the degree to which students attain requisite academic skills. Achieving this outcome has been an elusive task for educators, who have consistently observed evidence of insufficient academic development on the part of school children. The present chapter will offer evidence that with careful planning, goal setting, and application of behavioral principles, students can make outstanding academic gains. In the first part of the chapter, measurement considerations which supplement the ones that appeared in Chapter 3 will be presented in relation to teaching academics. Next, there will be a discussion of the importance and means of deriving behavioral objectives. Following this, will be a discussion of task analysis, which can be useful in teaching almost any academic task. The final three sections of the chapter will focus specifically on procedures for teaching reading, math, and language skills.

MEASUREMENT

Two of the most important characteristics of a competent teacher are that she teach students skills critical for community functioning and that she respond promptly and on the basis of reliable information when her students do not learn. Table 5-1 lists the essential steps a teacher must take if she is to use student performance as the basis for educational decision making and instruction. The present section will be devoted to an explanation of these steps.

DETERMINING ELIGIBILITY FOR SPECIAL SERVICES

When a student is referred for assessment, the need for special services is not yet established. Instead, the decision to provide special academic services is dependent upon assessment findings which reveal academic deficits. The use of traditional diagnostic tests often results in large inconsistencies in determining who receives special services. For instance, two sixth-grade students may each be reading on a third grade level according to achievement tests; one receives special services; the other does not. This simplified version of an often repeated occurrence serves to remind us that most school systems do not act consistently in determining who will be eligible for special services.

To enable school systems, parents, and teachers to quantitatively determine who is in need of special services, daily or weekly measures of performance as described in Chapter 3 are a necessary, but insufficient component in determining eligibility. In addition, a measure of a student's progress in the curriculum is essential.

The forthcoming discussion of measures of academic programs derives from the evaluation and training innovations of the University of Vermont's Consulting Teacher Training Program (Christie and McKenzie, 1974; McKenzie, Egner, Knight, Perelman, Schneider, and Garvin, 1970) and from the Data Based Program Modification Model (Deno and Mirkin, 1977; 1980).

A comparison of an individual student's level of progress in a particular academic area with the level of progress expected of any student

TABLE 5-1   Steps in Providing Data-based Instruction

1. State the curriculum in terms of essential objectives.
2. Compare the student's functional level of performance with the expected level of performance to determine eligibility for special services.
3. If the student is eligible for special services, project a learning rate which will increase the student's progress in the curriculum and reduce his academic deficit.
4. Project a performance rate for the next objective to be learned in the curriculum.
5. Select instructional procedures.
6. Specify a change criterion.
7. Implement instruction.
8. Evaluate intervention effectiveness.
9. If an academic deficit remains, return to steps four to nine.

will indicate the presence or absence of an academic discrepancy. It is the presence of a discrepancy between the level at which the student is functioning in a curriculum area and the expected level of functioning that quantitatively determines the need for instructional intervention. In order to make measures of a student's functional level meaningful, an objective should be written for each skill in the curriculum which is considered essential. Thus, the curriculum would be expressed as a collection of essential objectives. As will be discussed again in the objectives section of this chapter, the date by when each objective should be obtained by all students must be specified.

The progress graph illustrated in Figure 5-1 shows one application of this measurement procedure for establishing eligibility for special services. On the vertical axis (ordinate), the graph displays the numbers, 1.0 to 5.0, indicating the grade level in years and months at which the student is functioning in math. Each month of the school year represents one or more objectives in the academic area being measured. Indicated on the horizontal axis (abscissa) is the grade level in years and months which would be expected, given a student's chronological age. Regardless of the number of grades a student has repeated, his expected grade level is determined by the grade that is appropriate for his age and is identical to that of the student who has never repeated a grade in school. Finally, in constructing a progress graph, a diagonal line is drawn at a 45° angle to indicate the rate at which any student is expected to progress in the curriculum. This line, called the *minimum rate line*, indicates that a student is expected to make one year of progress for each year spent in school. Thus, the student who should have completed five years of school also should have mastered five years of objectives in the curriculum. This one-to-one

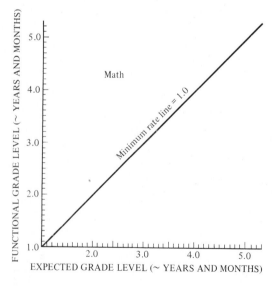

FIGURE 5-1 Progress graph showing the relation between the functional grade level (i.e., skills mastered in years and months) and the expected grade level for a student's math performance. The minimum rate line shows that for every year in school a student should make one year of progress.

ratio between years of objectives mastered and time spent in school indicates that a student who is performing at the expected level for the amount of time he has spent in school is learning at the minimum rate of 1.0.

Any student referred for a special-education evaluation first should be assessed according to his progress in all problematic academic areas considered essential for grade promotion. For each objective in a curriculum area (for example, math) a pretest and posttest should be constructed. Each pretest and posttest should be constructed so that it precisely reflects the content of its objective. To directly assess a student's functional level one administers a pretest prior to beginning intervention, for each objective within the student's range of performance. From the pretest results a teacher can not only determine the student's level of functioning, but can also obtain one baseline measure of performance for a particular skill. After instruction has been provided, the same test is readministered as a posttest to determine if the student has acquired the objective.

After administering and scoring pretests, the teacher notes the grade level of the most advanced objective that the student has mastered. She also determines the expected grade level of the student according to his chronological age. For example, the student in Figure 5-2 has spent two years in school (he should now be ready for the third grade) and in that time has only mastered one full year of math objectives. He is now ready to begin objectives at the second-grade level. This is depicted by point A. Point B represents the level of objective mastery the student was expected to attain after spending two full years in school. That is, he should be ready to begin third-grade work. The distance between points A and B represents a discrepancy in objective mastery of one year. Because point A is

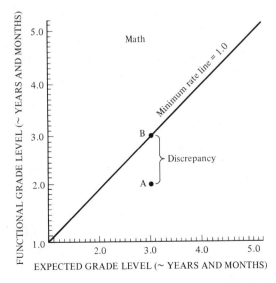

FIGURE 5-2 Progress graph showing a student who has spent two years in school and has made one year of progress in math. The distance between his present level of performance (Point A) and the grade level at which he should be performing (Point B) indicates the amount of his math deficit (i.e., one year).

below the minimum rate line, rather than on or above it, one knows that the student has an academic deficit and is in need of instructional intervention which will increase his learning rate and reduce the deficit. If this student continues to learn one year of objectives for every two years spent in school, a one-to-two ratio, it could be predicted that by the end of the fourth grade he will have mastered only two years of math objectives and will, therefore, have an academic deficit which has increased to two years. Similar graphs may be constructed for students with aspirations as diverse as entry into a sheltered workshop, teacher training programs, and auto mechanics.

At this point one might wonder how the minimum rate line is determined. In setting the minimum rate a decision must be made as to which objectives should be mastered at the end of each month of each school year. Two basic means of making this determination are available to school systems. They may do this by either looking at the performance of the average student or the performance of people judged to be competent in specific skill areas. The latter system is to be preferred (Van Houten, 1979).

PROJECTING LEARNING RATES

After the teacher has determined which objectives the student has met and has plotted his entry level on a progress graph, the rate at which the student is to learn as a result of instructional intervention must be projected. This decision is affected by a variety of factors such as the amount of the learning deficit and the number of years remaining in the student's schooling.

Studies at the University of Vermont indicated that students with academic deficits who received instruction based upon behavior analysis procedures were able to attain approximately two years of essential objectives in one year of time. Additional data from teachers participating in a training program at Simmons College in Boston, Massachusetts, revealed that the average learning rate of 143 students receiving similarly designed instruction was 3.4 years of skill acquisition in one year of time (Lew, Mesch, and Lates, 1982). Hence, gains of *at least* two years of academic skill for one year in school is a realistic goal.

To better understand projected learning rates, consider the math student who had made one year of progress during his two years in school (see point A in Figure 5-3). This student should have completed objectives up to the beginning of the third grade (see point B). If it were decided that the skill deficit was to be eliminated in one year's time, the student would need to learn not only the objectives up to the beginning of the third grade but also the objectives up to the beginning of the fourth grade (see point C). In other words two years of objectives would have to be mastered in one year's time if the student were to reach the minimum rate line in one year.

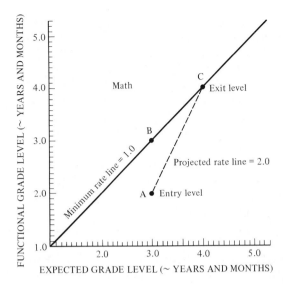

FUNCTIONAL GRADE LEVEL (~ YEARS AND MONTHS)

EXPECTED GRADE LEVEL (~ YEARS AND MONTHS)

FIGURE 5-3 Progress graph with projected rate line, indicating rate at which a student with a math deficit must learn in order to achieve the expected grade level performance in one year.

In Figure 5-3, a dotted line connects the student's entry level, point A, with the minimum rate line at point C. This line is called the *projected learning rate line* and represents the rate at which progress in the curriculum should take place as a result of instructional intervention. Because this student will be able to do without special services when his performance reaches the minimum rate line, point C is called the *exit level*. To quantify the projected learning rate, the following formula is used:

$$\frac{\text{Units of objectives to be mastered}}{\substack{\text{Units of time in which objectives} \\ \text{are to be mastered}}} = \text{The projected learning rate}$$

The units of objectives and time may be years, months, or weeks. In this example the units are measured in years. Thus, the projected learning rate of the math student can be calculated as follows:

$$\frac{2}{1} = 2.0$$

In other words, two years of objectives to be learned, divided by one year of time in which to learn them, means that the student is to learn at a 2.0 rate, or twice as fast as would be expected of a student who is performing at the expected rate of 1.0.

DETERMINING THE DATE BY WHICH OBJECTIVES SHOULD BE MET

Once the projected learning rate has been specified, the teacher must determine exactly which objectives are to be attained by the end of each month, since it is minimally on a monthly basis that a teacher should plot a data point to indicate the rate at which the student is learning. The means by which a teacher can determine which objectives a student should master by a specific date is illustrated in Figure 5-4. The program for the student for whom this graph was constructed contains phonics objectives to be learned at a projected rate of 2.0. This means that instructional intervention was planned so that this student could acquire two months of progress for every month in school. As should be obvious, a student who learns at a rate of 1.0 or less will never "catch up"; thus, a rate exceeding 1.0 must always be projected if a student's deficit is to be reduced or eliminated.

Shawn's functional level (point A) was plotted at a time when one would expect him to begin November of Grade 2 objectives (point C). At this time, however, his pretests indicate that he is ready for February of Grade 1 objectives (see the ordinate). To show how Shawn's functional level was plotted, lines have been drawn from November (N of Grade 2 on the abscissa) and from February (F of Grade 1 on the ordinate) until they intersect (point A). Thus, by November of Grade 2 Shawn has an academic discrepancy of seven months (the distance between points A and C).

In order for the teacher to know which objectives should be learned

FIGURE 5-4 Progress graph indicating the procedure for determining the months of phonics objectives which the student must master to progress at the projected rate.

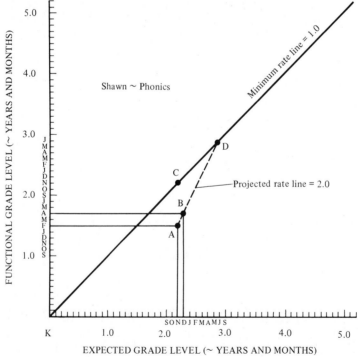

during the month of November, she then draws a straight line from December (D of Grade 2 on the abscissa) to the projected rate line (point B). From point B a line is drawn to the ordinate, at which point is indicated April objectives of Grade 1. By looking at the space between the two lines as they intersect the ordinate, one can see that during the month of November, Shawn must learn the objectives of February and March of Grade 1 in order to progress at the projected learning rate of 2.0.

To facilitate the planning of a student's progress in the curriculum a teacher might find it helpful to make a Planning and Progress Chart (Table 5-2). The first column contains the number of each objective written from the Grade 1 phonics curriculum sequence. In the second column are the dates by which each of those objectives would be met were a student progressing through the curriculum at the minimum rate of learning.

Shawn's data from Figure 5-4 will be used to illustrate how a teacher could identify exactly which objectives a student would need to master on a monthly basis. Shawn's pretests, which were administered at the beginning of November of Grade 2, indicated that he had mastered phonics objectives through January of Grade 1. A projected learning rate of 2.0 was planned so that Shawn would reach the minimum rate line by the beginning of June of Grade 2 (point D). According to Table 5-2, Grade 1 objectives which

TABLE 5-2 Planning and Progress Chart

Area: Phonics Grades 1 and 2			Shawn
Objective Number	Month of Objective Attainment at the Minimum Rate	Month of Objective Attainment at the Projected Rate	Date the Objective Was Attained
1	Oct.		
2	Nov.		
3	Nov.		
4	Dec.		
5	Jan.		
6	Jan.		
7	Feb.	Dec.	
8	Feb.	Dec.	
9	Mar.	Dec.	
10	Mar.	Dec.	
11	Apr.	Jan.	
12	May	Jan.	
13	May	Jan.	
14	June	Feb.	
15	Sept.	Feb.	
.	.	.	
.	.	.	
.	.	.	

All months refer to the first day of the month

Shawn had met by the end of January have the corresponding numbers of one through six. Beginning with objective number seven, however, instructional procedures are to be implemented which will enable Shawn to learn two months of objectives in one month's time, or at a projected rate of 2.0. As can be seen from the boxed portion of Table 5-2, the next two months of objectives which Shawn must master are objectives seven, eight, nine, and ten. Because Shawn's instructional intervention began at the beginning of November he should master these four objectives by the beginning of December as indicated in the third column.

This procedure of identifying the specific objective numbers which correspond to each two months of objectives to be taught in one month's time is continued through the objectives for Grade 2 (not shown) until the minimum rate line is reached. Once instruction has begun, the teacher should record the date each objective is actually attained in the fourth column. From this record of progress the teacher can then plot the student's actual learning rate on a monthly basis as illustrated in Figure 5-5.

By identifying how many objectives are to be learned during each

FIGURE 5-5 Progress graph indicating actual learning rate in phonics compared to the projected learning rate.

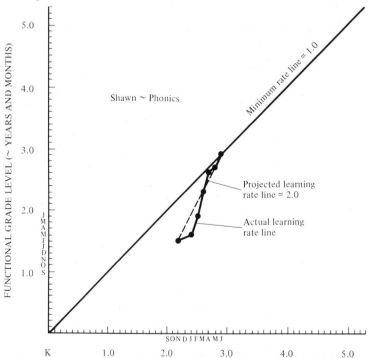

month of instruction, a teacher can estimate the number of days which can be spent teaching each objective.

PROJECTING RATES FOR PERFORMANCE OBJECTIVES

After the projected learning rate has been established whereby the attainment date of each objective can be determined (Table 5-2), the teacher should project the rate at which progress must be made on each individual objective as it is taught. In other words, a teacher must ask herself what rate of daily performance must be attained and how many days will be required in order for the student to reach each objective as scheduled. In order to establish a performance rate, two points of information must be known about each objective: (1) the student's pretest measure, and (2) the number of days within which the objective is to be attained. A teacher can estimate the number of days of instruction to be spent per objective by consulting her Planning and Progress Chart (Table 5-2). Thus, if four objectives are to be taught in one month's time, an average of one week may be spent on each objective.

It should be noted that if an objective calls for the student to demonstrate a skill for three consecutive days in order for the objective to be met, this amount of time must be included in the total amount of instructional time planned for that objective. For example, suppose a teacher has eleven days within which a student must attain mastery of an objective. The student's correct rate in reading is to increase from an average of seventy-five words per minute to 100 words per minute. If the criterion of the student's objective (see page 182) states that the correct rate will be maintained at a level of 100 words per minute for three consecutive days, then the teacher knows that she must allow one day for pretest, eight days to initially reach the correct rate and two days for maintenance of the correct rate. (Similar calculations must be made to depict the reduction of the error rate as indicated in the lower portion of Figure 5-6.) To construct the line which indicates the desired correct rate, one connects the pretest point (point A) with the first of three days of the desired correct rate (point B). The projected rate line formed by connecting points A and B will serve as the indicator of a daily performance rate which is necessary to enable the student to perform at the projected rate of progress in the curriculum. Following each day of intervention the teacher should plot the student's daily data and compare it to the projected rate line to determine the effectiveness of instructional procedures.

SELECTING INSTRUCTIONAL PROCEDURES

Only after it is known toward what end instruction will be provided can sound decisions regarding the content, duration, and setting of special

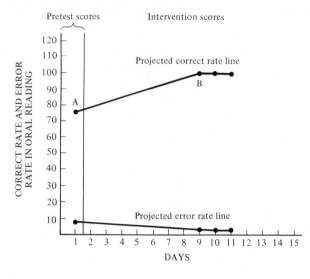

FIGURE 5-6 Performance graph indicating the projected correct rate and the projected error rate at which the student must perform in order to meet the projected rate line of the progress graph.

services be made. Unfortunately, these decisions are frequently made immediately after assessment results are reported, rather than after rates of learning and the objectives to be learned are determined. Therefore, instructional procedures often are not delivered in response to desired educational outcomes, but rather in response to assessment outcomes, only. As a result, educational decisions may not be responsive to a student's projected learning rate.

A more defensible order of decision making suggests that once the projected learning rate and objectives are determined, educators evaluate the diversity of instructional arrangements available to teach the objectives. They should then select options that conform to the following three standards:

1 Instructional procedures (such as feedback, modeling, token reinforcement) are expected to be sufficient to permit the projected learning rate to be maintained.

2 Instructional procedures are implemented in the regular classroom, rather than in a specialized setting.

3 Instructional procedures which are implemented in a specialized setting conform as closely as possible to procedures which can be implemented under regular classroom conditions. (By adhering to this practice, one would, hopefully, increase the prospects of regular class teachers assuming responsibility for the instruction of mainstreamed students.)

SPECIFYING CHANGE CRITERION

Although most instructional decisions should be based on student data, one decision essential to effective teaching must be made prior to the implementation of instructional procedures and the collection of data. As will be recalled, instructional effectiveness is *not* determined simply by whether the student demonstrates a desired skill, but whether that skill is acquired at the projected rate. Therefore, the teacher must decide precisely how long he will continue using an instructional procedure if the desired performance rate is not being maintained. The standard (for example, three days with an increase of less than five correct words per minute) which signals to a teacher the need for program modification, is known as the *change criterion.* An obvious advantage of using direct and daily measures is that this standard may be set in terms of days rather than in terms of months as one must do when standardized tests are employed. By daily comparing the student's actual performance with her projected rate of performance (Figure 5-6), a teacher can be continually informed of any discrepancy between desired and actual rates. Should a student, therefore, not perform at the projected performance rate for two to three days, the teacher should either modify the instructional technique, or select a new technique (Lovitt, 1978).

IMPLEMENTING INSTRUCTION AND EVALUATING INSTRUCTIONAL EFFECTIVENESS

On each day of instructional intervention, student performance is plotted on the performance graph and compared with the projected performance rate (Figure 5-7). Points on or above the projected rate line indicate that instructional procedures are effective and that the intervention procedure should be maintained. Three consecutive days of plots at the criterion level of performance indicate that the student has mastered the objective and is ready for the next objective in the curriculum. Performance which falls below the performance rate for the specified number of days in the change criterion indicates a need for modification or replacement of the intervention procedure.

In addition to daily measures of performance, progress in the curriculum should be recorded as it occurs on the Planning and Progress Chart (Table 5-2). This record will not only provide immediate feedback of objective attainment to a student, but will also provide a convenient reference for the teacher at the end of each month when progress data are plotted. From the information on this chart the progress graph can be plotted to illustrate the student's actual learning rate. When the actual rate is compared with the projected rate (Figure 5-5), one can then see the effects of daily instruction on a student's progress in the curriculum. It is

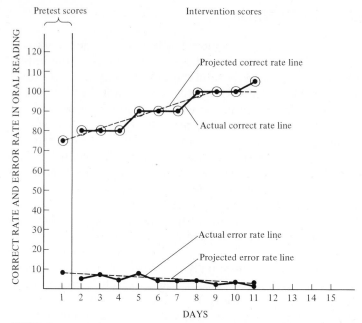

FIGURE 5-7 Performance graph indicating the actual correct rate and the actual error rate compared to the respective projected rates.

the actual learning rate of a student that provides a teacher with data from which to report student progress to parents throughout the school year, to consult with relevant educators, and to fulfill annual evaluation requirements.

WRITING BEHAVIORAL OBJECTIVES

With national trends toward accountability in education there has been an increasing emphasis in having teachers specify the educational outcomes their students should attain after receiving instruction. For some teachers this has resulted in a flurry of objective writing during which the rationale and benefits of objectives to both teacher and student may have been obscured. The intent of this section is not only to convey the professional and educational benefits of objectives, but to make objective writing an easier task for the teacher.

Before any discussion can begin, recognition must be given to Robert F. Mager who introduced objectives to education. The structure of objectives as well as the philosophical support for using objectives, basically remain unchanged since his early work (Mager, 1962). It is primarily from his incisive instruction that the content of this section is derived.

Although human behavior can not always be predicted without some error, a need does exist for parents and students to know what they minimally can expect for their tax dollar and for the time their children spend in school. Thus, behavioral objectives describe the intended outcomes of the teaching/learning process, that is, what the individual will "do at the conclusion of instruction" (Wheeler and Fox, 1972).

The specific behaviors that students will perform are usually derived after taking into account the overall goals of education. These goals, which describe long-term aspirations for competence in academic, vocational, and personal areas are usually stated in vague terms. Because people with identical goals for students may support highly varied outcomes, advocates for consumers of educational services have demanded that school systems make public their intended outcomes in the form of specific objectives. Objectives, unlike goals, permit consumers to design, implement, and precisely evaluate educational programs. In addition they disclose to public scrutiny precisely what will be taught and how one will know when it has been taught (Gilpin, 1962).

It would be erroneous to view behavioral objectives as benefiting only the consumer. For the teacher, objectives provide a clear target toward which his efforts can be directed. Once a teacher knows precisely to what end he is teaching, the selection and use of appropriate materials and instructional procedures become apparent. Behavioral objectives also provide teachers with a means of measuring the effectiveness of their programs. Only when a teacher knows the intended outcome of her efforts can she continuously monitor the effectiveness of her instruction in obtaining these outcomes. Continuously monitoring one's effectiveness enables teachers to maximally use instructional procedures and to modify ineffective procedures at an early point, thereby reducing student failure, and increasing success and pleasure in teaching.

Before beginning to write behavioral objectives, a few of their essential characteristics should be highlighted. First, behavioral objectives should describe in measurable, observable terms exactly what the student will do at the conclusion of instruction. To the concern voiced by some that many outcomes of education are intangible and therefore can not be evaluated, Mager (1962, p. 47) replies, "if you are teaching skills that cannot be evaluated, you are in the awkward position of not being able to demonstrate that you are teaching anything at all."

Behavioral objectives characteristically contain three parts: the "condition" under which the behavior will occur, the "behavior" in observable terms, and the "criteria" for successful performance of the behavior. Examples of behavioral objectives containing these three components appear in Table 5-3.

Although the three components of an objective are contained in a

TABLE 5-3

Condition	Behavior	Criteria
Given a set of 220 flash cards from the Dolch sight word list	the student will orally read each word	correctly within three seconds, on first attempt, for three consecutive days by September 14.
Given a worksheet with ten English measures of weight (in pounds and ounces) and the formula for conversion into metric units	the student will write the metric equivalents	with 90 percent accuracy within twenty-five minutes on two consecutive days by December 11.
Given any three selections from the text, *Be a Better Reader,* Level A,	the student will orally read	with a correct rate of at least 110 wpm and an error rate of no more than 4 wpm for two consecutive days by March 28.

single sentence (Table 5-3), one may express the same information in more than one sentence, as in:

> Given a list of five topics to choose from and a request to compose a story, the student will write the story such that an average of fifteen new verbs, eight new adjectives, and a total of eighty words are included. The assignment is to be completed daily within a thirty-five-minute period for two consecutive days by April 24.

The roles which the condition, behavior, and criteria play in describing the intended behavior of a student will be described in the succeeding pages. The instructions on how to write objectives are specific to academic objectives, though the basic procedures are similar for any area of human performance. Although the three parts of a behavioral objective usually appear in the order of condition, behavior, and criteria, when writing an objective it is usually easier to consider what you want to see the student do before considering the conditions and criteria for what he does. For this reason instruction in writing behavioral objectives will begin with the behavior.

BEHAVIOR

The behavior component of an objective is a statement of what the student will do, that is, what the teacher will see or hear the student do, as a result of instruction (for example, point, orally spell, or write). This may sound simple, yet many teachers have difficulty in arriving at terms which are observable and measurable. One way to approach this task is to begin with a goal or a vague description of what you want the student to do. For instance, you may want the student to "understand the relationship between the planets and sun in our solar system." Because the word "understand" has many connotations, you must go one step further, which is to ask yourself, "What will the student *do* to convince me that he 'understands' this relationship; what will I be able to hear or see him do?" Bearing in mind that you might answer this question differently from any other teacher (which is acceptable), you might decide that sufficient evidence of the student's "understanding" will be that he build a simulated solar system. The word "build" describes clearly what the student will be *doing*. If this is all that the student must do to assure you of his "understanding," you may proceed with writing the rest of the objective, that is, the condition and criteria. You may decide, however, that the student must do more than just build a simulated model of the solar system, that he must also orally define in his own words the terms "revolution," "rotation," and "gravity." Thus, it may be necessary that the student perform more than one behavior to demonstrate his "understanding." What this means is that a teacher should write as many behavioral objectives as is necessary to describe the major outcomes of goal attainment.

Because any two teachers may require different behaviors as evidence that a goal has been reached, another teacher might write an objective which specifies that the student must write the answers to comprehension questions (instead of building a model or orally defining terms) to demonstrate an understanding of the relationship of planets to the sun. Whereas, it is not necessary that people agree on which behavior to teach (unless they function as a team in making such decisions) it *is* essential that the behavior that is specified be replicable; that is, the behavior is the same regardless of which student performs it. The use of replicable terms not only provides clarity in communications between the student and members of the school, community, and family, but it also contributes to the continuity of programming, should a student change educational settings.

One more point to remember in selecting statements of behavior is that the behavior you teach should be the behavior you evaluate. For example, if you wish students to be able to identify the capitals of all states, teach them the capitals, and then test them on the same material. One example of a violation of this rule would be if a teacher were to construct objectives using any of the three previously stated behaviors for understanding a solar system, and then test the student by requesting that he write a description of the similarities and differences between a solar system and the structure of an atom. A second and more commonplace violation takes place when school systems report student achievement according to scores on standardized achievement tests which do not correspond directly with the scope and content of the texts and curriculum used by the teachers. Often the intent of teachers and school systems who test for skills other than those specified in the objectives is to determine which students in the class are generalizing from material that has been taught to material that has not been taught. Although generalization of this type is desirable it should be planned with the knowledge of students and parents and obtained as a result of teaching.

The term the teacher selects to describe student performance in an objective also describes the behavior toward which both evaluation and instructional procedures (for example, modeling, prompting) will be directed. If you have chosen an acceptable word to describe your students' performance following instruction then you will find that the term selected represents a behavior which:

1 Is measurable and observable, that is, it describes what you will see or hear the student doing

2 Can be reliably measured by another teacher

3 Is the behavior toward which instructional procedures will be designed and implemented, and

4 Is the only behavior you will evaluate

In situations where it is difficult to identify a term which precisely describes the relevant student behavior, you might consult a list of directly observable verbs and compare them with the terms you are interested in using (see Table 5-4, adapted from Wheeler and Fox, 1972).

CRITERIA OF ACCEPTABLE PERFORMANCE

Once a teacher has identified a behavior to be performed by a student as evidence of achieving a goal, she must decide exactly how well the student

TABLE 5-4 Three Categories of Verbs, A Modified Excerpt from Wheeler and Fox (1972)

Verbs that are directly observable

will write	will orally read	will tell
will orally count	will label	will put on
will point to	will name	will state

Ambiguous verbs

will idenfity	will subtract	will locate
will read	will supply	will use
will measure	will play	will perform
will summarize	will find	will select

Verbs that are not directly observable

will understand	will develop	will infer
will analyze	will concentrate	will apply
will distinguish	will solve	will determine
will learn	will feel	will be aware

Adapted with permission of the publishers.

must perform that behavior. The portion of a behavioral objective which quantifies the minimum level of performance acceptable to the teacher is called the *criteria*. These are the standards toward which she will teach, by which she will determine whether the student has met his objectives, and by which she may evaluate the effectiveness of her own instructional procedures. Without the criteria, a teacher will be unable to determine whether the behavior was performed acceptably.

The criteria of most academic objectives should contain three parts: (1) rate of performance, for example, correct and error rates; (2) the duration of performance, that is, the amount of time in days or weeks that the behavior must be performed at the specified rate, and (3) the date by which the objective is to be attained. The italicized portion of the following objective provides an example of complete criteria:

> Given a worksheet of twenty problems the student will multiply three-digit by three-digit numbers requiring carrying, for example, 365 × 873, *with a correct rate of at least thirty problems per ten minutes and an error rate of no more than three per ten minutes for three consecutive school days by January 31.*

As can be seen, the components of the criteria indicate that in determining whether a student has met an academic objective, one must measure both the student's performance in a specific behavior (see p. 178) and his progress in the curriculum (see p. 174). A closer examination of the three components of the criteria (rate, duration, and date) may better explain the unique contribution of each to describing a student's behavior. As discussed in Chapter 3, rate conveys more information about a behavior than does percent accuracy. There *are* a few instances when a teacher may find that a measure of accuracy may be a more appropriate measure than rate. An example is reading comprehension. In most instances, however, the omission of correct and error rates renders an academic objective meaningless in describing the level of competency the student is to attain. Take, for instance, the two fourth-grade students who each made 90 percent on an assignment of twenty identical multiplication problems. The first student required forty minutes and the second student required twenty minutes to complete the same assignment. The first student's correct and error rates were exactly twice those of the second student. These obvious differences in levels of proficiency would not have been reflected, had percent accuracy scores alone, been used. Rate, therefore, is a succinct means of expressing accuracy in the context of time. Inasmuch as time is an essential factor in the performance of most academic skills, its inclusion in the criteria of academic objectives is also essential.

The designation of rates at which a student is to perform a skill should not, of course, be arbitrarily decided upon. Rates of performance may be determined by one of two standards. The rate may be based either on the average performance of peers or the average performance of highly competent individuals. The latter approach is recommended for developing skills prerequisite for successive levels of learning (Van Houten, 1979).

The second part of the criteria, duration of performance, is frequently omitted by teachers. Its role is to specify the amount of time a student must perform an academic task at the specified rate. It is the duration of an acceptable rate of performance that convinces the teacher that a skill has been learned. In other words, the correct and error rates of performance, plus the amount of time during which they must be sustained, define for a teacher and the student what is meant by the word "learned." For example, the student who reads with a correct rate of 100 and an error rate of three for *one* day has not yet sustained that level of performance long enough to reasonably assure the teacher that her reading fluency will be high tomorrow. If the same student maintains that level of performance for two or three consecutive days, however, the teacher would be better assured that the student is ready to move to a higher level of instruction. The inclusion of the required duration of performance with rates, not only defines for the student and teacher what the criteria for movement to the next level of instruction must be, it also helps assure that the student does not stay at a skill level too long, nor move prematurely to ultimately encounter failure.

The final portion of the criteria, the date of attainment, is perhaps more important than either of the other two elements of the criteria. It alone enables a teacher, parent, or student to determine if the student's overall rate of progress in the curriculum will allow the student to "catch up." As will be recalled, this element of the criteria is determined, not arbitrarily, but by first establishing the rate of progress the student will make in the curriculum of a specific area (such as math) and then determining the date by which that rate indicates each objective should be met. For a more complete review of the procedure by which one determines the date of attainment, refer to "Projecting Learning Rates" (see p. 170).

CONDITION

After teachers and parents decide precisely what they want the student to do and the standard to which that behavior will be performed, they need to consider the conditions under which the behavior will occur. A statement of conditions, which often introduces a behavioral objective, describes the specific situation in which instruction *and evaluation* will take place. A teacher should state the conditions so specifically that another teacher will have no difficulty in replicating them precisely. Conditions for academic behaviors often include a description of the materials to be used, for example:

Given a description of experimental procedures, necessary equipment, and a forty-five-minute lab period. . . .

Given any three selections, of 200 words each, from the 4^2 reader of the Bank Street Readers. . . .

Conditions might also describe a restriction or the absence of an undesirable prompt, as in:

Given a worksheet with twenty-five addition facts and instructions not to count on her fingers. . . .

Conversely, the wording of a condition might assure specific prompts, for instance:

Given a workbook exercise of five story problems in subtraction of two-digit numbers with regrouping and a calculator. . . .

Occasionally, one may need to include a definition or an example in the condition to assure effective communications with parents and, in particular, with the student as in these two examples:

Given ten minutes of "free time" per day, that is, time without teacher instruction or an assignment. . . .

Given a worksheet with twenty-five problems which require subtraction of three-digit numbers with regrouping (borrowing), for example,

$$565$$
$$-467$$

When conditions would be wordy or difficult to characterize, a teacher might reference the conditions to the materials he will use to assure replicability, as in:

Given twelve Spanish idioms from p. 98 of *Spain, Its Language and Its People*. . .

It is important to note that the condition component of a behavioral objective describes the circumstances that will occur during both the instruction *and* evaluation of student performance. Often teachers test students under a different set of conditions from which they taught them. This is done in order to test their ability to generalize. A student's ability to generalize, in this case, to perform the same behavior under a variety of conditions, is a highly desirable outcome of instruction. If generalization is to be tested, however, the teacher is responsible for identifying generalization as the desired outcome (in terms the student will understand) and for specifically implementing instructional procedures which will assure its attainment. Consider, for instance, the disillusionment of the student who is allowed to do homework assignments in physics with his book open, but is not permitted to open his book during an examination. Tests should measure a student's behavior only under the conditions provided during instruction. Otherwise, questions of fairness, as well as effectiveness and efficiency of instruction can legitimately be raised.

Frequently in testing, generalization is confused with the skill of a student predicting a teacher's "test-giving" behavior. If this is regarded as an important study skill, then it should be taught separately and directly, not included surreptitiously in a testing situation. That is, a student should be free of "second guessing" a teacher as to assessment conditions while demonstrating a skill learned under a different set of conditions.

TASK ANALYSIS

Teachers will occasionally find that normally effective instructional procedures have little effect on the academic progress of a few students. Frequently the problem is in the difficulty of the task.

A closer examination of the task may reveal that it is composed of not one, but several smaller steps which occur in a specific order. It is often in the completion of one or more steps or in the sequencing of steps that the problem lies. The process of breaking down a task into its component steps and listing them in the order of their occurrence is called *task analysis*. This process makes three specific contributions to the preparation of instruction. First, it enables a teacher to determine where in the sequence of steps intervention should be applied. Second, it enables the teacher to precisely identify the next skill the student is to learn. Third, a task analysis outlines, step-by-step, the content and sequence of the teacher's instruction. It is these three aspects of teaching preparation which determine in large part the extent to which the use of subsequent instructional procedures can be effective.

The uses of task analyses extend to all areas and levels of human performance, from instruction in daily living skills, sports, reading, and math, to the management of industry and the design of college-level textbooks. Among the most commonly used task analyses, however, are the recipes of cookbooks, which specify in sequence each of the steps a person must perform to prepare a meal. Teachers, too, are daily breaking academic tasks into smaller steps, such as those required to complete a long division problem (see Figure 5-8).

Many teachers are familiar with how to analyze a task. It should be understood, however, that task analysis is *not* a teaching procedure as are

STEP 1

Round the divisor to the nearest tens.

$67 \approx 7$ tens

STEP 2

Estimate how many times the rounded number will go into the first two digits of the dividend.

$36 \div 7 \approx 5$

STEP 3

Write the estimate over the hundreds place of the dividend.

$$\begin{array}{r} 5 \\ 67\overline{)3642} \end{array}$$

STEP 4

Write the product of the estimate times the divisor under the first three numbers of the dividend

$$\begin{array}{r} 5 \\ 67\overline{)3642} \\ 335 \end{array}$$

STEP 5

Subtract 335 from the first three digits of the dividend.

$$\begin{array}{r} 5 \\ 67\overline{)3642} \\ 335 \\ \hline 29 \end{array}$$

STEP 6

Bring down the ones of the dividend.

$$\begin{array}{r} 5 \\ 67\overline{)3642} \\ 335 \\ \hline 292 \end{array}$$

STEP 7

Repeat step 1.

FIGURE 5-8 The first seven steps of a task analysis of the division of a four-digit number by a two-digit number, for example, 67 $\overline{)\,3642}$. (*Adapted from R. E. Eicholz, P. G. O'Daffer, and C. R. Fleenor,* Mathematics in Our World (Workbook), *Menlo Park, Calif.: Addison-Wesley, 1978, p. 64. By permission of the publishers.*)

shaping and fading, but rather a tool for identifying learning problems and a guide to determining the order of presentation of units of instruction. Whereas instructional procedures are generally enhanced if their use is preceded by an analysis of the task, the use of a task analysis without the accompaniment of effective instructional procedures may be of no instructional value at all.

TASK ANALYSIS AND PROBLEM IDENTIFICATION

Upon completion of a task analysis the teacher should compare the student's work with the task analysis, to precisely identify the learning problem. Task analysis can be used to reveal two types of errors: (1) incorrect completion of the steps of a task; or (2) incorrect sequencing of the steps of a task.

Incorrect completion of a step, in turn, may be caused by any of three errors. First, the student may not have the prerequisite skills to complete a step as shown below:

$$\begin{array}{r} 63 \\ 67\overline{)3642} \\ 344 \\ \hline 202 \\ 178 \\ \hline 24 \end{array}$$

As is evident from the incorrect products, the student has yet to master multiplication facts—a skill prerequisite to long division. The absence of prerequisite skill mastery may not always be so evident. A teacher may find that a student is accurate in performing long division, yet requires excessive time to complete an assignment. In such a case, a teacher should check first to see if the student can write answers to multiplication (and subtraction) facts at an acceptable rate before proceeding with instruction in long division. Were instruction provided in long division while the student lacked proficiency in multiplication facts, for example, the student would be attempting the mastery of two skills rather than one. That is, the student would be trying to learn to multiply while also learning to divide. The effectiveness of teaching is increased and much confusion eliminated when a student is presented with only one skill to learn at a time (Van Houten, 1980).

A second reason for incorrectly completing a step occurs when a student has the prerequisite skills, but does not perform a specific step in the task presently being taught. For example, a student who performs a task as follows:

$$\begin{array}{r} 5 \\ 67\overline{)3642} \\ \underline{335} \end{array}$$

may have acquired prerequisite multiplication skills, but has not learned where to place the first number of the quotient. This problem might be solved by providing information through models and verbal explanations, or by introducing a contingency.

Third, a student may have acquired prerequisite skills and know how to perform each step of a task, but still may not perform the step. Such students are sometimes called "lazy," or "unmotivated." The solution to such a problem is often to reinforce the desired behavior.

Whereas some students do not correctly complete the steps of a task, other students perform the steps of a task correctly, yet do so in an incorrect sequence. This problem is evident in the illustration of the student's attempt to write her name, "Karen," as follows:

KAERN

Although each step of the task has been included, the sequencing of the steps (letters) presents the learning problem. Incorrect sequencing may also explain the confusion of the chemistry student who diligently completed each step of an experiment only to find that his results differed from those of his classmates. A possible solution to the sequencing problem is given below.

TASK ANALYSIS AND CHAINING

Once a teacher has identified a problem in the acquisition of a step or in the sequencing of steps, she should decide in which order to teach a task. As indicated in Chapter 1, forward or backward chaining may be used to sequentially teach the steps of a task. An advantage of backward chaining is that a child who successfully performs the required steps experiences the reinforcer of observing a completed task.

As will be recalled from Chapter 1, each step in a task is an S^D for the next step. Thus if a student skips or incorrectly performs a step in a task, the correction procedure should be to prompt performance of the steps in the correct order. This recommendation is often disregarded, when teachers return a paper to a student with the request to cross each "t". In so doing the student has not learned the correct sequence of events. What is necessary is that the teacher prompt the student to cross the ʟ immediately after the final letter of the word containing the ʟ has been written. The correct sequence of steps might be attained with a prompt such as "Remember to cross each t as soon as you have completed a word containing a t."

TASK ANALYSIS AND PROMPTS

The use of prompts such as written models (that is, examples) and verbal reminders may encourage the successful performance of either a step or the sequencing of steps. For instance, to assist a student in the performance of Step 3 of the long division task analysis (Figure 5-8), the teacher could tape an example of the problem on the student's desk. Additional assistance might be provided if the teacher highlighted the correct placement of the first numeral of the quotient with a yellow marker and offered the verbal prompt, "Look at the model before you write your answer." Models may also be used to assist students who have mastered the individual steps of a task, yet perform them in the incorrect order. Flow charts posted in the front of the room listing the sequence of steps of an experiment, direct chemistry students to correctly complete steps which they may already know how to perform, but tend to perform in an incorrect order.

TASK ANALYSIS AND FADING

Once a student can sequentially perform the steps of a task at a high and stable rate, prompts should be faded out. Thus, for the student working the division problem (Figure 5-8), a model without the yellow highlight could replace the model containing the highlight. If performance remains high, that model could then be removed from her desk and shown to her only at the time the assignment was made. Eventually, that model, too, would be withdrawn. In conducting the laboratory experiment, the flow chart could be removed from the front of the room and posted in a less conspicuous place. Later, it too could be permanently removed, if the student were performing at a proficient level. The accompanying verbal reminders for each task might be provided less and less frequently until the teacher says, "Please begin your work now." Through the gradual, systematic removal of prompts, students are likely to acquire greater independence in the performance of a task.

TASK ANALYSIS AND SHAPING

Like other instructional procedures, shaping may be used to teach either the steps of a task or the sequencing of the steps. For the student who prints the name, DAVID, DAVID , acceptable formation of the letter, "V," could be shaped, that is reinforcement could be contingent upon successively closer approximations of V to "V." Shaping is frequently used, too, to teach a sequence of steps. The teacher of a student who counts "1,3,2,5,4,7,6,10,8,9" could shape correct sequencing using forward chaining by contingently reinforcing the correct ordering of only the first two numbers: 1,2. When the sequencing of these two steps is mastered, the same reinforcer could be made contingent upon counting of the first three numbers, and so on, until correct sequencing of the numbers, one through ten, had been shaped. The use of task analysis is especially important in facilitating a shaping procedure, for it shows the teacher the precise steps to be followed and the points at which prompts and reinforcment should be provided.

TEACHING READING

The importance of reading in contemporary society is incalculable. Virtually every academic, vocational, and many pleasurable pursuits depend on an ability to read. Reading is probably the most critical academic skill that schools can impart to their students. The present section will concentrate on a few procedures which address the reading problems most frequently confronting teachers. An effort was made to select procedures which are easily replicable in classroom settings. For these reasons the topics selected will be limited to an overview of current procedures in the areas of oral reading, word recognition, and reading comprehension.

PLACEMENT

Implementation of a successful reading program begins with the placement of students at their instructional levels of reading. A modified version of the placement inventory developed by Lovitt and Hansen (1976a) suggests six steps to be followed in determining reading placement for students who have some ability to read and understand short passages. First, a teacher should choose a series of books such as a set of basal readers which have graduated levels of difficulty. Second, the teacher should select and duplicate three passages, one each from the beginning, middle, and end of each reading text in the series. The passages selected should be long enough (at least 100 words) to permit uninterrupted oral reading for one minute and sufficient in length and content for the teacher to compose four to six comprehension questions.

Next, comprehension questions should be constructed. Six questions should be designed for each passage taken from a reader at the first- through third-grade levels—two recall, two sequence, and two interpretation. For texts above the third-grade level, four questions should be designed: one recall, one sequence, one interpretation, and one vocabulary. (Duplicates of reading passages and questions should be referenced to the materials from which they were taken and filed by grade level for easy access when a new student arrives.)

In order to find the grade level at which to begin oral reading and comprehension assessment for a student, the teacher should begin with the text that corresponds to the grade level the student is in. For example, a student in the fifth grade should read from a fifth-grade text during this assessment even though it is suspected that placement will be much lower. A system to be described later will adjust for any inequity.

In the fourth step, the teacher presents one reading passage a day to the student for three consecutive days. The distribution of data collection over three days, instead of only one or two, assures the teacher that an "off day" or "good day" did not produce scores which would misrepresent the student's typical performance. A stopwatch or second hand is used to time the student for exactly one minute of oral reading from each passage. The teacher should place a check mark over each word read incorrectly, as the student reads from her passage. A student should not be penalized for incorrectly reading proper names and places. The number of errors made during a one-minute reading becomes the error words per minute for that passage. The number of errors subtracted from the total number of words read constitute the correct words per minute. Some teachers may want to obtain an analysis of errors in order to determine the prevalence of hesitations, omissions, substitutions, and so on. An error analysis at this point, however, may be unnecessary in that a general intervention procedure often eradicates many of these errors (see p. 192). Thus, it is recommended that an error analysis be conducted only if subsequent instruction proves to be ineffective in reducing errors. For purposes of placement, however, only the notation of an error, regardless of type, is necessary. Teachers interested in using a notation system for specific types of oral reading errors are referred to Hansen and Eaton (1978, p. 53).

Following the oral reading of each passage the student should be permitted to complete any remaining portion of the passage over which the comprehension questions have been composed. No timing is needed at this point. Comprehension questions are posed to the student in the mode of response to be used in subsequent classroom instruction. Thus, if the student will be expected during classroom instruction to read comprehension questions with multiple choice answers from a worksheet and to circle correct answers, the placement activities likewise should require reading and circling responses. The teacher notes correctly or incorrectly answered comprehension questions for each passage, from which a percent accuracy score is then determined.

In the fifth step the teacher averages the three days' scores for each of the three measures—correct rate, error rate, and comprehension. The correct rate score should be rounded to the nearest unit of five. Placement can now be predicted from these three averages. If the correct rate is below the recommended instructional level of 45 to 60 correct words per minute (Hansen and Eaton, 1978), the teacher should lower the reader one level for every five points (that is, words) which must be added to the student's score to reach a score of fifty. For example, if the student reads forty correct words per minute in a 5^2 reader, her predicted placement would be two levels lower, that is, she would be placed in a 4^2 reader. (Remember to account for two levels per grade.)

Confirmation of placement is the sixth and final step in the placement process. Instruction should begin if the student's performance in the predicted reader meets the following criteria: correct rate is between forty-five and sixty words per minute, error rate is between four and eight words per minute, and reading comprehension accuracy is between 50 and 75 percent. If all three of the student's scores do not fall within the recommended ranges, the student's correct rate score should be the determinant of placement (Hansen and Lovitt, 1976).

ORAL READING

Once the student has been appropriately placed in reading materials a teacher may choose to address oral reading as a general area for improvement or to focus on one of several types of oral reading errors. A straightforward, general approach to oral reading problems was presented in a study of three students by Willis (1974). During baseline, tutors provided praise for correct reading and assistance for errors. Systematic intervention was then introduced whereby tutors provided feedback to the students in the form of green chips for each correctly read sentence. A red chip was dispensed for an error. Following each reading session chips were counted and the total numbers of red and green chips were recorded on a posted graph by each child. The results clearly indicate that the combination of feedback, public posting, and self-charting was effective in increasing the number of correctly read sentences. This procedure offers at least three advantages. First, it permits a teacher to possibly reduce an oral reading problem without investing valuable time in analyzing and arranging intervention for smaller specific reading errors. A second feature of this procedure is that young children as well as adolescents can serve as tutors provided they are competent readers. A teacher would find this procedure quite manageable in that minimal training and monitoring would be required of the tutors. Third, because tutors can be used, many students can receive individual feedback on a daily basis.

Another general procedure which improves reading fluency and which also may employ tutors is known as "previewing." Over the years teachers have used various previewing techniques to familiarize students with reading assignments prior to having them read their lessons orally. In a study of eight students, ages nine to seventeen years, Eaton, Lovitt, Sayre, and Lynch (1974) compared silent previewing, previewing by listening, and oral previewing both with and without feedback. During silent previewing the student inaudibly read the assigned reading at his desk. Previewing by listening required the student to follow the reading passage while the teacher read aloud. Oral previewing provided the student with an opportunity to read aloud to the teacher. Feedback provided during oral reading was to assist the student with error words. During all types of previewing, students were encouraged to seek teacher help with difficult words. Findings of the study indicate that oral previewing plus feedback yielded the greatest reductions in error rates. Previewing by listening, on the other hand, produced the greatest increases in correct rate.

After implementation of a general procedure to reduce oral reading errors a teacher may find that a particular type of error accounts for the majority of oral reading errors. In such a case a more specific type of intervention is required. Such was the case in a study by Haupt, Magee, Axelrod, Coben, and Price (1977) in which students would correctly read the initial consonant of a word but would then complete the word incorrectly. This type of error resulted in words such as "mat" being read as "mad." During the baseline condition, an experimenter made no comment while listening to each student read. Following baseline, a drill procedure was introduced in which each student was required to read twenty pairs of words prior to each oral reading session. Members of each pair of words differed in their final consonants. Each word in the pair consisted of a single consonant in the initial position, with a vowel in the medial position, followed by a single consonant or consonant cluster in the final position. Examples of word pairs included gun/gum and lung/lush.

Prior to the oral reading lesson pairs of words, printed on cards, were flashed until the student could read nineteen out of twenty correctly. Results of the study indicated that the drill procedure, preceding oral reading, rapidly reduced the type of reading errors described above.

Every teacher who listens to a student read must decide which type of response will best prompt a student to correct her errors. Many teachers will simply read the word for the student. However, correction strategies may be used that give a student an opportunity to correct her errors with less teacher assistance. Hansen (1975) suggests that the teacher adhere to the following hierarchy when correcting a student's oral reading errors:

1   Tell the student to try a different way (that is, to select her own method of error correction).
2   Tell the student to complete the sentence and then attempt the word.
3   Tell the student to divide the word into segments and pronounce each.
4   Cover portions of the word and ask the student to read each part.
5   Ask the student what sound '———' (letters) make.
6   Tell the student the word.

Hansen found that error correction which began with step 1 and proceded, when necessary, through step 6, produced more independent readers than error correction which used only steps 4 and 5. It would appear that by posting the hierarchy, students, tutors, and teachers would have a readily accessible prompt to facilitate error correction.

WORD RECOGNITION

Research has found that practice in identifying words in isolation can increase a student's oral reading rate. In a study conducted by Eaton and Haisch (1974) the effects of drill on new words were compared with the effects of drill using error words. New words were selected from words just introduced into the series by the publisher. Error words were words read incorrectly the preceding day. Six students between the ages of six and eight who were deficient a year or more in reading were selected for the study. During baseline, students were not drilled on either new or error words. During the condition requiring drill on new words the teacher instructed the students to listen to and record five new words on a language master for three minutes. The drill on error words was similarly carried out with the exception that five error words instead of five new words were used. It was generally found that drill on error words was superior to drill on new words and that either type of drill produced better results than no drill at all.

The relationship between word recognition and oral reading fluency demonstrated in this study would suggest that teachers also might find word drill procedures employing flash cards to be effective. A flash-card procedure designed by Egner, Burdett, and Fox (1972) has indicated high success rates among students of all ages, especially for those who persistently err on basic sight words. When teaching the flash-card procedure presented below, a learned word may be defined as a word read correctly on the first attempt, within three seconds of presentation, for three consecutive sessions.

The following eight steps of the flash-card procedure combine the measurement and instructional procedures a teacher must carry out. To facilitate implementation of the procedure a list of these steps should be kept close at hand until the sequence is mastered.

A teacher implementing the flash-card procedure for the first time should not be surprised if a student initially complains about the large number of 0's she receives. Students who are told before the procedure is begun that two or three days may be required before many plusses are likely to be recorded and that four or five days may lapse before a word is learned, usually express less dissatisfaction with the activity. Once the

Flash-Card Procedure

1 *Compose a list of words to be learned.* Use words from sources such as basic sight word lists, words commonly missed in oral reading, or new words to be introduced into a basal series.
2 *Determine which words are known and which are to be learned.* Flash all words allowing the student *no more* than three seconds to read each word. Place all words read incorrectly on the first attempt or those read after the three-second interval in a stack labeled "words to' be learned." Eliminate all correctly read words from future drill activities.
3 *Select any ten cards from the "words to be learned" stack and write the words in any order on the response sheet.*
4 *Flash all ten cards in sequence three times each and record the data for each response.* (See Figure 5-9.) Record a "+" *immediately* and praise the student if the word is read correctly. Record a "0" for any word read incorrectly, and say, "No, the word is _____. Now you read it." If a student first reads a word incorrectly and then corrects his own error, still record a "0" and say, "You are right, but you must read the word correctly the first time." If a student takes more than three seconds to respond, record a "0" and tell him the word. Make certain the student is looking at the card as it is re-read. If necessary, say, "Look at the word and read it." It is important that the teacher record the "0" *before,* rather than after the student correctly re-reads the word in order to avoid the risk of punishing a correct response.
5 *Have the student plot the number of newly learned words on a cumulative graph (post).* Count the number of learned words, that is, those with nine consecutive plusses, and let the student plot her own graph. The teacher should draw a line through each word on the response sheet as it is learned to avoid confusion in data recording.
6 *Deliver back-up reinforcers if additional contingencies have been established and if a sufficient number of words has been learned.*
7 *Replace each card of the learned words with a new card, maintaining ten cards at all times.*
8 *Prepare a response sheet, if necessary, for the next day's lesson.* When all squares on the response sheet have been filled or when there is no more space to record a "+" or "0" for any one word, take a new response sheet and list the ten words currently being flashed. Paper clip all old response sheets behind the one in current use for easy reference when determining whether a sufficient number of plusses have been recorded to warrant dropping a word or delivering a reinforcer.

Flash-Card Procedure Data Sheet   *Student:* _____

No.	Word	Session 1 Date:	2 Date:	3 Date:	4 Date:	5 Date:	6 Date:	7 Date:
1.	fast	0 0 +	+ 0 0	0 + +	+ 0 +	+ + 0	+ + +	+ + +
2.	~~and~~	0 + +	+ + +	+ + +	+ + +			
3.	come	0 0 0	0 0 0	0 + 0	+ + 0	0 0 +	+ + +	+ + +
4.	~~get~~	0 0 +	+ 0 +	+ + +	+ + +	+ + +		
5.	work	0 0 +	0 + 0	+ 0 +	+ 0 +	+ + 0	+ + +	+ + +
6.	said	0 0 0	+ 0 0	0 + 0	+ + 0	0 + 0	+ + 0	+ + +
7	surprise	0 0 +	0 + +	+ + 0	+ 0 +	+ + 0	+ + +	+ + +
8.	this	0 0 +	0 0 +	+ 0 0	+ + +	0 + +	+ + +	0 + +
9.	~~want~~	0 + 0	0 + 0	+ + +	+ + +	+ + +		
10.	chair	0 0 +	+ 0 +	+ 0 0	+ + +	+ 0 +	+ + +	+ + +
11.	home					0 + 0	+ + 0	+ + +
12.	happy						0 + 0	+ 0 +
13.	cake						0 0 +	+ 0 +

FIGURE 5-9 Data sheet for correct and incorrect responses for flash-card procedure. (*Adapted from A. N. Egner, C. S. Burdett, and W. L. Fox,* Observing and Measuring Classroom Behaviors, Austin, Tex.: Austin Writers Group, 1972, p. 16. By permission of the authors.)

learned words have begun to accrue, students frequently have been heard to beg teachers to use their flash cards.

If a student's learning rate is slower than desired, the teacher may modify the procedure in one of two ways. One strategy suggested by Neef, Iwata, and Page (1977) is to mix known words in with the unknown words. If this procedure were employed, one would still keep the total number of words presented at any one time at ten. Another strategy is to increase the criterion for a learned word. One teacher required a student prone to "forgetting" to correctly read a word for five instead of three consecutive sessions over as many days to assure skill maintenance. It should be noted with respect to the response-interval criterion, that the three-second time limit should not be extended except in the event that an articulation problem accounts for the need for additional time. If success is occurring at a low rate, another strategy is to increase the strength of the reinforcer or enrich the schedule of reinforcement rather than to extend the time limit for the response. Remember, *mastery is a matter of rate, not just accuracy.*

The biggest hurdle in implementing the procedure is the teacher's mastery of the steps. Students who have participated in the activity quickly learn to assume the role of the teacher and become excellent tutors of their peers. A pleasant way to get students on-task immediately upon entering a classroom is to arrange for a daily tutorial session of five to ten minutes. In the meantime the teacher is free to circulate around the room and reinforce tutors for accurately recording data and appropriately responding to their tutees.

Whereas the two previously described procedures for teaching sight words lend themselves to one-to-one instruction, a third procedure developed by Kirby, Holborn, and Bushby (1981) is more appropriate for group instruction where teacher preparation time is at a premium. In the study, the game of bingo was modified to teach sight words to students ranging from eight to ten years of age. Each bingo card was constructed with twenty-five boxes, including one "free" box in the center. Twenty-four words selected for instruction were randomly printed on each card. Thus, while all cards contained the same twenty-four words, they all differed in the placement of the words on the cards. The teacher also constructed another set of cards, each of which contained one word. Prior to each game, the teacher shuffled the cards, drew one from the top of the deck, and called out the word. When necessary the teacher also showed the word to the students. Students then covered the word on their bingo cards with a plastic chip. Throughout the game the teacher encouraged students to help each other locate words on their cards. Upon attaining a predetermined configuration for winning (for example, chips in a diagonal line across the card) the student called out, "Bingo!" When words had been correctly identified, the teacher stamped a star beside the name of the winning student on a chart. The students then cleared their cards and began a new game. If, however, a student had covered an incorrect word, the word was uncovered and the game resumed. Word-game bingo was played approximately six times per day for forty-five minutes, Monday through Thursday. On Fridays, game time was reduced to fifteen minutes to allow the students time to redeem their stars for a variety of activity reinforcers. Results of this procedure indicated that the word-game bingo increased word recognition an average of 30 percent. In addition to effects being immediate, post-treatment effects were found to be quite high. As can be seen, this procedure combines not only simplicity of preparation, broad student appeal, and adaptability to varying group sizes, but also peer modeling and feedback. Increasingly, teachers should select and use instructional procedures that combine advantages such as these.

READING COMPREHENSION

A teacher's first line of defense in solving either group or individual problems should always be to use a direct, uncomplicated teaching procedure. The use of feedback proved to meet this criterion in a study conducted by Van Houten, Hill, and Parsons (1975) in teaching reading comprehension. The feedback procedure involved having the teacher post each child's daily reading comprehension score and note when a new high had been reached. As a result, the number of comprehension problems worked correctly nearly doubled.

Only if a teacher determines that an individual student or group of students does not improve sufficiently through a feedback procedure should additional steps be taken. Before procedural changes are made, however, a check should be conducted to determine if the student is placed at her instructional level. Colavecchia (1975) found that students answer more comprehension questions correctly when reading at rates of sixty to 100 words per minute than when reading at rates of fifteen to thirty words per minute. Therefore, if a student's correct rate of oral reading is exceptionally low or the error rate is very high, one could lower the student's placement and use a feedback procedure. Should performance then prove to be less than desired, a reinforcement procedure, for example, points for exceeding the previous highest score, might be instituted.

A challenging problem occasionally encountered by all reading teachers is presented when a student reads fluently, yet performs considerably below that level in answering comprehension questions. This problem was successfully managed by Hauck, Metcalfe, and Bennett (1975) by requiring small increments of student progress. Prior to intervention, the student averaged 60 percent correct on comprehension questions. The questions included a combination of categories such as factual recall, sequence, retelling, main idea, and inference. During intervention a sequence of five prompts ranging from picture cues to written questions was used to teach one specific aspect of a comprehension question at a time. As a result of the cumulative addition of different types of comprehension questions the student's level of accuracy was increased to 84 percent. Though this procedure requires a systematic and somewhat arduous fading in of comprehension prompts, the effort is worthwhile in that a student who might have continued to fail was ultimately able to perform at an acceptable level.

When students are one or more years below grade level in reading, some accelerative procedures may prove insufficient to bring them to the performance level of their age mates. Reading each page in a text may actually impede the progress of such students, rather than maximally advance their development. A study by Lovitt and Hansen (1976b) allowed students to skip large portions of their reading books for meeting specific criteria in oral reading and comprehension. Students read 500-word segments and received comprehension questions each day. If their correct rate, error rate, and reading comprehension scores were at least 25 percent better than the previous day's score, they were allowed to skip one quarter of their reading book. If they did not meet this criterion for several consecutive days they received a drill technique. The combination of procedures resulted in substantial improvement in reading comprehension, as well as in oral reading rate.

TEACHING MATHEMATICS SKILLS

In order to function successfully in society some ability to apply mathematical operations is necessary. Yet, many individuals exhibit difficulties in performing even simple mathematical applications. The purpose of the present section is to suggest instructional procedures that will allow teachers to provide their students with essential mathematical skills.

NUMBER FACTS

Students can unnecessarily spend years learning basic math facts. They may receive reams of worksheets and requests to practice flash cards at home, frequently to little avail. When analyzed, one often finds that the procedures used to teach math facts are characterized by an absence of three known components of effective teaching—systematic practice, prompt feedback, and contingency management.

The flash-card procedure, described on page 195 as a method of teaching sight words, lends itself to an integration of these three components. Modification of the procedure for math facts is done simply by substituting facts for words. Procedures for implementation do not vary. A teacher can permit students to choose permanent buddies and establish a ten-minute period of time each day for reciprocal tutoring. One advantage of the procedure in teaching math facts is that a tutor can effectively implement it without actually knowing the answers, provided the answers are written on the backs of the cards. Thus, a student in the process of learning his subtraction facts may be a competent tutor for a student learning her multiplication facts. Because cross-level tutoring with the flash card procedure can be mutually beneficial and easy to manage, a teacher can often engage the entire class in tutoring activities at one time.

A brief procedure which would be a suitable follow-up to peer tutoring was described by Van Houten (1980). To implement the procedure, the teacher prepares a worksheet of 100 randomly arranged number facts with ten items per line to facilitate scoring. Duplicates are made for daily repetition of the exercise. Students are given a worksheet with the instructions to complete as many problems correctly as they can within one minute. At completion of a timed one-minute interval the teacher says, "pencils up" or "stop." The teacher can then read aloud the answers while the students make corrections in a different medium, such as ink. At the top of the sheet, the student notes the total number of problems worked correctly before submitting the paper to the teacher.

One advantage to the drill procedure, in addition to its effectiveness, is that all students can work at the same time, and yet, be learning different facts. The procedure has been used with students working on addition, subtraction, multiplication, and division facts simultaneously. Scoring can be done with answer keys and pens.

Another drill procedure, presented by Van Houten and Thompson (1976), requires a series of one-minute timings and offers an effective alternative to students' plodding through practice worksheets. Participants in the study were twenty second-grade students who had histories of poor school performance. Each day during baseline the teacher surreptitiously timed the class for thirty minutes as students alternately completed addition- and subtraction-fact worksheets. During this phase the students' correct rate averaged 3.5 problems per minute. During intervention, the teacher set a timer for thirty minutes and told the class that all work would end when they heard the bell. In addition, she told the students that during the thirty minutes she would repeatedly time them with a stopwatch for one-minute intervals. Prior to each one-minute timing the teacher would say, "Pencils up, ready, begin." When the minute was up, the teacher would stop the students and request that they draw a line after the last problem completed. Thus, the procedure involved nothing more than timing the students as they completed their worksheets. The teacher did not program for positive reinforcement or feedback; nevertheless, students nearly doubled their correct rates while maintaining high levels of accuracy. As a corrollary, the teacher noticed a substantial reduction in the students' use of finger counting and other aids. As one can see, this procedure increased instructional efficiency for a large group of children while requiring minimal instructional effort.

To further enhance performance, however, Van Houten (1980) recommends the public posting of individual and group scores. The attainment of an "all time high" correct rate score or an "all time low" error rate score for an individual or for the entire class should be noted on the chart by the teacher, and enthusiastically applauded by the students.

Even though a fact worksheet is timed, some students, nonetheless, can be observed counting on their fingers or using some other form of computational assistance. Timing worksheet activities does not always efficiently reduce this restrictive practice. Adolescents have been observed counting rapidly on their fingers in order to attain higher rates of performance. At risk is the reinforcement of fast finger counting. Finger counting places an unacceptable upper limit on a person's rate of performance. It is recommended, whenever possible, that a flash-card procedure be used to teach number facts to students with prolonged histories of finger counting before introducing timed worksheets. Not only is the flash-card procedure structured in such a way as to offer immediate feedback for each unknown fact, but it also places time constraints on responses to *individual* facts, thus making finger counting impossible. Once facts have been orally acquired without finger counting, timed worksheets can then be introduced to increase the student's rate of unassisted written responses.

MATHEMATICAL OPERATIONS

Although a student may be adept at number facts, overall performance may break down in his carrying out more complex types of addition, subtraction, division, and multiplication problems. This difficulty is frequently seen in students who err in carrying out a sequence of several steps such as that found in multiplication with decimals.

Two procedures for remedying this type of error are backward chaining and modeling. In backward chaining the teacher prepares a worksheet of problems in which all but the final step of each problem has been completed. The student's only task is to complete the final step of each problem. When mastery of this step has been achieved, the teacher prepares worksheets with the last two steps remaining to be finished. Backward chaining not only introduces only one step to be learned at a time, it also increases the likelihood that each problem attempted will be completed. Table 5-5 presents an example of backward chaining applied to multiplication of three-digit numbers. The procedure can similarly be used with addition, subtraction, and division, as well as algebraic equations.

Modeling also serves as an invaluable tool in teaching computational steps. Maximizing the value of a prompt such as modeling often entails more than just providing an example or showing the student how to work a sample problem. A study by Smith and Lovitt (1975) shows the combined effects of demonstration and modeling for a group of students in carrying out a specific type of problem. The intervention consisted of the teacher describing the computational steps of a problem while writing the problem on a sheet of paper. The demonstration and provision of a permanent model preceded requests for the students to do any work. When students

TABLE 5-5 Examples of Problems Which Would Appear on a Series of Worksheets to Teach Multiplication of Three-Digit Numbers

Example from Worksheet 1	Example from Worksheet 2
427	259
×341	×197
427	1813
1708	2331
1281	

Example from Worksheet 3	Example from Worksheet 4
635	884
×391	×673
635	

received a demonstration and were permitted to work with the model nearby, effects were immediate and enduring. Increases from zero to 100 percent in accuracy were not unusual.

Should demonstration and provision of a permanent model not prove sufficient for some students, a teacher should immediately follow these prompts with a request that the student also work a sample problem before beginning her assignment. Praise should be provided for correct imitation and additional prompting should be given for incorrect responding. The teacher should have the student continue to work examples until the computational steps can be performed without teacher assistance. When this point is reached the student may then begin his assignment with an example of a problem on the board or taped to his desk for reference. As the student works, the teacher should occasionally monitor his progress by walking around the room to provide feedback and verbal praise for correct responding. Should teacher time not permit this level of individual attention, a peer tutor sitting nearby could easily be taught to carry out this sequence of instructional steps.

Full attention to the rate at which students complete multistep math problems, such as long division, should be given only after fact attainment is at a proficient level and computational steps are consistently and accurately carried out. Math teachers have several effective procedures from which to choose, when modifying students' correct and error rates. The use of antecedents, such as instructions and timing, and the use of consequences, such as feedback and contingent reinforcement, have been proved successful in bringing about desired rate changes.

An uncomplicated procedure developed by Smith and Lovitt (1974) used an antecedent event to increase the average correct rate for seven boys 24 percent over baseline level. During all conditions the boys were given one minute of time to work problems from a worksheet. Effective intervention consisted of simply writing at the top of each page: "Please do this page faster."

Correct rate has also been demonstrated to be amenable to the consequence of oral and graphic feedback (Lovitt, 1978). The procedure consisted of a teacher telling each child his correct rate for the day, how it compared to the previous day's rate, and the desired correct rate. A graph illustrating the same information was also provided. The combination of oral and graphic feedback resulted in improved correct rates for all eight boys in the study with attainment of the desired rate for two of the boys.

The use of another type of consequence, contingent positive reinforcement, has also been effective in increasing correct rates. Lovitt (1978) demonstrated that, in general, contingent free time with access to toys and games, as well as contingent points redeemable for toy models, were effective in increasing correct rate performance.

A third type of consequence, response cost, was contingently applied to the erratic performance of a student working subtraction problems. This procedure was selected, in part, because of the teacher's inability to identify any pattern in the student's errors. Intervention consisted of subtracting one minute of recess time from the total recess time of ten minutes for each incorrect response. Results demonstrated that the response cost contingency resulted in performance near 100 percent, whereas baseline performance was often near zero (Lovitt and Smith, 1974).

WRITTEN COMPOSITION

School curricula generally suggest a hierarchy of skills in the areas of math and reading. Such a progression, however, is less evident in the area of written composition. This may be due to the difficulty educators have had in quantifying and ordering the components of a well-constructed composition. As behavior analysis research is increasingly applied to isolating the variables of written composition, teachers are finding that skills in composition writing, like those in reading and math, may be acquired through systematic instruction. Components of written language which have been found to affect the overall quality of written communication include the organization of a composition into paragraphs, and the use of proper spelling, correct punctuation, and specific elements of composition content. In the following pages, several procedures will be described which teachers have found effective in improving students' ability to communicate through written language.

HANDWRITING

A major problem in teaching handwriting skills is developing a measurement procedure that will conveniently and accurately measure student output. Jones, Trap, and Cooper (1977) showed that this task could be accomplished with student participation. The study involved first-grade students who learned to use plastic overlays to score their own manuscript letters. Instruction in self-scoring was shaped by first requiring the students to align overlays with copy paper. In the second step, students were presented with incorrect letters and overlays and were asked to tell why each letter was incorrect (for example, too long). In the third step, students self-scored their own letters from practice sheets with the use of overlays and self-recording sheets. During each handwriting lesson, students received worksheets containing ten letters. Following a demonstration by the teacher at the chalkboard, they copied the letters. After the lesson was completed, students aligned an overlay to their worksheet to determine which letters were correctly written. To indicate to the teacher which letters had been correctly formed, the students traced corresponding dotted letters on a self-recording sheet. In the corner of the sheet the student wrote the total number of correctly written letters. The study showed that the students' and teachers' scoring of letters were in high agreement. This means that a large number of students in a classroom can receive daily feedback on the accuracy of letter formation without requiring teacher scoring.

Trap, Milner-Davis, Joseph, and Cooper (1978) expanded on the previous study in order to demonstrate the effects of feedback on the quality of manuscript writing. During baseline, students copied letters modeled by an experimenter and received no feedback on the accuracy of letter production. In the next stage the students received visual feedback from overlays and verbal feedback from the experimenter on the accuracy of letter formation. They also received praise for correctly written letters. The third stage was the same as the second, except that students were required to rewrite letters that were incorrect. In the final stage, students could receive a certificate by meeting an individualized criterion for correct letters. Each stage produced progressively higher percentages of correctly formed letters.

An additional study which effectively increased printing and cursive writing was conducted by Hopkins, Schutte, and Garton (1971) and is described earlier in the book (see pp. 80–81).

SPELLING

There are several procedures available to teachers who are interested in improving their students' spelling performance. One approach, used by Christie (1971), is to provide reinforcing consequences for outstanding spelling achievement. The study involved twenty-four fourth-grade children most of whom were doing poorly in spelling. Each Tuesday the teacher gave the students a new eighteen-word spelling list and tested the children on the words the next week. During Baseline₁, 24 percent of the students had perfect papers. In the second stage of the study, the teacher made a list of the children's favorite activities. Included were being captain of the gym team, washing chalkboards, and so forth. The teacher informed the students that any child who received 100 percent on a test would be able to engage in one of his favorite activities that afternoon. During this phase 65 percent of the children received 100 percent on their weekly spelling test—40 percent more than Baseline₁. Although the study was effective, teachers should be aware that setting such a high criterion may be too difficult initially for some students and that shaping procedures may need to be used.

An alternative approach to teaching spelling was introduced by Rieth,

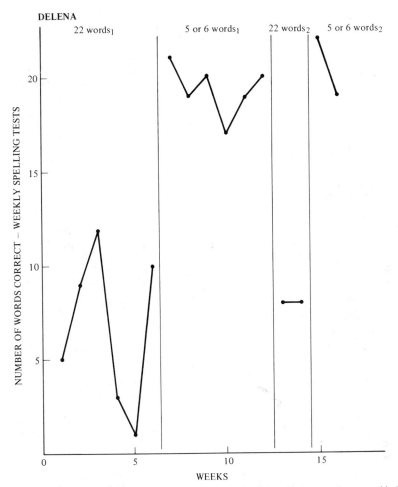

FIGURE 5-10 The number of words a seventh-grade girl spelled correctly on weekly twenty-two-word spelling tests. *(From H. Rieth, S. Axelrod, R. Anderson, F. Hathaway, K. Wood, and C. Fitzgerald, "Influence of Distributed Practice and Daily Testing on Weekly Spelling Tests," Journal of Educational Research, 68, p. 74, 1974. By permission of the publishers.)*

Axelrod, Anderson, Hathaway, Wood, and Fitzgerald (1974). The authors challenged the traditional practice of presenting all spelling words at the beginning of the week and testing students at the end of the week. Instead, they presented students with a portion of the words one day and tested them the next day. Students then received a spelling test on all words at the end of the week. The data for one student, Delena, are presented in Figure 5-10. During the first phase of the study, the teacher presented twenty-two words to Delena at the beginning of each week. During the week she performed workbook assignments involving the spelling words. At the end of the week she received a spelling test on all twenty-two words. The average number of words spelled correctly was seven. In the second stage the teacher divided the twenty-two words into four lists of five or six words. The teacher gave Delena five or six new words each day and tested her on the words the following day. Delena continued to complete assignments from the workbook each day. On the final day of the week she took a review test on all twenty-two words. Her average on the review test increased to nineteen words per week, from the initial level of seven.

CAPITALIZATION AND PUNCTUATION

Students frequently have difficulty applying the rules for capitalization and punctuation in composition writing. In fact such problems are frequently maintained into adult life. A study by Leach and Graves (1973) showed that by providing students with immediate feedback on the sentences they composed, such problems could be alleviated. Two students, Betty and Jane, were having problems with the appropriate use of capitalization and punctuation. Each day they were asked to write ten sentences. During Baseline₁ the teacher graded the students' papers and returned them the following day. Figure 5-11 shows that Betty averaged 54 percent and Jane received 61 percent during the Baseline₁ phase.

In the second phase (Immediate Correction₁) the teacher continued to

FIGURE 5-11 The percentage of correctly written sentences by two seventh-grade girls. The youngsters wrote ten sentences daily for a language arts assignment. (*From D. M. Leach and M. Graves, "The Effects of Immediate Correction on Improving Seventh Grade Language Arts Performance," in A. Egner (ed.),* Individualizing Junior and Senior High Instruction to Provide Special Education within Regular Classrooms. *Burlington, Vt.: University of Vermont, 1973, p. 17. By permission of the publishers.*)

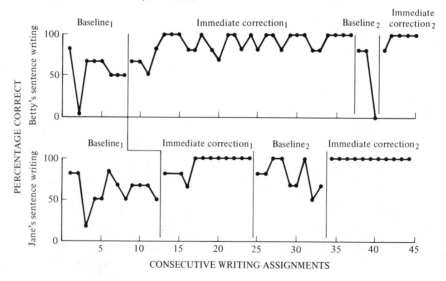

request that the girls write ten sentences but immediately graded the papers and returned them to the girls. After three days the scores of each of the girls increased to high levels, with Betty reaching an average of 90 percent and Jane an average of 93 percent. On sixteen of the twenty-nine days Betty had a perfect score and on eight of eleven days Jane's scores were perfect. When baseline and immediate correction were reinstated during the third and fourth stages of the study, the remarkable effect of immediately correcting papers was verified. Desirably, the effectiveness of the immediate-correction procedure will encourage teachers to grade students' papers soon after they are completed. Teachers who find this task difficult to implement should consider using aides and volunteer parents as graders. It may also be possible to train students to perform the grading tasks.

PARAGRAPHING

Another basic skill in composition writing that rarely receives systematic attention is paragraphing. Van Houten and Nau (1978; cited by Van Houten, 1980) conducted a study in a regular fifth-grade classroom in which the teacher held ten-minute writing sessions daily. The purpose of the study was to determine the effects of two different types of comments on the accuracy of paragraph placements. Designated peers delivered the comments to their classmates during the ten-minute writing period. One type of comment was termed a "performance comment" and consisted of a student saying, for example, "I wrote three paragraphs today." The apparent purpose of the performance comment was to set a standard for other children. The second type of comment was a "preferential comment," such as, "I really like to write paragraphs in my stories." Results showed that performance comments greatly increased the accuracy of paragraph usage, whereas preferential comments were ineffective.

COMPOSITION CONTENT

Even when a composition is technically correct, teachers are still concerned about the quality of the content. Van Houten, Morrison, Jarvis, and McDonald (1974) showed that by increasing the rate of words students wrote, the quality of student compositions also improved. The study involved twenty-one second graders who were given ten minutes to write a composition each afternoon. Teacher records indicated that the students tended to write sentences with few words and that the quality of the work was poor.

Each day the teacher wrote a topic on the board and instructed the students to write as many words as they could, without using repetitious statements. A graduate language major rated the quality of the compositions without knowing that she was grading the papers for an experiment. As shown in Figure 5-12, the students averaged about thirty words per ten-minute session. Quality ratings taken during baseline (not shown) averaged six out of a possible twenty-five. On the first day of the second phase, the teacher showed the children a chart displaying the greatest number of words each of them had written during Baseline₁. She also informed students she would be timing them for ten minutes on future compositions and encouraged them to beat their own previous high score. After the composition period, the teacher counted each student's words and placed the total on the top of his paper. On the following day, scores on the chart were changed when the student reached a new high. The procedure more than doubled the number of words the students wrote and produced quality scores twice as high as Baseline₁.

Further procedures for increasing composition content are described in the final chapter of this book in the discussion on creativity.

FIGURE 5-12 The number of words twenty-one second graders wrote on English composition assignments. *(From R. Van Houten, E. Morrison, R. Jarvis, and M. McDonald, "The Effects of Explicit Timing and Feedback on Compositional Response Rate in Elementary School Children,"* Journal of Applied Behavior Analysis, 7, p. 551, 1974. By permission of the publishers.)

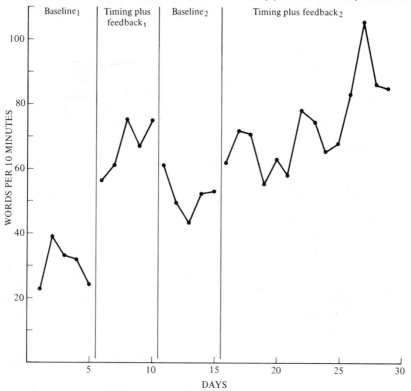

SUMMARY

In teaching academic subjects it is important to measure the student's level of performance in the curriculum, set objectives for him, and to analyze the academic tasks which he is to perform. Once these steps have been taken, the teacher has a basis on which to choose instructional techniques to teach subjects such as reading, math, and composition writing. The measurement process continues throughout instruction to determine the effectiveness of teaching procedures.

In order to determine whether a student is in need of special services for a given academic subject, her current level of functioning is compared with that which is expected of her age peers. If her level of learning is below expectation her eligibility for special services is established. The teacher then projects a learning rate that will enable the student to catch up with her peers. Instructional procedures are chosen according to their ability to produce the desired learning rate. Student performance is monitored to determine whether progress is sufficient or whether a change in instructional procedures is called for. The final measure of the effectiveness of an instructional procedure is determined by whether the student's rate of progress is sufficient to meet both short- and long-term program objectives.

The role of objectives in instruction is to enable a teacher to specify not only what she will teach, and at what rate, but also to determine when the objective has been achieved. A behavioral objective specifies the conditions under which behavior will occur, describes the behavior in measurable terms, and establishes the criteria for acceptable performance. The criteria specify the rate or accuracy of performance, the duration (for example, number of days) over which the skill must be demonstrated, and the date by which the objective is to be obtained.

A task analysis breaks down a behavior into steps that are required to teach an objective. An ability to perform task analyses will help a teacher to identify tbe specific problem a student has in learning a behavior. This in turn will allow the teacher to choose the appropriate instructional procedure and the next behavior to be taught.

QUESTIONS AND ACTIVITIES

1   Suppose that it is October 1 and you discover through pretests that a student in your sixth-grade math class has mastered objectives only through the fourth grade, fifth month. After consultation with his parents and other educators it is decided that instruction should be provided so that he will learn at a rate of 2.0, that is, two months of objectives for each month in school. Draw a progress graph containing the minimum rate line and this student's projected learning rate of

2.0. At this rate of learning when will the student "catch up" to grade level performance (that is, the minimum rate line)?

2 Select one student who you suspect is reading below grade level. For three consecutive days, time the student for one minute as she orally reads from the reading book in which she is now placed. Determine her average correct rate per minute and her average error rate per minute. Is she correctly placed in her present reader? If not, at what level should she be placed?

3 Obtain a student's math workbook and select three problems that have been worked incorrectly. Based on a task analysis of how each problem should be worked, identify the errors in terms of incorrectly completed steps or incorrectly sequenced steps. Recommend instructional procedures (or prerequisite skills) and provide a rationale for the selection of each.

4 Suppose you have a student who is five months below grade level in reading comprehension (or any other area of your choice). You would like to plan reading instructional procedures so that he could make a ten-month gain during the next five months in school. Write objectives for that period of time. Also, note the page number on which the student will be working at the end of each of the five months. What new instructional procedures will you need to use in order that the student can maintain a 2.0 learning rate?

5 Select a student who you believe would be capable of doing better in spelling if only he tried harder. Assume that he will not receive help from home to practice his spelling words at night. Make and post a feedback chart such as the one on page 22. Publicly post weekly spelling grades for at least three weeks. Compare individual and group performance using feedback with spelling scores acquired prior to the use of feedback. Continue to use the better procedure.

6 First, describe the criteria you believe students on any specific grade level should meet when writing a composition. Specify the percentage of verbs, new adjectives, and the total number of words you expect the students to write during a specified period of time. Next, ask a student whom you suspect is functioning below grade level to write a composition. Allow only the specified amount of time. Compare his performance levels with your criteria. If he does not meet all the criteria, design an instructional procedure which will shape his performance to the criteria.

7 Select a student who counts on her fingers or uses some other form of assistance. Ask her to identify a student with whom she can work quietly as a tutor. Teach the tutor the flash-card procedure and chart the tutee's progress.

8 Describe how one might adapt the flash-card procedure for teaching a student how to spell orally.

9 Make multiple copies of a math worksheet containing 160, one-digit by one-digit multiplication problems. Addition or subtraction problems could be used in place of the multiplication problems. Individual problems, of course, will need to be repeated and randomly arranged. Give one copy of the problems to the school principal and a copy to each student who is in the process of learning the facts. Time everyone for two minutes and ask that they draw a line after the last problem attempted. Post the correct rate and error rate for everyone. Continue timed drills and daily posting of student's correct rates and error rates until each can beat the principal's score.

10 How does a projected progress line help a teacher to determine whether or not her daily procedures are effective?

REFERENCES

Christie, L. S.: "Improving Spelling Accuracy for a Fourth-Grade Class," in E. A. Ramp and B. L. Hopkins (eds.), *A New Direction for Education: Behavior Analysis—1971* (Lawrence, Kan.: Support and Development Center for Follow Through, Department of Human Development, University of Kansas, 1971), pp. 164-166.

Christie, L. S., and H. S. McKenzie: *Minimum Objectives: A Measurement System to Provide Evaluation of Special Education in Regular Classrooms* (Burlington, Vt., Special Education Area, College of Education and Social Services, University of Vermont, 1974), ED 102 786.

Colavecchia, B.: "The Relationship Between Oral Reading Rate and Reading Comprehension." Unpublished master's thesis, Dalhousie University, 1975.

Deno, S. L., and P. K. Mirkin: "Data Based IEP Develop: An Approach to Substantive Compliance," *Teaching Exceptional Children,* **12**, pp. 92–97, 1980.

Deno, S., and P. Mirkin: *Data Based Program Modification: A Manual* (Reston, Va.: Council for Exceptional Children, 1977).

Eaton, M., and L. A. Haisch: "A Comparison of the Effects of New vs. Error Word Drill on Reading Performance." Working paper No. 23, Experimental Education Unit, Child Development and Mental Retardation Center, University of Washington, 1974.

Eaton, M., T. Lovitt, E. Sayre, and V. Lynch: "The Effects of Previewing on Oral Reading Rate." Working paper No. 22, Experimental Education

Unit, Child Development and Mental Retardation Center, University of Washington, 1974.

Egner, A. N., C. S. Burdett, and W. L. Fox: *Observing and Measuring Classroom Behavior* (Austin, Tex.: Austin Writers Group, 1972).

Eicholz, R. E., P. G. O'Daffer, and C. R. Fleenor: *Mathematics in Our World* (Menlo Park, Calif.: Addison-Wesley, 1978).

Gilpin, J. B: "Foreword," in R. F. Mager, *Preparing Instructional Objectives* (Palo Alto, Calif.: Fearon Publishers, 1962).

Hansen, C. L: "Corrective Cues vs. Aided Oral Feedback in Word Attack Strategies." Unpublished manuscript, Experimental Education Unit, Child Development and Mental Retardation Center, University of Washington, 1975.

Hansen, C. L., and M. D. Eaton: "Reading," in N. G. Haring, T. C. Lovitt, M. D. Eaton, and C. L. Hansen (eds.), *The Fourth R: Research in the Classroom* (Columbus, Ohio: Charles E. Merrill, 1978), pp. 41–92.

Hansen, C. L., and T. C. Lovitt: "The Relationship Between Question Type and Mode of Reading on the Ability to Comprehend," *Journal of Special Education*, **10**, pp. 53–60, 1976.

Hauck, B., J. Metcalfe, and P. Bennet: "Teaching Early Comprehension Skills: A Case Study." Unpublished manuscript, Experimental Education Unit, Child Development and Mental Retardation Center, University of Washington, 1975.

Haupt, E. J., J. W. Magee, S. Axelrod, M. Coben, and M. Price: "Rapid Reduction of Graphically Similar Substitution Errors in Oral Reading with a Drill Procedure," *Journal of Educational Research*, **71**, pp. 114–116, 1977.

Hopkins, B. L., R. C. Schutte, and K. L. Garton: "The Effects of Access . to a Playroom on the Rate and Quality of Printing of First- and Second-Grade Students," *Journal of Applied Behavior Analysis*, **4**, pp. 77–87, 1971.

Jones, J. C., J. Trap, and J. O. Cooper: "Students' Self-Recording of Manuscript Letter Strokes," *Journal of Applied Behavior Analysis*, **10**, pp. 509–514, 1977.

Kirby, K. C., S. W. Holborn, and H. T. Bushby: "Word Game Bingo: A Behavioral Treatment Package for Improving Textual Responding to Sight Words," *Journal of Applied Behavior Analysis*, **14**, pp. 317–326, 1981.

Leach, D. M., and M. Graves: "The Effects of Immediate Correction on Improving Seventh Grade Language Arts Performance," in A. Egner (ed.), *Individualizing Junior and Senior High Instruction to Provide Special*

Education within Regular Classrooms (Burlington, Vt.: University of Vermont, 1973), pp. 15–21.

Lew, M. B., D. J. Mesch, and B. J. Lates: "The Simmons College Generic Consulting Teacher Program: A Program Description and Data Based Application," *Teacher Education and Special Education*, **5**, pp. 11–16, 1982.

Lovitt, T. C.: "Arithmetic," in N. G. Haring, T. C. Lovitt, M. D. Eaton, and C. L. Hansen (eds.), *The Fourth R: Research in the Classroom* (Columbus, Ohio: Charles E. Merrill, 1978), pp. 127–166.

Lovitt, T. C., and C. L. Hansen: "Round One—Placing the Child in the Right Reader," *Journal of Learning Disabilities*, **9**, pp. 347–353, 1976a.

Lovitt, T. C., and C. L. Hansen: "The Use of Contingent Skipping and Drilling to Improve Oral Reading and Comprehension." *Journal of Learning Disabilities,* **9**, pp. 481–487, 1976b.

Lovitt, T. C., and D. D. Smith: "Using Withdrawal of Positive Reinforcement to Alter Subtraction Performance." *Exceptional Children,* **40**, pp. 357–358, 1974.

McKenzie, H. S., A. N. Egner, M. F. Knight, P. F. Perelman, B. M. Schneider, and J. S. Garvin: "Training Consulting Teachers to Assist Elementary Teachers in the Management and Education of Handicapped Children," *Exceptional Children*, **37**, pp. 137–143, 1970.

Mager, R. F.: *Preparing Instructional Objectives* (Palo Alto, Calif.: Fearon Publishers, 1962).

Neef, N. A., B. A. Iwata, and T. J. Page: "The Effects of Known Item Interspersal on Acquisition and Retention of Spelling and Sightreading Words," *Journal of Applied Behavior Analysis*, **10**, p. 738, 1977.

Rieth, H., S. Axelrod, R. Anderson, R. Hathaway, K. Wood, and C. Fitzgerald: "Influence of Distributed Practice and Daily Testing on Weekly Spelling Tests," *Journal of Educational Research*, **68**, pp. 73–77, 1974.

Smith, D. D., and T. C. Lovitt: "The Influence of Instructions and Reinforcement Contingencies on Children's Abilities to Compute Arithmetic Problems." Paper presented at the Fifth Annual Conference on Behavior Analysis in Education, University of Kansas, October 1974.

Smith, D. D., and T. C. Lovitt: "The Use of Modeling Techniques to Influence the Acquisition of Computational Arithmetic Skills in Learning-Disabled Children," in E. Ramp and G. Semb (eds.), *Behavior Analysis: Areas of Research and Application* (Englewood Cliffs, N. J.: Prentice-Hall, 1975), pp. 183–308.

Trap, J. J., P. Milner-Davis, S. Joseph, and J. O. Cooper: "The Effects of Feedback and Consequences on Transitional Cursive Letter Formation," *Journal of Applied Behavior Analysis*, **11**, pp. 381–393, 1978.

Van Houten, R: *Learning Through Feedback* (New York: Human Sciences Press, 1980).

Van Houten, R: "Social Validation: The Evolution of Standards of Competency for Target Behaviors," *Journal of Applied Behavior Analysis*, **12**, pp. 581–591, 1979.

Van Houten, R., S. Hill, and M. Parsons: "An Analysis of a Performance Feedback System: The Effects of Timing and Feedback, Public Posting, and Praise upon Academic Performance and Peer Interaction," *Journal of Applied Behavior Analysis*, **8**, pp. 449–457, 1975.

Van Houten, R., E. Morrison, R. Jarvis, and M. McDonald: "The Effects of Explicit Timing and Feedback on Compositional Response Rate in Elementary School Children," *Journal of Applied Behavior Analysis*, **7**, pp. 547–555, 1974.

Van Houten, R., and P. Nau: "The Effects of Peer Comments on the Academic Behavior of Elementary School Children." Paper presented at the Association for Advancement of Behavior Therapy, Chicago, 1978.

Van Houten, R., and C. Thompson: "The Effects of Explicit Timing on Math Performance," *Journal of Applied Behavior Analysis*, **9**, pp. 227–230, 1976.

Wheeler, A. H., and W. L. Fox: *Behavior Modification: A Teacher's Guide to Writing Instructional Objectives* (Lawrence, Kan.: H & H Enterprises, 1972).

Willis, J.: "Effects of Systematic Feedback and Self-Charting on a Remedial Tutorial Program in Reading," *The Journal of Experimental Education*, **42**, pp. 83–85, 1974.

6

Commonly Asked Questions about Behavior Modification and One Person's Answers

Prospective and practicing teachers often feel uncomfortable about the idea of using behavior modification procedures in their classrooms. This is hardly surprising since most teachers attend or have graduated from programs in which the doctrines of theorists such as Freud, Dewey, and Piaget were emphasized. As a result some teachers hesitate or refuse to use behavior modification procedures because they feel they are treating a surface problem rather than the real one; or they feel that they are bribing children who should be inherently motivated toward success; or they feel that they are being manipulative, when a more natural course would likely solve an existing problem. The final chapter presents twelve questions commonly asked about behavior modification and provides the author's response to each question. The reader should note that the author is expressing his own opinion on each of the subjects, although he has made use of the comments of other authors in the field.

HOW ARE REINFORCERS DIFFERENT FROM BRIBES?

This is probably the most frequently asked question about behavior modification. The problem is that many teachers (and other adults) do not feel comfortable reinforcing children "for what they're supposed to do." They feel that learning should be a self-satisfying process and that children should behave properly because it is expected of them. Some educators believe that when teachers reward students, they are artificially motivating them to engage in behaviors for which they should be intrinsically (that is, naturally) motivated. The use of rewards is then seen as a bribe to children for fulfilling their expected roles.

There is at least one similarity between positive reinforcement and bribery. In both cases one person is trying to encourage another person to behave in a certain manner, by offering a bonus. The difference is that bribery also involves the notion that the individual is being influenced to perform an immoral act. Webster's (1970) primary definition of bribery, for example, is the giving or promising of anything "to induce a person to do something illegal or wrong" [p. 176]. Clearly, the examples of positive reinforcement presented in this book do not involve immoral behavior. The goals of teaching children to read, spell, perform arithmetic operations, and refrain from aggression are hardly behaviors that can be considered immoral.

Even if the practice of reinforcement does not conform to dictionary definitions of bribery, many teachers still find the process of rewarding children abrasive to their teaching philosophy. They should realize, however, that they themselves work under a reinforcement system. Teachers readily accept their paychecks as payment for their duties and would cease teaching if their checks were not forthcoming. Similarly, teachers are delighted when they receive merit increases, and enter into collective bargaining with school districts to establish higher pay scales. Teachers are expected to educate effectively, but still they want to be reinforced for their efforts; and they wish to be reinforced, not merely at a subsistence level, but at a level that will afford them the pleasures of life (that is, their M&M's). Risley and Baer (1973) point out that what has developed is a double standard in which adults insist on pay for their work but criticize children for behaving in the same manner. Since children will ultimately have to function under the same capitalist reinforcement system as adults do, one can only wonder what value there is in enforcing the double standard.

Homme (1969) indicates that some adults find it "immoral to reward today's child for doing assignments that earlier generations had to do 'or else'" [p. 20]. He points out, however, that youngsters learn better and more willingly if reinforcers are provided for academic achievement; they are enthusiastic about learning and delight in achieving a task and receiving reinforcement; they are not characterized by timidness and aggressiveness as are children being coerced by the "do it or else" standard, nor do they demonstrate the "spoiled" traits of youngsters who receive privileges and treats independently of their behavior. Admittedly, many adults adequately learned academic tasks without the benefit of programmed reinforcement procedures. That does not mean, however, that modern children should be denied superior teaching methods when they become available any more than it means that they should be denied improved dental and medical developments just because their parents survived without them.

A concern related to the claim that reinforcement is bribery, is the notion that changes brought about with positive reinforcement are not "real" (Kazdin, 1980). That is, when the reinforcer is removed, the behavior will disappear. Research on this position has been ambiguous. As will be discussed in a later section, however, with appropriate planning, such behavioral changes can become long-term alterations. It should also be understood that learning that occurs with procedures other than positive reinforcement can also disappear. (Try to recall the names of five battles that took place during the American Revolutionary War.)

It would be a happy state of affairs if all children were naturally motivated to perform academic assignments and to refrain from inappropriate behavior. Unfortunately, experience has shown that often this is not the case. This does not mean that we should abandon our efforts to educate such children. To do so would be to forsake a large segment of our student population. It would also ignore the fact that some academic tasks become self-satisfying only after a reinforcement program has motivated the children to engage in the tasks. It has been found, for example, that some poor readers must initially be motivated by a reinforcement procedure to engage in reading activities. Once accomplished, the reinforcement procedure can often be removed without a decrement in student performance (Axelrod and Piper, 1975).

Horowitz (1975) points out that if children are learning in a classroom using reinforcement procedures, and one criticizes such a practice as a matter of principle and advocates its discontinuation, one should offer alternative techniques which are at least as effective; "Otherwise, one is saying here is something that works, but I don't like it for philosophical reasons, so stop doing it—I don't have anything to substitute for it right now, but when I do I am sure it will be better and will not be philosophically objectionable [pp. 8–9]." She further states that such a position is socially irresponsible and that it is ironic that only those individuals who have greatly benefited from "adequate education have the luxury of opposing educational techniques on theoretical grounds" [p. 9].

WHAT GIVES TEACHERS THE RIGHT TO MODIFY STUDENT BEHAVIOR? BY DOING SO ARE THEY NOT DEPRIVING CHILDREN OF FREEDOM OF CHOICE?

A number of people admit to the effectiveness of behavioral techniques, but object to the notion that in applying them to children, teachers are determining what youngsters should learn and are deciding how the learning process will take place. Cote (1973), for example, protests that a big human being is managing the behaviors of a little human being. He also claims that when a student's motivation and achievement are low, she is communicating that something may be wrong with the curriculum and therefore, he asserts, she should not be forced to adjust to it. Other authors have also expressed concern that behavioral procedures might be so effective that children will not be free to choose their objectives, nor learn to control their own behavior.

First, it must be understood that behaviorists should not be singled out for accountability on the freedom of choice issue. Other approaches are also concerned with procedures that will alter human behavior. The fact that terms such as "guide," "counsel," and "enlighten" are used, does not nullify this issue. Also, more radical approaches to modifying behavior, such as electroconvulsive therapy, seem to be less criticized for arbitrarily controlling human behavior (Roos, 1974).

One analysis of the issue is that behavioral procedures have been effective in educational endeavors to an extent that is unmatched by other techniques. Thus, although behavior modification has great potential for producing large improvements in student behavior, it also has the potential for abuse by overcontrolling student behavior. Although there may be some merit to this position it must be recognized that teachers have gained control of student behavior in the past through such devices as the dunce cap, the paddle, and suspension. Given the choice between the reinforcer and the dunce cap, the reinforcer is an easy winner.

In one sense it cannot be denied that behavior modification programs have deprived children of certain freedoms. Successful behavior modification techniques have deprived children of the freedom to hit their classmates, to destroy their property, and to sit placidly in class without participating in academic activities. In a larger sense, however, effective behavior modification procedures have given children an increased amount of freedom. As children are taught to respect the rights and possessions of other youngsters, many of them become capable of developing friendships that were previously impossible. Self-controlled, the youngsters can choose to spend their free time alone or with other children. Physically destructive children have no choice but to spend most of their free time without playmates.

Similarly, Cohen (1969) points out that illiterate people do not have the freedom to make choices that literate people have. People who can read and write have job opportunities, educational opportunities, and many pleasures of life available to them because of their skills. Illiterate people will find their choices in these areas more limited. Even if successful behavior modification procedures initially deprive children of some freedoms, their ultimate effect is to increase the individual's social and academic choices. The ideal of giving children freedom should not be seen as giving them license to do "their own thing" without regard to the consequences. Children who fail to meet certain standards of conformity have a great chance of finding themselves in such freedom-depriving establishments as institutions and jails.

Although the behavioral approach has been accused of depriving children of free choice, it can also be seen as the most liberating philosophy and technology in existence. First, there is the assumption that all human beings can learn. This is not unusual. What is unusual is that behaviorists provide a precise description of how the learning process takes place. Labels such as emotionally disturbed and mentally retarded are ignored in the teaching process. Instead, students are taught according to relevant learning characteristics. Baseline is taken on an individual's *own* behavior. Reinforcers are chosen according to his *own* preferences. Requirements are changed according to the individual's *own* performance. Nowhere is there the assumption that the learning pattern of children follows a normal curve in which some students will learn and others will not (Smith, 1973). Rather, the assumption is that *all* children can learn.

The reader should understand that behavior modifiers did not invent the principles which influence human behavior—they merely discovered them (perhaps "rediscovered" is a better description). The principles were always there, and they have always affected the behavior of humans. Risley and Baer (1973) point out that the contribution of behavior modifiers is that, rather than letting the principles operate randomly, they have systematically employed the principles in such a manner as to produce desirable behaviors. Educators may reject the notion of programming behavioral principles, but they should not do so under the assumption that somehow the principles will disappear and that some mysterious process will take place and automatically make children into freer, more independent human beings.

AREN'T YOU AFRAID THAT UNETHICAL PEOPLE WILL USE OPERANT-CONDITIONING TECHNIQUES?

Almost any time a useful invention or discovery occurs, certain dangers are present. This is true whether one is talking about penicillin, power lawnmowers, or positive reinforcement. Since behavioral principles are powerful and act independently of morality (Sulzer-Azaroff and Mayer, 1977) concerns that unethical people will abuse them are understandable. Questions have been raised as to whether aversive procedures can be unethically used and whether it is possible to coerce a person to perform behaviors she does not wish to engage in (Kazdin, 1980).

Hively (1971) points out that although the danger of exploitation is a serious one, its solution is reasonably simple. He suggests that individuals employing operant-conditioning procedures be required to make public the techniques they will use, the behaviors they wish to alter, and the intended long-term benefits for the students. The system would thus be subject to public scrutiny and pressure for change. This recommendation should be relatively easy to implement since behavior modifiers are already oriented toward clearly defining target behaviors and specifying remedial procedures. Hively states that in cases in which the benefit to the student is dubious, the community served by the teacher can decide whether or not it is desirable to maintain, alter, or eliminate the techniques.

The suggestion that Hively made has become more formalized in recent years through the practice of informed consent and the formation of human-rights and peer-review committees. *Informed consent* is a practice in which an individual (sometimes through his parent or guardian) agrees to engage in a remedial program with full information on the nature of the program, the benefits, risks, expected outcomes, and alternatives (Kazdin, 1980). *Human-rights committees* are interested community members of various backgrounds who make recommendations on the necessity, quality, and social acceptability of programs that have been proposed. *Peer-review committees* consist of professionals who make judgments on whether proposed programs are appropriate, given existing knowledge. One benefit of all such practices is that it becomes increasingly difficult to use socially repugnant procedures or produce unacceptable behaviors. Another benefit is that it helps behavior modifiers to shed the image that they operate in coercive and covert ways.

It might be argued that the greatest danger posed by behavior modifiers is that they develop punishment procedures that can be adopted by unethical people. Indeed, punishment procedures can be abused. Nevertheless, categorically prohibiting the use of punishment could have negative repercussions in a variety of situations. Consider the case histories of numerous institutionalized retarded individuals who continually bang their heads and bite and pinch themselves. Many such people are kept under restraint in order to prevent serious injury. Attempts to modify self-abusive behaviors with positive reinforcement and extinction have often met with failure. To the contrary, punishment procedures have frequently led to quick and permanent elimination of the deviant behaviors, thus freeing the person from a life of restraint. This does not mean that people should be quick to use a punishment procedure when alternatives are available. As Morrow and Gochros (1970) point out, however, "If a carefully controlled aversive technique can eliminate severely disruptive, handicapping behavior when other procedures have proved ineffectual, it seems unethical not to use the aversive technique" [p. 303]. Again, by requiring public disclosure of procedures and goals, one should be able to derive the advantages and avoid some of the difficulties associated with a punishment tactic.

The fear that *unethical* people might use behavioral procedures is understandable. What I fear more is that *ethical* people will not use them. At a time when inner-city schools are reporting high rates of illiteracy and violence, when retarded children are unjustifiably kept in restraints, and when malingerers are being pitied, the well-intentioned but unskilled teacher who fails to employ effective behavioral procedures might be causing more harm through the acts of omission, than the immoral person does through acts of commission. As has often been stated, "Not to decide, is to decide."

IT SEEMS THAT IF TEACHERS USE BEHAVIOR MODIFICATION PROCEDURES, THEY WILL BE MECHANICAL AND COLD

The practices of measuring behavior, precisely applying consequences, and using experimental design operations are exercises that many educators find offensive. It seems to some that the art is being taken out of teaching and that is being replaced with an unappealing version of science. Yet, it is precisely those scientific operations which prevent teachers from becoming mechanical. When a teacher is using a procedure to increase reading levels or decrease outbursts and the data indicate that the technique is ineffective, a teacher has no choice but to change his procedure. A teacher who has not used scientific operations may mechanically apply the same ineffective procedures to children day after day. Scientific procedures *force* a teacher to be responsive to his students—to his preference for certain reinforcers, to his learning rate, and so on.

A correlated concern is that in using behavior modification procedures, teachers do not become personally involved with their students and instead develop into "cold" dispensers of consequences. Those who make that claim should first examine research which has shown that teachers using traditional procedures are more likely to reprimand their students than praise them. Walker (1979), for example, described a study in which teachers used fifteen times as many reprimands as praise statements! (Other studies on the topic are described in the positive-reinforcement section of Chapter 1.) Second, one should note the huge body of literature indicating the benefits of social-reinforcement procedures which behaviorists have developed. While watching a teacher smile at, compliment, and hug a youngster, it is hard to see how the teacher can be considered "cold."

Presently the term "burn out" is being increasingly heard in the schools. Large numbers of teachers are leaving education claiming that they don't have the energy to go on. The speculation here is that teachers are burning out not so much because of the effort required in teaching, but because of the lack of appreciation they receive for their efforts. An environment devoid of social reinforcers *is* a cold environment. Teachers who have been in a system for many years will claim that they have never received a complimentary note from their principals and are praised no more than a few times a year. Principals could produce a warmer and more productive climate for teachers with frequent notes and compliments. Lest the argument become too one-sided, however, teachers could help create the same atmosphere by socially reinforcing their principals, and each other, more often.

Even if social-reinforcement procedures are not considered mechanical and cold, one might raise the question as to whether other techniques, such as token reinforcement tactics, can be so characterized. Yet, a study by Breyer and Allen (1975) showed that when a teacher gave students tokens for being on-task, there was a concomitant increase in the number of times she praised the youngsters. A similar finding was made by Mandelker, Brigham, and Bushell (1970).

Finally, many teachers find it difficult to be warm and kind to students who are continually misbehaving and showing little interest in developing basic skills. Teachers are as human as anyone else, and it is understandable that they become frustrated and unsociable toward children when their teaching efforts repeatedly fail. To the degree that behavior modification procedures can produce teaching success, they should help facilitate warm personal relationships between students and teachers.

MUST TEACHERS AND OTHER EDUCATORS USE SCIENTIFIC PROCEDURES?

Educators who have read the measurement and design chapter might shrug their shoulders and say, "All that scientific stuff is fine, but what has it got to do with me? I am only interested in what works, and besides, who has time to go around measuring behavior and using reversal designs?"

In response to such questions, I would first like to state that all *I* am interested in is what works. The problem is that unless a teacher is systematic and objective, she cannot be certain whether a particular procedure or philosophy is worthwhile or not. In the absence of adequate evaluative techniques, a teacher must make important decisions on the basis of "what seems right." Decisions made according to such a standard may be inaccurate as the result of a variety of factors. It is possible, for example, that a teacher will be enthusiastic about the prospects of a certain technique producing an improvement in her students' academic performance. Without objective data, her enthusiasm may convince her that her students have made gains when, in fact, they have not. Hence, she will continue to use ineffective procedures. Conversely, it is feasible that a teacher will implement a technique that produces a gradual but definite improvement in behavior. In the absence of accurate data, the teacher might not realize that gains have been made and might abandon a procedure which she should maintain. In any event, the problem of persuading teachers to use behavior modification procedures is an important and difficult one.

As mentioned earlier, most practicing teachers received their training from education departments that did not teach, or were opposed to, behavior modification procedures. In order for such teachers to become convinced of the value of behavior modification techniques, they will need definitive evidence of the effectiveness of the procedures. This can best be achieved by measurement and design considerations which leave no doubt that a certain procedure improved a behavior. Similarly, teachers can more readily convince their principals to adopt certain large-scale teaching strategies when they present data demonstrating that their practices have been effective.

Teachers with a scientific orientation are able to participate in the development of the field of education. By using appropriate experimental methods teachers can provide convincing evidence that they have devised solutions to important problems. They can transmit the relevant information by word of mouth or by publishing the results in school newsletters, journals, or books. Teachers can test their own ideas, and the field can benefit from the insights of educators who spend their days in classrooms rather than depending on professional researchers who spend relatively small periods of time in classrooms.

In the absence of adopting a scientific methodology, the field of education has been characterized by a continuous stream of cycles and fads. Risley (1970) points out that a particular approach is proposed, accepted, and applied. Later the approach is dropped and another one replaces it. The earlier approach might have had much merit, whereas the latter one might be detrimental; nevertheless, new fads continue to rise and fall independently of their worth. Risley also indicates that modern-day behavior modifiers are using procedures remarkably similar to those employed in the eighteenth and nineteenth centuries by educators such as Rousseau, Itard, and Seguin. One might be tempted to laud the efforts and foresight of the early educators, but perhaps this would be a mistake. In the absence of providing of convincing evidence of the value of their work to the educational communities of their times, these initial efforts were not continued by succeeding educators. Instead, other philosophies prevailed, and it became necessary to rediscover the same principles a century and a half later.

The use of the scientific method has provided information that can be used to counter the claim that there is nothing new about behavior modification—that people have always used it. While admitting that behavior modification has historically been used to deal with human behavior, Kazdin (1980) points out that due to scientific methodology, our understanding of human behavior has progressed. Thus, even though people have always reinforced, punished, or extinguished each other's behavior, it has only been with research that we have been able to find out the effects of partial-reinforcement schedules, how to teach self-control, and how to get behavior to generalize to new situations. Through science the field has developed from a haphazard, rudimentary endeavor to a more sophisticated one.

DOES BEHAVIOR MODIFICATION STIFLE CREATIVITY?

It should not be surprising that many people will see behavior modification procedures as encouraging conformity rather than creativity. Certainly the practices of measuring behavior, specifying rules, and reinforcing behavior that conforms to the rules, conjure up notions of sameness, rather than innovativeness. Nevertheless, when creativity is defined in concrete terms, and when the definition is applied to specific creative behaviors, the behaviors can be broken down into smaller units which can be taught. An endeavor which teaches a behavior surely does not stifle it.

Although there are various notions as to what creativity is, one common aspect of all definitions is the property of novelty. Goetz and Baer (1973), for example, define creativity as behavior which has *not* been previously displayed in a given setting. Similarly, Maloney and Hopkins (1973) define creative behavior as different responses to the same situation.

With this general definition one can begin to teach creative behavior. The first step is to determine the components of creativity for the behavior of interest. Next a teacher can apply reinforcement procedures to the target behavior in the same manner as one would reinforce other behaviors. Goetz and Salmonson (1972), for example, were interested in teaching three preschool girls to be more creative in easel painting. They had found that all three youngsters tended to use a low number of forms in their painting. The authors identified and defined twenty-five types of painting forms. These included "blended color" (any hue formed by mixing two or more colors on paper), "diagonal line" (a straight line at least three inches long, forming a 10° to 80° angle), and so on. After a baseline period the teacher praised a student each time the student painted a form she had not previously made during the period. If a student blended colors for the first time in a period, the teacher might say, "That is very nice. I like the way you mix colors." The next time the student blended colors, the teacher *would not* make a comment; she *would* praise the child, however, if she made a diagonal line for the first time. For all three girls the social-reinforcement procedure produced increased diversity of painting forms as compared with baseline rates.

Sulzer-Azaroff and Mayer (1977) point out that one of the most difficult problems in teaching creativity is determining the components of the behavior. To deal with this problem they recommend that one contact a subject-matter expert. For example in asking an artist for the components of an excellent specimen of art, one might learn that elements of line, mass, space, light, color, and texture, and the principles of unity, variety, contrast, balance, rhythm, and emphasis are critical. Presumably, the elements and principles can all be taught.

An example of consulting the work of an expert was provided by Glover and Gary (1976). The authors were interested in teaching eight fourth and fifth graders to create novel uses of objects such as boxes, cans, and so on. They noted an article by Torrance (1966) which claimed that there were four components to creativity—fluency, flexibility, elaboration, and originality. Fluency refers to the production of a large number of ideas, whereas flexibility is a large variety of ideas. Elaboration is the development of ideas. Originality is considered to be an unusual application of an idea. Glover and Gary set up a game with two teams, in which the members with the greater score could start recess ten minutes early. First students could earn points for fluency, then flexibility, elaboration, and originality. In each case there were substantial increases in the component of creative behavior that the game rewarded. (The interested reader should see a study by Campbell and Willis, 1978, in which students learned creative essay writing with a procedure that reinforced fluency, flexibility, and elaboration.)

There has always been a mystique surrounding the creative person. The image of a wild-haired artist or writer who passionately pours out her soul in a manuscript or on a canvas, needing neither nutrients nor human support, is a common one. Yet, an examination of the work habits of famous writers should help dispel this myth. Novelist Irving Wallace (Wallace, 1977) reports that in order to be productive he would set deadlines for himself and reward himself with rest if he finished early. He would also publicly post charts giving the date at which he started a chapter, how many pages he completed each day, and the date at which he finished the chapter. Not so mysteriously, his writing patterns followed a fixed-ratio schedule.

Wallace indicated that he was initially embarrassed to reveal his work methods, but later did so when he found that other novelists used similar procedures. In fact, he revealed that Victor Hugo sometimes forced himself to work by removing all his clothes, entering his studio, and ordering his servant not to return the clothes until his writing chores were completed for the day.

WHAT HAPPENS WHEN BEHAVIOR MODIFICATION PROCEDURES ARE WITHDRAWN?

The present question arises because many teachers are willing to invest the energy required to conduct a behavior modification procedure for a limited period of time, but do not wish to carry out special procedures indefinitely. The issue that has been raised is one of "maintenance," or the degree to which behavioral gains persist after formal programming is terminated and reinforcement is no longer provided.

There are times when maintenance occurs even though no special procedures are used to produce it. Thus, a student who learns to read when a token reinforcement program is in effect, may continue to read after the token program is discontinued. Nonprogrammed maintenance is also likely to occur when a student is taught a new behavior which she finds enjoyable (such as using playground equipment), or when the behavior is one that derives much reinforcement from the environment (for example, reading and walking). In most cases, however, one should not expect maintenance to occur automatically.

When maintenance does not occur, teachers are often disappointed and assume that the procedure has failed. Walker (1979) argues against this conclusion. He proposes, instead, that behavior modification programs involve two stages. In the first stage a procedure is used to change the behavior to a desired level. In the second stage, procedures are implemented to assure long-term maintenance. Programs that involve only the first stage are not considered to have failed, but to be incomplete.

A number of procedures have been used or suggested to increase the probability that maintenance will occur. First, since maintenance involves resistance to extinction, it is suggested that training end on a thin partial-reinforcement schedule. Thus a student might receive reinforcement after every correct behavior at the beginning of training. After the behavior improves to a high, stable level, the teacher might deliver a reinforcer after an average of every two responses, then three, five, and so on. Second, the teacher can move a student from an immediate reinforcement procedure to one that programs increasingly longer delays of reinforcement. With both procedures, the differences between the final intervention techniques and its absence are small, making it difficult for the student to notice that reinforcement is no longer occurring.

Walker (1979) recommends that in order to achieve maintenance, procedures involving tangible reinforcers be gradually replaced by procedures involving social reinforcers. This can be done through a respondent conditioning program in which praise always precedes the delivery of the tangible reinforcer. For example, a teacher can say "Nice going" and then deliver a tangible reward. In this way the praise statement becomes a conditioned reinforcer and maintains the behavior even after the delivery of the tangible reinforcer ceases. When this is done, Walker suggests that surprise tangible rewards be delivered occasionally to act as a "booster shot" for the operation.

A further suggestion that Walker makes is that components of programs involving multiple procedures be gradually removed. Thus if a program involves praise and time out, the time-out component can be removed once substantial improvement has occurred. Similarly, in a program involving home and school rewards, either component can be removed after change takes place.

Kazdin and Mascetelli (1980) used an interesting technique to achieve maintenance of behavior change. They were working with two special-education students who were on a token reinforcement program designed to increase their attentiveness. Tokens were backed up with various consumables. When the children were given the opportunity to work their way off the token system, their behavior rose to higher levels than had occurred with just the tokens. Thus, the children increased their efforts so as not to be receiving rewards for their behavior! One possible explanation for their paradox is that it was considered prestigious *not* to be on the token program.

There are some procedures that are associated with maintenance of gains even when special efforts are not made. Van Houten (1980) reports that in most studies involving feedback, gains are maintained even after the procedure is removed. Similar findings have occurred with self-control procedures.

Two other points about maintenance are worth noting. First, before implementing a behavior modification program, teachers should consider how much student resistance they are likely to encounter, if they gradually remove the procedure. It is relatively easy to gradually increase a DRO5 (minute) schedule to higher levels (for example DRO7, DRO10, and so on). It is more difficult to switch from a program in which students earn extra free time every day, to one in which they earn free time every other day. In the former case the change is less noticeable than in the latter case. Second, maintenance can be considered a type of generalization in which behavior occurring in one set of circumstances (for example, reinforcement), generalizes to another set of circumstances (for example, a time period in which reinforcement is not occurring).

IF A BEHAVIOR MODIFICATION PROCEDURE KEEPS CHILDREN QUIET AND IN THEIR SEATS—DOES THAT MEAN THEY WILL LEARN MORE?

The concern has been raised by various sources, including teachers, administrators, parents, and both proponents and opponents of behavior modification practices. The question is whether students are benefiting academically from programs that increase their attentiveness and decrease their disruptiveness or whether the sole effect of such operations is to produce docile, less mobile youngsters (Winett and Winkler, 1972). It would appear that some light could be shed on the question by studies which improved classroom deportment and measured the collateral effects on academic behavior. Yet, a review of research on the question conducted by Shapiro and Klein (1980) did not reveal any consistent findings.

An approach favored by many behavior modifiers is to directly reinforce academic behavior on the assumption that incompatible, inappropriate behavior will automatically decrease. The feasibility of this approach was demonstrated in studies by Ayllon, Layman, and Burke (1972) and Ayllon and Roberts (1974). In fact the results of one of the studies led Ayllon et al. (1972) to conclude, "the impressive progress made by all four children suggests that the time has come for behavioral engineers to be satisfied with nothing less than academic objectives. . . . While disruptive behavior and discipline in the classroom are the major, and often the immediate, objectives of the classroom teacher, behavioral applications cannot in good conscience be exploited to foster classroom conformity" [p. 323].

Nevertheless, in a later study, Ayllon and his colleagues (Ayllon, Garber, and Pisor, 1975) found that reinforcing students for academic behaviors did *not* reliably reduce disruptiveness. They then devised a program that focused directly on reducing disruptiveness and were extremely successful. Therefore, it appears that there are at least some situations in which a teacher's initial concern must be to establish classroom order.

This conclusion should not be seen as a license to modify disruptive behavior to the neglect of programming for academic improvement. Teachers may benefit from a quiet classroom, but students will gain little from order if they do not simultaneously develop academic skills. The main purpose of the schools is to teach academic skills. Sometimes it might be necessary to first establish order, but the main part of a teacher's day should be devoted to developing academic behaviors. If would be an abuse of behavior modification procedures to have a teacher use the procedures simply to produce compliant children.

The ideal classroom is not one in which there is total quiet, but one in which students are actively participating in classroom assignments, volunteering answers, and making presentations. Some teachers may fear that "if they give students an inch they will take a mile" (Sloane, 1976), but this fear can be greatly minimized in cases where teachers have sufficient management skills that they can gain control of a disorderly class.

WHEN A TEACHER APPLIES A BEHAVIOR MODIFICATION PROCEDURE TO ONE STUDENT, HOW DO THE OTHER STUDENTS REACT?

Educators are often concerned that when a teacher singles out one or two students for a behavior modification program, other children will either misbehave in order to be placed on the program, or will object to the program so vociferously, that teaching becomes unpleasant.

Studies investigating the former question have generally not verified their concern. Broden, Bruce, Mitchell, Carter, and Hall (1970), for example, found that when a teacher praised the attending behavior of one boy, the attending behavior of his seatmate also increased. Similarly, Drabman and Lahey (1974) found that when a feedback procedure reduced the disruptiveness of a ten-year-old girl, her classmates also became less disruptive. One might suspect that the outcomes of both studies were due to the fact that tangible rewards were not programmed for the students of concern. Yet, Christy (1975) found that when a teacher gave a selected number of students praise and food for being in their seats, the in-seat behavior of their classmates also increased.

The results of the above studies may surprise some readers. Nevertheless, two points should be kept in mind. First, when a disruptive student behaves properly, her classmates have one less student to inappropriately socialize with. Secondly, students who are behaving appropriately are sometimes annoyed by their disruptive classmates and are pleased to see them behaving properly. In fact, Drabman and Lahey (1974) found that when the student of concern became less disruptive, her popularity, as measured by a sociometric test, improved.

Even if students do not imitate the misbehaviors that caused their classmates to be placed on special programs, there are many cases in which students will complain about the special attention that others receive. (See, for example, Christy, 1975; Boyd, Keilbaugh, and Axelrod, 1981.) In such cases, a number of procedures can be used:

1   The teacher can explain to all students, *in advance*, that a youngster in the class has a particular problem and that a special program will be implemented in his behalf. She should also point out that the student will be receiving special rewards and that she would appreciate the help of all students in conducting the program. Although this solution might appear somewhat naive, it has worked with children at a variety of grade levels. The teacher can also offer the children group rewards for their cooperation.

2   In cases in which the first suggestion is largely effective but a small number of children continually voice objections, the teacher should ignore the complaints. Ignoring is effective with a variety of other behaviors and will often reduce complaints.

3   The teacher can have all youngsters share or participate in the rewards earned by the student of concern. In one situation that I am familiar with, a student refused to wear his eyeglasses, presumably because his classmates taunted him with derogatory names such as "four eyes," "goofy," and "professor." The teacher instituted a behavior modification procedure in which she periodically checked to see if the youngster was wearing his glasses. If he was, all students received extra free time. Immediately after the tactic was implemented, the students ceased the name-calling and instead complimented their breadwinner with comments such as, "You're really looking cool today with your specs on." Hence, the students lent their support to the procedure rather than undermining it or being hostile to it.

4   The child can receive his rewards in a setting outside the classroom, such as the home. Children will usually not object to having a classmate receive the special attention associated, for example, with the awarding of points. They are more likely to object to a classmate who sticks his tongue out at them while he skips out of class with a new game under his arms. Teachers might provide cooperative parents with a report on the number of points their child has earned each day. The parents can then translate the points into an allowance or a special privilege without the knowledge of their child's classmates.

5   Whenever feasible, the teacher should use social rather than tangible reinforcers. Children object less to having a classmate receive social reinforcement than they do to the sight of one child receiving tangible reinforcers or special privileges. Also, even though one child may be a particular problem, there is no reason why the teacher cannot grant

social reinforcement to other children who are well behaved. This can be done by reinforcing individual children or by complimenting the entire group.

6 If several children perform the same misbehavior, a group contingency procedure involving all students might be in order. Since the same rules apply to all children, no particular child is singled out for rewards. The teacher might be most concerned about the misbehaviors of one student, but still wish to see the behavior of all students improve.

There is at least one other matter with which a teacher must concern herself if she singles out one child for a behavior modification program—not neglecting other students in the class. There is no doubt that a teacher's attention can be reinforcing to a child, and that the time she spends with a student can assist him in the learning process. But what happens to the rest of the class when this occurs? A study by Scott and Bushell (1974) was concerned with the relationship between the amount of time a teacher spent with one student and the on-task rate of the other students during mathematics class. The authors found that contacts of long duration with one child caused a substantial decrease in the on-task rate of his classmates. With contacts of shorter duration, the on-task rate of his classmates was much higher. A major conclusion of the study was that the duration of a teacher's contact should be long enough to help a particular student, but not so long that the teacher neglects the responses (such as hand raises) of the other students.

WHEN A CHILD DOES NOT LEARN, BEHAVIOR MODIFIERS PLACE THE BURDEN ON THE TEACHER TO DEVISE ALTERNATIVE PROCEDURES THAT WILL BE EFFECTIVE. DON'T THEY EVER TAKE INTO ACCOUNT THAT CULTURAL AND PHYSIOLOGICAL FACTORS MIGHT BE INTERFERING WITH A YOUNGSTER'S ABILITY TO LEARN?

Certainly physiological and cultural factors are important in the learning process of any child. The difficulty is that such factors are not under the control of educators. Educators cannot modify the genetic makeup of a child, nor can they prescribe medicine for ailments that might affect a student's academic performance. Similarly, educators cannot alter the family size of students, nor can they change parents' educational background. Educators must begin their work where physiological and cultural factors leave off. Nevertheless, their efforts are often fruitful. With appropriate teaching, children from diverse cultures learn to read, blind children develop mobility skills, and withdrawn children become more sociable.

Perhaps because of the pervasive influence of Freud, many parents, educators, and psychologists are bothered by the fact that behavior modifiers do not probe into an individual's past before attempting to remediate his difficulties. There are several reasons for this. First, the problems in correctly reconstructing one's past are immense. Accuracy depends on the individual's ability to precisely recall the past as well as the degree to which he reports the events truthfully. Accuracy also depends on the actions of his therapist. Some therapists expect clients to report or interpret events in certain ways and will reinforce them with smiles and nods when they do; they will also withdraw reinforcement when the client does not make the expected report. The fact that a therapist does not approve of behavioral procedures does not mean that she is not applying them—knowingly or unknowingly.

Another objection that behavior modifiers have to probing a child's past is that the factors that originally *caused* a problem are not necessarily the same as the ones that are *maintaining* the problem. A one-year-old child, for example, might start crying at night because he is ill. After a few nights, his illness might be cured. Nevertheless, he continues to cry because he has learned that crying brings his anxious parents running into his bedroom. His illness was the original *cause* of his crying, but his parents' attention is *maintaining* the problem; it is his parents' attention, rather than the illness, that must now be modified.

Cultural and physiological processes might make the job of the behaviorally oriented teacher easier or more difficult. Regardless, she enthusiastically and optimistically attacks every school problem as if it can be solved. In her efforts to remediate a problem, she often fails and tries again. If she never finds an appropriate solution to a problem, she does not conclude that the child is incapable of learning, but rather that she has not *yet* developed the skills to address the problem or that educational technology has not developed far enough to deal with such situations. In assuming that all problems can be solved, a teacher is often incorrect. Still it is better to make the error of believing a problem can be solved, and find out it cannot be, than to assume a problem cannot be solved, when it can be.

IF YOU ELIMINATE ONE INAPPROPRIATE BEHAVIOR, ISN'T IT POSSIBLE THAT A WORSE ONE WILL REPLACE IT?

The concern expressed in this question emanates from the medical model of human behavior proposed by Freud and other proponents of the psychoanalytic school. One of the basic tenets of this school is that human behavior can be explained in terms analogous to physical medicine. Just as germs and viruses operating within an individual lead to a disease and its associated symptoms, aberrant human behavior is seen as a symptom of an underlying psychological disease. Being only a symptom of a deeper disorder, it is claimed that one should not attempt to directly alter the behavior which is manifested but should probe further for the underlying cause of the problem. Psychoanalytic psychologists claim that the maladaptive behavior that is exhibited is the most economical and least harmful one the individual could have adopted under unfavorable conditions. They further propose the "hypothesis of symptom substitution," which states that if one maladaptive behavior is improperly removed, a more pathological one will replace it. It is, therefore, contended that if parents use a procedure to eliminate thumb-sucking, problems such as bed-wetting and temper tantrums might substitute for the original disorder. Freudian psychologists claim that in order to achieve the appropriate kind of change, there must be cognitive and emotional growth, and that an individual must have increased insight into the original cause of his problems.

In responding to this claim, it is important to note that when behaviorists treat a problem, they do not believe they are merely treating a "symptom" of the problem. Cooke and Cooke (1974) assert that a basic element of a behavioral approach is that all behaviors, whether adaptive or maladaptive, are learned through environmental contingencies. Thus, a student who calls out for attention has been reinforced for the behavior in the same way as a student who raises her hand for attention. The task for the teacher who is confronted with maladaptive behavior is to restructure the environment so as to strengthen the desired behavior (for example, by praising hand raises and ignoring call-outs). To behaviorists the symptom *is* the problem and when the symptom no longer exists, neither does the problem (Cooke and Cooke, 1974).

It should also be noted that behaviorists reject the term "symptom substitution." One reason is that the word "symptom" implies that behavioral disorders have an underlying medical origin—a notion which lacks experimental validation. Another reason is that the hypothesis states that the new behavior will necessarily be worse than the one it replaces. In fact, in those cases in which novel behaviors have emerged, they have sometimes been found to be desirable behaviors. The term preferred by behavior modifiers is *side effects,* or a particular kind of side effect, known as *response substitution*— the increase in the frequency of one behavior that occurs when another behavior is reduced.

As was indicated in Chapter 1, Newsom, Favell, and Rincover (1983) reported instances of undesirable side effects of punishment, such as crying, screaming, aggression, and disrupted social relationships. They also reported incidents of desirable side effects such as increased alertness, toy play, eye contact, and social behavior. The authors concluded that most punishment studies have not found undesirable side effects and that in cases where they have been noted, the effects tend to be short-lived or can be treated with standard behavioral procedures. Some perspective on the question was further provided by Baer (1971) who noted, "Behavior modifiers eliminated a few thousand tantrums in children who did not subsequently explode into psychopathology. Instead, they looked very much like children they had been previously, but without tantrums. Many of them, shorn of their one weapon of parent abuse, began to seem like children again to those parents, and pleasant, family-like things often happened subsequently" [p. 359].

There has been an aura of mystery surrounding the topic of "symptom substitution." In fact the idea that when one response disappears, another may replace it, can be understood in common sense terms. When a person no longer receives reinforcement for a certain behavior, he may perform another behavior to receive it. This behavior may be desirable or undesirable. If it is desirable it should be reinforced. If it is undesirable, it should be reduced as would any other inappropriate behavior. Better yet, when teachers apply procedures to reduce the level of one behavior, they should concurrently program for the desired behavior, and not leave the question of positive or negative side effects to chance.

I'VE TRIED EVERYTHING INCLUDING BEHAVIOR MODIFICATION AND NOTHING WORKS. WHAT AM I DOING WRONG?

Books and journal articles tend to publish reports of successful applications of behavior modification principles. This is important because teachers should be aware of techniques that are effective. On the other hand, it is frustrating to many teachers that their procedures do not work, despite repeated efforts. The present section describes some of the most common problems teachers encounter in setting up behavior modification procedures and suggests ways to avoid the difficulties. Some of the material is adapted from Fine, Nesbitt, and Tyler (1974):

1 Some programs fail because behaviors have not been clearly defined. Unless both students and teachers know exactly what the target behavior is, ineffective programming can result. Once an adequate definition is derived, it should be written down and, where appropriate, posted in the form of rules before the class or on a student's desk.

2 Teachers are sometimes unsuccessful because their measurement or implementation procedures are too difficult to conduct. Teachers should gather only enough data to get a good estimate of student performance. Similarly teachers should look for powerful, uncomplicated remedial techniques.

3 Desiring to tackle a long-standing problem with a procedure they believe will be effective, many teachers will neglect to collect baseline data. Several days later they may improperly abandon their procedure, because they are uncertain of its effectiveness. It is almost always worthwhile to collect baseline data.

4 Some teachers will collect data, but not graph it. As such their decisions are not sufficiently based on available data.

5 Teachers will sometimes try to change too many behaviors at once or will require too large a change in a given behavior. It is better to proceed slowly and set individual rather than absolute standards.

6 Sometimes teachers choose reinforcers according to what *most* children like, rather than on the basis of what the *present* child likes. As effective as praise has been, Varenhorst (1969) found that praising a seventeen-year-old boy caused a great deterioration in his behavior. The selection of reinforcers must be individualized and sometimes varied.

7 Sometimes delays in reinforcement are too long to sustain behavior. Waiting for a party on Friday afternoon may be too long for a student who leaves his seat an average of once every two minutes. In these cases it may be necessary to program more frequent, smaller reinforcers (such as extra free time) three times a day, or praise every fifteen minutes, and gradually build up to the longer delays.

8 In attempting to extinguish a behavior, teachers frequently do not wait long enough for the behavior to disappear or do not eliminate all sources of reinforcement. Extinction is slow and must be carried out with patience.

9 In applying punishment procedures, teachers should be certain not to reinforce a student *immediately after* punishing her, but should be certain to reinforce the desired behavior *at other times*.

10 Properly applied, time-out procedures are usually effective. Two common problems are allowing the time-out area to be too interesting, or permitting the time-out procedure to remove the student from an activity he dislikes.

11 Behavioral programs can fail because teachers lack a general understanding of behavior modification principles. As such they are capable of carrying out a specific program until an unexpected event occurs. When teachers have a general understanding of behavioral principles, they can respond appropriately to unanticipated events.

12 The best behavior modification programs can fail if teachers are not properly organized. Therefore, data sheets should be readily accessible, tokens and backup reinforcers should be conveniently located, and time-out rooms should be set up, in advance, for student placement.

13 Teachers sometimes use more intrusive procedures than are necessary. Consequences, for example, can be more difficult to apply than other procedures. Therefore, teachers might try to motivate students with more interesting materials or by changing seating arrangements before considering more intrusive techniques (Fine, 1970).

14   Programs are sometimes undermined because relevant individuals were not given advance notice of their occurrence. Whenever appropriate, teachers should inform parents, colleagues, and administrators that a special program will be implemented, and should attempt to elicit the support of such individuals.

15   Teachers often attempt to devise their own solutions to problems they encounter. In many cases it is profitable to consult published literature for procedures that have already proved effective.

A FINAL WORD

At the time of this writing the gigantic efforts of the 1960s and 70s to improve the educational lot of children are a matter of history. Such efforts are being declared a failure. It now appears that state and federal governments will decrease their financial contributions to the schools; it is even possible that public apathy will replace public interest. As such, it is all the more important that educators commit themselves to educational philosophies that will most benefit school children.

There have been repeated demonstrations that behavior modification procedures can effectively deal with social and academic problems, from preschool through high school, whether mild or severe. In some fields demonstrations of effectiveness would cause a rush to use the methodology. Not so in education. It is ironic that an endeavor that has frequently admitted to and complained about its ineffectiveness, often recoils when presented with a useful methodology. At some point we must reorder our priorities, so that teachers do not have a right to choose approaches solely on the basis of personal appeal. At some point our ethics must demand that students be taught according to whatever technology benefits them most. Students have a right to the best education that existing knowledge permits.

REFERENCES

Axelrod, S., and T. J. Piper: "Suitability of the Reversal and Multiple-Baseline Designs for Research on Reading Behaviors." Paper presented at the meeting of the Association for the Advancement of Behavior Therapy, San Francisco, Calif., December 1975.

Ayllon, T., S. Garber, and K. Pisor: "The Elimination of Discipline Problems Through a Combined School-Home Motivational System," *Behavior Therapy*, **6**, pp. 616–626, 1975.

Ayllon, T., D. Layman, and S. Burke: "Disruptive Behavior and Reinforcement of Academic Performances," *The Psychological Record*, **22**, pp. 315–323, 1972.

Ayllon, T., and M. D. Roberts: "Eliminating Discipline Problems by Strengthening Academic Performance," *Journal of Applied Behavior Analysis*, **7**, pp. 71–76, 1974.

Bear, D. M.: "Behavior Modification: You Shouldn't," in E. Ramp and B. L. Hopkins (eds.), *A New Direction for Education: Behavior Analysis, 1971* (Lawrence, Kan.: Support and Development Center for Follow Through, Department of Human Development, University of Kansas, 1971), pp. 358–369.

Boyd, L. A., W. S. Keilbaugh, and S. Axelrod: "The Direct and Indirect Effects of Positive Reinforcement on On-Task Behavior," *Behavior Therapy*, **12**, pp. 80–92, 1981.

Breyer, N. L., and G. J. Allen : "Effects of Implementing a Token Economy on Teacher Attending Behavior," *Journal of Applied Behavior Analysis*, **8**, pp. 373–380, 1975.

Broden, M., C. Bruce, M. A. Mitchell, V. Carter, and R. V. Hall: "Effects of Teacher Attention on Attending Behavior of Two Boys at Adjacent Desks," *Journal of Applied Behavior Analysis*, **3**, pp. 199–203, 1970.

Campbell, J. A., and J. Willis: "Modifying Components of 'Creative Behavior' in the Natural Environment," *Behavior Modification*, **2**, pp. 549–564, 1978.

Christy, P. R.: "Does Use of Tangible Rewards with Individual Children Affect Peer Observers?" *Journal of Applied Behavior Analysis*, **8**, pp. 187–196, 1975.

Cohen, S. A.: *Teach Them All To Read: Theory, Methods, and Materials for Teaching the Disadvantaged* (New York: Random House, 1969).

Cooke, T. P., and S. Cooke: "Behavior Modification: Answers to Some Ethical Questions," *Psychology in the Schools*, **11**, pp. 5–10, 1974.

Cote, R. W.: "Behavior Modification: Some Questions," *Elementary School Journal*, **74**, pp.44–47, 1973.

Drabman, R. S., and B. B. Lahey: "Feedback in Classroom Behavior Modification: Effects on the Target and Her Classmates," *Journal of Applied Behavior Analysis*, **7**, pp. 591–598, 1974.

Fine, M. J.: "Some Qualifying Notes on the Development and Implementation of Behavior Modification Programs," *Journal of School Psychology*, **8**, pp. 301–305, 1970.

Fine, M. J., J. A. Nesbitt, and M. M. Tyler: "Analysis of a Failing Attempt at Behavior Modification," *Journal of Learning Disabilities*, **7**, pp. 70–75, 1974.

Glover, J., and A. L. Gary: "Procedures to Increase Some Aspects of Creativity," *Journal of Applied Behavior Analysis*, **9**, pp. 79–84, 1976.

Goetz, E. M., and D. M. Baer: "Social Control of Form Diversity and the Emergence of New Forms in Children's Blockbuilding," *Journal of Applied Behavior Analysis*, **6**, pp. 209–217, 1973.

Goetz, E. M., and M. M. Salmonson: "The Effect of General and Descriptive Reinforcement on 'Creativity' in Easel Painting," in G. Semb, D. R. Green, R. P. Hawkins, J. Michael, E. L. Phillips, J. A. Sherman, H. Sloane, and D. R. Thomas (eds.), *Behavior Analysis and Education—1972* (Lawrence, Kan.: Support and Development Center for Follow Through, Department of Human Development, University of Kansas, 1972), pp. 53–61.

Hively, W.: "What Next?" in E. Ramp and B. L. Hopkins (eds.), *A New Direction for Education: Behavior Analysis, 1971* (Lawrence, Kan.: Support and Development Center for Follow Through, Department of Human Development, University of Kansas, 1971), pp. 311–322.

Homme, L.: *How to Use Contingency Contracting in the Classroom* (Champaign, Ill.: Research Press, 1969).

Horowitz, F. D.: "Living among the ABAs: Retrospect and Prospect," in E. Ramp and G. Semb (eds.), *Behavior Analysis: Areas of Research and Application* (Englewood Cliffs, N. J.: Prentice-Hall, 1975), pp. 3–15.

Kazdin, A. E.: *Behavior Modification in Applied Settings.* (Homewood, Ill.: Dorsey Press, 1980).

Kazdin, A. E., and Mascitelli, S.: "The Opportunity to Earn Oneself off a Token System as a Reinforcer for Attentive Behavior," *Behavior Therapy*, **11**, pp. 68–78, 1980.

Maloney, K. B., and B. L. Hopkins: "The Modification of Sentence Structure and Its Relationship to Subjective Judgments of Creativity in Writing," *Journal of Applied Behavior Analysis*, **6,** pp. 425–433, 1973.

Mandelker, A. V., T. A. Brigham, and D. Bushell: "The Effects of Token Procedures on a Teacher's Contacts with Her Students," *Journal of Applied Behavior Analysis*, **3**, pp. 169–174, 1970.

Morrow, W. R., and H. L. Gochros: "Misconceptions Regarding Behavior Modification," *The Social Service Review*, **44**, pp. 293–307, 1970.

Newsom, C., J. E. Favell, and A. Rincover: "Side Effects of Punishment," in S. Axelrod and J. Apsché (eds.), *The Effects of Punishment on Human Behavior* (New York: Academic Press, 1983).

Risley, T. R.: "Behavior Modification: An Experimental-Therapeutic Endeavor," in L. A. Hamerlynck, P. O. Davidson, and L. E. Acker (eds.), *Behavior Modification and Ideal Mental Health Services* (Calgary, Alberta, Canada: University of Calgary Press, 1970), pp. 103–127.

Risley, T. R., and D. M. Baer: "Operant Behavior Modification: The Deliberate Development of Child Behavior," in B. Caldwell and H. Ricciuti (eds.), *Review of Child Development Research, vol. III: Social Action* (Chicago: University of Chicago Press, 1973), pp. 283–329.

Roos, P.: "Human Rights and Behavior Modification," *Mental Retardation*, **12**, pp. 3–6, 1974.

Scott, J. W., and D. Bushell: "The Length of Teacher Contacts and Students' Off-task Behavior," *Journal of Applied Behavior Analysis*, **7**, pp. 39–44, 1974.

Shapiro, E. S., and Klein, R. D.: "Self-Management of Classroom Behavior with Retarded/Disturbed Children," *Behavior Modification*, **4**, pp. 83–97, 1980.

Sloane, H. N.: *Classroom Management: Remediation and Prevention* (New York: John Wiley and Sons, 1976).

Smith, A. B.: "Humanism and Behavior Modification: Is There a Conflict?" *Elementary School Journal*, **74**, pp. 59–67, 1973.

Sulzer-Azaroff, B., and G. R. Mayer: *Applying Behavior Analysis Procedures with Children and Youth* (New York: Holt, Rinehart, and Winston, 1977).

Torrance, E. P.: *Torrance Tests of Creative Thinking* (Princeton, N. J.: Personnel Press, 1966).

Van Houten, R.: *Learning Through Feedback* (New York: Human Sciences Press, 1980).

Varenhorst, B. B.: "Reinforcement that Backfired," in J. D. Krumboltz and C. E. Thoreson (eds.), *Behavioral Counseling: Cases and Techniques* (New York: Holt, Rinehart, and Winston, 1969), pp. 49–51.

Walker, H. M.: *The Acting-Out Child* (Boston: Allyn and Bacon, 1979).

Wallace, I.: "Self Control Techniques of Famous Novelists," *Journal of Applied Behavior Analysis*, **10**, pp. 515–525, 1977.

Webster's New World Dictionary of the American Language, 2d college ed. (Englewood Cliffs, N. J.: Prentice-Hall, 1970).

Winnett, R. A., and R. C. Winkler: "Current Behavior Modification in the Classroom: Be Still, Be Quiet, Be Docile," *Journal of Applied Behavior Analysis*, **5**, pp. 499–504, 1972.

Glossary

Abscissa the points along the horizontal axis, usually depicting a measure of time, such as days, weeks, or sessions. See also Ordinate.

Actual Learning Rate the rate at which a student either progresses in the curriculum or performs on a daily basis as a result of instructional intervention. See also Progress Graph.

Alternating Treatment Design See Multi-element Design.

Antecedent Event any event occurring before a behavior that may influence the probability of the behavior occurring. A common example is the use of instructions.

Back-up Reinforcer the items or activities for which tokens may be exchanged. Examples might include trinkets and the opportunity to be the classroom messenger. See also Token Reinforcer.

Backward Chaining See Chain.

Baseline the level (e.g., frequency) of a behavior before initiating special procedures. Baseline is typically the initial phase of a reversal or multiple-baseline design.

Behavior any observable act an individual performs; synonymous with the term "response." Included are both operants and respondents.

Behavior Chain See Chain.

Behavioral Objective a statement containing a specific condition, behavior, and criteria which describe the expected performance of the student following instruction. See also Criteria.

Chain a series of behaviors occurring in a specific order that compose a larger act. In a *forward chaining* procedure a teacher teaches the first link in the chain of behaviors, then the second, the third, etc. In a *backward chaining* procedure, the teacher first teaches the last link in the chain, followed by the next to last link, etc.

Change Criterion a standard (e.g., number of days) used by a teacher to determine when a change in instructional procedures is warranted. For example, a teacher might determine that if a student is not performing at the level specified by the projected learning rate line after eight school days, then the instructional procedure which was used will be changed in an effort to find a more effective method of teaching.

Classical Conditioning See Respondent Conditioning.

Conditioned Reinforcer an event that owes its reinforcing capacity to an association with other reinforcers. For example, by frequently patting a child on the back and then giving her a favored food, the pat on the back is likely to become a conditioned reinforcer. See also Unconditioned Reinforcer.

Consequence any event that follows a behavior. Such events may increase or decrease the future rate of the bahvior.

Consequence Sharing a group contingency

arrangement in which the behavior of one student determines the consequence for all other students. An example would be reading all students a story if a classmate finishes his work on time. See also Group Contingency.

Contingency Contract a written agreement between a teacher and student specifying the reinforcers a student will receive for acceptable performance. The contract should be attained through negotiation.

Contingent Observation a time-out procedure in which a student is moved a short distance from an activity after misbehaving, but is able to observe classmates engaging in the behavior appropriately. See also Time Out.

Contingent Relationship a relationship indicating that *if* a certain behavior occurs *then* a consequence will follow. Examples include: *if* a student raises her hand in class *then* the teacher will call on her; or *if* a student is tardy *then* he will miss a portion of his free play time.

Continous Measurement any measurement operation that occurs frequently (e.g., daily). A teacher, for example, might measure a student's reading performance each day.

Continous Reinforcement Schedule a reinforcement schedule in which each occurrence of a certain behavior is reinforced. See also Schedule of Reinforcement.

Correct Rate See Rate.

Correlation a measure of the degree to which two variables have a tendency to change together.

Criteria that portion of a behavioral objective which specifies three aspects of intended student performance. Contained in the criteria should be the intended (a) rate or accuracy of performance, (b) duration of performance at a specified rate, accuracy, or frequency, and (c) the date by which the behavior is to be performed, at the two previously stated criteria. See also Behavioral Objective.

Cross-Age Tutor a tutor from a higher grade than the tutee. See also Peer Tutor.

Cumulative Graph a graph in which the score for each session is added to all previous scores.

Differential Reinforcement of Low Rate of Response (DRL) a schedule of reinforcement in which a reinforcer is delivered if a

behavior occurs at or below a certain rate. For example, students might receive five extra minutes of free play time, if they talk out eight or fewer times in a morning.

Differential Reinforcement of Other Behavior (DRO) a schedule of reinforcement in which an individual or group receives a reinforcer for completely refraining from a behavior. An example would be allowing a student to change her desk if she did not throw spitballs for an entire week.

Direct Measurement any measurement procedure in which a teacher measures the exact behavior which is a target for modification. In a program designed to improve math skill, for example, a direct measure would involve noting the number of problems answered correctly on a daily math test. Performance on a math achievement test would be an *in*direct measure.

Discrimination a situation in which a behavior is occurring in some circumstances, but not in others. For example, if a student gives an answer when called on, but does not give answers at other times, a discrimination has been formed. In this case being recognized by the teacher is a discriminative stimulus to give an answer; all other situations are S^Δ. See also Discriminative Stimulus and S^Δ.

Discriminative Stimulus (S^D) any cue indicating that a certain behavior may be reinforced.

Duration Recording an observational record of how long a behavior lasts. A duration record might indicate that it took a student 32 minutes to complete an assignment.

Exclusion Time Out a time-out procedure, following a misbehavior, in which a student is removed from an activity, remains in the general area, but *cannot* observe the activities of classmates. See also Time Out.

Exit Level the point on the minimum rate line which indicates that the student is performing the skills expected of any student of the same chronological age and, therefore, is no longer eligible for special services. See also Functional Level, Progress Graph, and Projected Learning Rate.

Extinction a procedure to reduce the rate of behavior that involves the discontinuation of the reinforcement that follows a behavior. Extinction has taken place if a teacher stops attending to a student's profanities, and profanities decrease in rate. See also Extinction Burst, Resistance to Extinction, and Spontaneous Recovery.

Extinction Burst the temporary increase in behavior that frequently occurs with an extinction procedure. See also Extinction.

Fading the gradual removal of prompts that help a student to perform a behavior. Often, many prompts are necessary in the early stages of learning a behavior, but can be systematically removed as competence increases.

Feedback any kind of information indicating whether a behavior was correct or incorrect. Feedback can be provided by a reinforcer, a punisher, grades, charts, etc.

Fixed-Interval Scallop the low rate of response during the early portion of the interval, and the high rate of response during the latter portion of the interval, on a fixed-interval schedule of reinforcement. See also Fixed-Interval Schedule.

Fixed-Interval Schedule (FI) a schedule of reinforcement in which a behavior is reinforced following the passage of a standard amount of time. On an FI 10 minute schedule, for example, exactly 10 minutes must have elapsed since the previous behavior was reinforced, for reinforcement to be available.

Fixed-Ratio Schedule (FR) a schedule of reinforcement in which a reinforcer is delivered following an unvarying number of responses, since the previous reinforcement. On an FR 10 schedule, for example, a student would be reinforced after *exactly* ten responses.

Forward Chaining See Chain.

Frequency Record an observational record indicating the number of times a behavior occurs. A student, for example, may hit a classmate at a frequency of three times on a given day.

Functional Level the level at which a student is functioning in a specific skill area, e.g. multiplication, as indicated by the highest level objective which the student has mastered. See also Exit Level, Progress Graph, and Projected Learning Rate.

Functional Definition any definition of behavior that describes the environmental effects of the behavior. See also Topographical Definition.

Generalization See Stimulus Generalization.

Generalized Reinforcer a conditioned reinforcer that is associated with many other reinforcers. Examples include tokens and money. See also Conditioned Reinforcer.

Group Comparison Design a research design in which a sample of students is randomly selected from the population and then randomly assigned to different experimental groups.

Group Contingency an arrangement in which student consequences depend, to some degree, on the behavior of one, or more, other students. A competitive game is an example of a group contingency. See also Consequence Sharing and Interdependent Group Contingency.

Home-Based Programs a reinforcement procedure in which teachers rate student behavior and send home reports on a frequent basis. Parents are responsible for providing reinforcers in accordance with the reports.

Imitation learning that takes place by observing the behavior of another individual. The learner's behavior is the same as the model's. See also Model.

Incorrect Rate See Rate.

Informed Consent a practice in which students (or their parents or guardians) are given all information relevant to participation in a study, before agreeing to become involved in the study.

Interdependent Group Contingency a group contingency in which the behavior of all students determines the consequence for all group members. An example would be giving an entire class extra free time if all students complete their homework. See also Group Contingency.

Intermittent Reinforcement Schedule a reinforcement schedule in which some occurrences of a certain behavior are reinforced and other occurrences are not. See also Schedule of Reinforcement.

Interval Recording an observational record indicating whether or not a behavior occurred during a specified time interval (e.g., during a 10-second interval).

Maintenance of Behavior the degree to which a behavior remains at an improved level, once a successful procedure is removed.

Mean Score the average of several data points.

Measurement of Lasting Products the

measure of a student's work output in which a tangible product is involved. Examples include a math paper graded as having 37 correct answers or an English composition with a "B" grade.

Median the middle point of several data points arranged from lowest to highest, or highest to lowest.

Minimum Rate Line a line drawn at a 45° angle on a progress graph which indicates the 1:1 ratio which exists between a month (or year) spent in school and a month (or year) of skills learned. This line represents the rate of 1.0 at which any student should learn. Thus a student whose progress is less than 1.0 should be eligible for special services. See also Progress Graph.

Model the individual whose behavior is imitated by another individual. See also Imitation.

Momentary Time Sampling an observational record indicating whether or not a behavior was occurring at the *end* of a time interval.

Multiple-Baseline Design an experimental design in which baseline data are taken on different behaviors. A procedure is then applied to one behavior, later to a second, a third, etc. If the behavior consistently changes when the procedure is applied to it, it is clear that the procedure *caused* the change in behavior. The design can also be applied across different settings or across different individuals.

Multi-element Design an experimental design in which baseline and interventions alternate from one session to the next. For example, a student could receive a reinforcement procedure the first day, an extinction procedure the second, baseline on the third day, extinction on the fourth, etc. After several exposures to each procedure, data would be examined to determine which procedure was most beneficial for a certain behavior.

Negative Reinforcement the process by which events that are removed following a behavior, increase the future rate of the behavior. The events are called "negative reinforcers." A possible example would be an increase in chemistry test performance after a teacher announced that all students with an average above 90% would not have to take the final examination. In this case the examination is the negative reinforcer. See also Positive Reinforcement.

Negative Reinforcer See Negative Reinforcement.

Observational Recording any procedure used to obtain a record of transitory student behaviors (e.g., calling out, out of seat) that do not leave a product. See also Duration Recording, Frequency Recording, Interval Recording, and Momentary Time Sampling.

Operant Behavior a behavior whose occurrence is controlled by its consequences. Such behaviors are considered "voluntary" and are "emitted" by the individual. Examples include hand raising, writing down assignments, and reading aloud.

Operant Conditioning the process by which the consequences of a behavior increase or decrease the future rate of the behavior. See also Operant Behavior.

Ordinate points along the vertical axis, usually consisting of a measure of a behavior (e.g., number of words spelled correctly). See also Abscissa.

Overcorrection one of two types of punishment procedures: (a) *Restitutional Overcorrection*—used when an individual disturbs the environment. The offending individual is first required to restore the environment to its original state and then to improve it beyond this state. (b) *Positive Practice Overcorrection*—used when there is no environmental disturbance, but a behavior is performed incorrectly. The student is then required to perform the correct behavior repeatedly.

Peer Tutor a tutor in the same grade as the tutee.

Performance Graph a graph which permits a daily comparison of the rate and direction in which academic performance should change in order for a specific objective to be met, with the level (e.g., correct rate, or accuracy) at which the student actually performs. See Progress Graph.

Positive Practice Overcorrection See Overcorrection.

Positive Reinforcement the process by which events that are presented after a behavior, increase the future rate of the behavior. The events are called "positive reinforcers." An example would be an increase in hand raising after a teacher praised a student for raising his hand. See also Negative Reinforcement.

Positive Reinforcer See Positive Reinforcement.

Post-Reinforcement Pause the temporary decrease in the rate of a behavior following the delivery of a reinforcer, on a Fixed-Ratio Schedule. See also Fixed-Ratio Schedule.

Postchecks measures of a behavior taken some time after a procedure is shown to be effective. Postchecks typically occur less frequently than measures conducted during the study (e.g., weekly, rather than daily).

Previewing one of several procedures whereby a student becomes familiar with a reading assignment before reading orally. Previewing techniques include: previewing by listening, oral previewing both with and without feedback, and silent previewing.

Primary Reinforcer See Unconditioned Reinforcer.

Progress Graph a graph which permits a comparison of a student's overall progress in a curriculum area (e.g., math) with both her projected learning rate and the minimum rate of learning which is expected of any student. See also Actual Learning Rate, Exit Level, Functional Level, Minimum Rate Line, and Projected Learning Rate.

Projected Learning Rate a term used to indicate either the rate at which a student must progress in the curriculum, or the rate of daily performance necessary for an objective to be met at a predetermined time. The projected learning rate for progress in the curriculum is determined by the formula:

$$\frac{\text{units of objectives to be mastered}}{\text{units of time in which objectives are to be mastered}} = \text{projected learning rate}$$

On the progress graph the projected learning rate line connects the plot for the functional level with the plot for the exit level. On the performance graph the projected learning rate is automatically determined by the number of days allowed for the attainment of each specific objective. See Exit Level, Functional Level, Performance Graph, and Progress Graph.

Prompt any antecedent event used to initiate a behavior. Examples include hints, instructions, and a gentle push in the right direction.

Punishment any change in the environment following a behavior that decreases the future rate of that behavior. Events that can serve as punishers include reprimands, and reducing a child's opportunity to earn reinforcers.

Rate the frequency of a behavior per unit of time. A student may read at a rate of 40 words per minute or call out at a rate of four times per hour. A teacher might measure the number of correct responses per unit of time (*correct rate*) or the number of incorrect responses per unit of time (*incorrect rate*).

Reinforcement a process by which the consequence of a behavior increases the future rate of the behavior. The consequence can involve the presentation of something desirable (e.g., a preferred seating arrangement) or the removal of an undesirable event (e.g., a final examination). See also Negative Reinforcement and Positive Reinforcement.

Reinforcement Menu a description of the reinforcers available to the students.

Reinforcement of Incompatible Behavior a procedure to reduce behavior that involves reinforcing a behavior that cannot coexist with the undesirable behavior. An example would involve a principal who reduced truancy by reinforcing students for coming to school.

Reliability a measure of the degree to which independent observers agree on the occurrence of a behavior.

Reprimand a punishment procedure involving an expression of disapproval. A reprimand may either be verbal or gestural.

Research Design the operations used to demonstrate that a procedure *caused* a change in behavior. See also Group-Comparison Design, Multi-Element, Multiple-Baseline, and Reversal Design.

Resistance to Extinction the number of behaviors an individual performs once reinforcement is no longer forthcoming. The more intermittent the schedule of reinforcement, the greater the resistance to extinction. See also Extinction.

Respondent a reflexive or involuntary behavior; a behavior which is elicited by an identifiable, antecedent stimulus. Examples include salivation, knee jerks, and eye blinks.

Respondent Conditioning a conditioning procedure in which a neutral stimulus acquires the ability to elicit a reflexive behavior. The neutral stimulus attains this capacity through an association with an unconditioned stimulus that can elicit the response automatically.

Response Cost a punishment procedure in which a portion of a student's positive reinforcers are removed following a behavior. An example would be removing a token from a student after he hit a classmate.

Restitutional Overcorrection See Overcorrection.

Reversal Design an experimental design in which a procedure is withdrawn after being associated with an improvement in behavior. Typically the design consists of a baseline phase, followed by intervention, and then by a return to baseline conditions. The second baseline period is known as the *reversal* phase.

SD (pronounced "ess delta") any cue indicating that a certain behavior will *not* be reinforced.

S^D See Discriminative Stimulus.

Schedule of Reinforcement a specification of the number of behaviors that must occur, or the amount of time that must pass, in order for a response to be reinforced. See also Fixed-Interval Schedule, Fixed-Ratio Schedule, Variable-Interval Schedule, Variable-Ratio Schedule.

Seclusion Time Out a time-out procedure in which a student is physically removed from an activity and placed in an area devoid of reinforcers. See also Time Out.

Self-Control any procedure an individual undertakes in order to modify some aspect of her behavior. See also Contingency Contract and Self-Recording.

Self-Recording an attempt to change one's own behavior by attaining a record of it. This might involve a student graphing the number of days he completed his homework assignments each week.

Shaping the process of teaching a new behavior by reinforcing behaviors that progressively resemble the desired behavior. Each of the behaviors that approaches the target behavior is called a "successive approximation."

Side Effects any changes in behaviors which were *not* the intended targets for modification.

Spontaneous Recovery the recurrence, following an extinction procedure, of a behavior that had ceased for a period of time. The phenomenon does not always occur and is usually temporary. See also Extinction.

Stimulus any observable change in the environment that may affect behavior. A stimulus may come before a behavior (i.e., a discriminative stimulus) or after a behavior (e.g., a reinforcer).

Stimulus Generalization a situation in which a behavior that has been reinforced in one situation also occurs in situations in which it has not been reinforced. An example of stimulus generalization is a case in which a student is reinforced for improved table manners in the school cafeteria and exhibits the same improved manners at home.

Successive Approximation See "Shaping."

Task Analysis the process of breaking down a task into its component steps and listing them in the order of their occurrence. For example, a task analysis might consist of the steps a given student would need to perform in order to complete a division problem.

Time Out a punishment procedure in which a student experiences a less reinforcing environment following a behavior. The procedure can involve making the existing environment less reinforcing or placing the student in a less reinforcing environment. See also Contingent Observation, Exclusion Time Out, and Seclusion Time Out.

Token Reinforcer a tangible or symbolic event that can be exchanged for a back-up reinforcer. Examples of tokens include poker chips and checkmarks. See also Back-up Reinforcer.

Topographical Definition any definition of behavior that describes the actions an individual performs. See also Functional Definition.

Unconditioned Reinforcer a reinforcer

that can strengthen behavior independently of an association with other reinforcers. Common examples include food, water, and sexual activities. See also Conditioned Reinforcer.

Variable-Interval Schedule (VI) a schedule of reinforcement specifying the average amount of time that must elapse before reinforcers are available. The amount of time, however, varies from one reinforcer to the next.

Variable-Ratio Schedule (VR) a schedule of reinforcement specifying the average number of responses that must occur before a reinforcer is delivered. The number of responses, however, varies from one reinforcer to the next.

Name Index

Subject Index